JOURNAL FOR THE STUDY OF THE NEW TESTAMENT SUPPLEMENT SERIES
102

Executive Editor
Stanley E. Porter

JSOT Press
Sheffield

Other Followers of Jesus

Minor Characters as Major Figures in Mark's Gospel

Joel F. Williams

Journal for the Study of the New Testament
Supplement Series 102

To Becky, for her love and patience

Copyright © 1994 Sheffield Academic Press

Published by JSOT Press
JSOT Press is an imprint of
Sheffield Academic Press Ltd
343 Fulwood Road
Sheffield S10 3BP
England

Typeset by Sheffield Academic Press
and
Printed on acid-free paper in Great Britain
by Bookcraft
Midsomer Norton, Somerset

British Library Cataloguing in Publication Data

A catalogue record for this book is available
from the British Library

ISBN 1-85075-489-6

CONTENTS

ACKNOWLEDGMENTS

This work is a revision of my doctoral dissertation that was completed in the summer of 1992 at Marquette University. My interest in the subject began in a seminar on Mark led by Dr Richard Edwards. In that class, I became intrigued by the narrative analysis of the Gospels and by Mark's portrayal of minor characters. I am grateful to Dr Edwards, who served as my dissertation advisor, for starting me on this project and for helping me to finish it. In addition, I received helpful critiques and encouragement from the other members of my dissertation committee, Revd William Kurz, SJ, Dr Julian Hills, Dr Carol Stockhausen and Dr Ronald Feenstra. The completion of my doctoral program overlapped with my initial years of teaching, and I would not have brought this project to an end without understanding and gracious supervisors. Therefore, I am indebted to Dr Harold Hoehner, Dr Buist Fanning, Dr Gary Meadors and my present academic dean Dr Ralph Enlow of Columbia Bible College and Seminary. The person most responsible for moving this work from a dissertation to a book is Dr Elizabeth Struthers Malbon. I am grateful to her for taking an interest in my work and for recommending it for publication.

Although many have provided me with help along the way, my family supplies my joy. My parents, Forrest and Rachel Williams, pray for me without ceasing. My children, Anna and Matthew, are patient with a father who works too much and plays too little. Most of all, I am thankful for my wife, Becky, for her love, friendship and partnership in ministry.

ABBREVIATIONS

AB	Anchor Bible
AsSeign	*Assemblées du Seigneur*
BAGD	W. Bauer, W.F. Arndt, F.W. Gingrich and F.W. Danker, *Greek–English Lexicon of the New Testament*
BBB	Bonner biblische Beiträge
BDF	F. Blass, A. Debrunner and R.W. Funk, *A Greek Grammar of the New Testament*
Bib	*Biblica*
BNTC	Black's New Testament Commentaries
BR	*Biblical Research*
BTB	*Biblical Theology Bulletin*
BZNW	Beihefte zur *ZNW*
CBQ	*Catholic Biblical Quarterly*
CGTC	Cambridge Greek Testament Commentary
EBib	Etudes bibliques
EKKNT	Evangelisch-katholischer Kommentar zum Neuen Testament
EvQ	*Evangelical Quarterly*
ExpTim	*Expository Times*
FFNT	Foundations and Facets: New Testament
FRLANT	Forschungen zur Religion und Literatur des Alten und Neuen Testaments
HNT	Handbuch zum Neuen Testament
HTKNT	Herders theologischer Kommentar zum Neuen Testament
HTR	*Harvard Theological Review*
ICC	International Critical Commentary
Int	*Interpretation*
IRT	Issues in Religion and Theology
JAAR	*Journal of the American Academy of Religion*
JBL	*Journal of Biblical Literature*
JR	*Journal of Religion*
JSNT	*Journal for the Study of the New Testament*
JSNTSup	*Journal for the Study of the New Testament* Supplement Series
JSOT	*Journal for the Study of the Old Testament*
JSOTSup	*Journal for the Study of the Old Testament* Supplement Series
JTS	*Journal of Theological Studies*
LB	*Linguistica Biblica*

LSJ	Liddel–Scott–Jones, *Greek–English Lexicon*
MM	J.H. Moulton and G. Milligan, *The Vocabulary of the Greek Testament*
NCB	New Century Bible
Neot	*Neotestamentica*
NICNT	New International Commentary on the New Testament
NovT	*Novum Testamentum*
NTD	Das Neue Testament Deutsch
NTS	*New Testament Studies*
RB	*Revue biblique*
RelSRev	*Religious Studies Review*
RNT	Regensburger Neues Testament
SANT	Studien zum Alten und Neuen Testament
SBLDS	Society of Biblical Literature Dissertation Series
SBLSS	Society of Biblical Literature Semeia Studies
SJT	*Scottish Journal of Theology*
SNT	Studien zum Neuen Testament
SNTSMS	Society for New Testament Studies Monograph Series
TDNT	G. Kittel and G. Friedrich (eds.), *Theological Dictionary of the New Testament*
THKNT	Theologischer Handkommentar zum Neuen Testament
TynBul	*Tyndale Bulletin*
TZ	*Theologische Zeitschrift*
WBC	Word Biblical Commentary
ZNW	*Zeitschrift für die neutestamentliche Wissenschaft*
ZTK	*Zeitschrift für Theologie und Kirche*

Chapter 1

INTRODUCTION

The disciples, the opponents of Jesus and the crowd are the main character groups in Mark's Gospel. In addition, Mark includes in his narrative a number of minor characters.[1] Some of these secondary characters, such as Andrew or Peter, are disciples, while others, such as the high priest or Pilate, oppose Jesus. Mark also presents a series of individuals who function neither as Jesus' disciples nor as his opponents. Instead, these minor characters come from the crowd.[2] They appear in the narrative when they meet with Jesus, and then after their encounter with him they generally disappear from the narrative. Mark portrays these minor characters as suppliants, those who come to Jesus for help, or as exemplars, those who exemplify the teaching of Jesus, or as both suppliants and exemplars.[3] The task of this study is to examine Mark's presentation of the minor characters from the crowd. The specific contribution of this work lies in its analysis of the way

1. In Chapter 2, an attempt is made to describe the real author, the implied author and the narrator of Mark's Gospel. For the sake of convenience, the term 'Mark' is used frequently in this study for the implied author of the Gospel of Mark.

2. The minor characters from the crowd in Mark's Gospel include: the man with an unclean spirit (1.21-28), Simon's mother-in-law (1.29-31), the leper (1.40-45), the paralytic (2.1-12), the man with the withered hand (3.1-6), the Gerasene demoniac (5.1-20), Jairus (5.21-24, 35-43), the hemorrhaging woman (5.25-34), the Syrophoenician woman (7.24-30), the deaf man (7.31-37), the blind man of Bethsaida (8.22-26), the man with the possessed boy (9.14-29), the rich man (10.17-31), blind Bartimaeus (10.46-52), one of the scribes (12.28-34), the poor widow (12.41-44), the woman who anoints Jesus (14.3-9), Simon of Cyrene (15.21), the centurion (15.39, 44-45), the women followers (15.40-41, 47), Joseph of Arimathea (15.42-47), the women at the tomb (16.1-8).

3. For the use of the terms 'suppliants' and 'exemplars' see E.S. Malbon, 'The Jewish Leaders in the Gospel of Mark: A Literary Study of Markan Characterization', *JBL* 108 (1989), p. 277.

that Mark uses his characterization of these individuals to influence the reader.[1]

These minor characters are from the crowd in the sense that they belong to the general population, the group of people who are not numbered among the disciples or opponents of Jesus. They are not specifically called and commissioned to be Jesus' disciples, and they do not align themselves with the religious and political establishments that oppose Jesus and seek to destroy him. Instead, these characters come from the crowd in the broad sense of that term.

The crowd is a diverse and shifting character group in Mark's Gospel. Mark's favorite designation for the crowd is ὄχλος, although he also employs other terms, such as πᾶς, πολλοί, πλῆθος, λαός, or simply an undefined subject of a plural verb.[2] In Mark's Gospel, references to the crowd normally indicate a specific gathering of people who come together at a particular time and location. In general, the crowd gathers around Jesus, although this is not always the case (9.14; 12.41; 14.43; 15.8, 11, 15). The crowd in Mark's narrative is an amorphous and shifting group which changes in its makeup from scene to scene.[3] The crowds, the large gatherings of people, are often the recipients of Jesus' ministry, his teaching, healing and feeding.[4]

Although Mark normally uses the term 'crowd' for a specific gathering of people around Jesus, he also makes use of the term in a broader sense to refer to people in general or to the masses of humanity outside the disciples and opponents of Jesus. For example, in Mk 7.14, Jesus is present on the scene along with his disciples and the religious leaders. In the midst of his dispute with the religious leaders over the actions of his disciples, Jesus summons the crowd.

1.　Unless otherwise noted, the term 'the reader' is used in this study for the implied reader. Chapter 2 includes an explanation of the concept of the implied reader.

2.　For a list of references to the crowd in Mark's Gospel along with the terms used see E.S. Malbon, 'Disciples/Crowds/Whoever: Markan Characters and Readers', *NovT* 28 (1986), pp. 126-30. On the terms used for the crowd in Mark's Gospel see also E. Best, 'The Role of the Disciples in Mark', *NTS* 23 (1977), pp. 390-91; T.J. Weeden, *Mark—Traditions in Conflict* (Philadelphia: Fortress Press, 1971), p. 22.

3.　Weeden (*Traditions in Conflict*, p. 22) defines the crowd as 'the amorphous gathering of humanity'.

4.　Malbon, 'Disciples/Crowds/Whoever', p. 113.

The picture is not that there is a previously formed gathering of people off to the side who are simply waiting to be called. Instead, when Jesus summons the crowd, he is calling to himself people beyond his opponents and disciples. Therefore, in Mk 7.14, 'crowd' refers to people among the general population who do not belong to the company of Jesus' disciples or opponents. A similar use of ὄχλος is found in Mk 8.34. After talking privately with his disciples concerning his identity and destiny, Jesus summons the crowd. In other words, Jesus calls to himself other people beyond his disciples. The term 'crowd' is also used in a broader sense in Mk 11.32 and 12.12. In both verses, Mark states that the religious leaders held back from their desired words and actions, because they feared the crowd. Their fear is not directed toward a specific gathering of people around Jesus, since Mark gives no indication that such a crowd is present on the scene. Instead, the religious leaders are afraid of the general population, which regarded John as a prophet and responded positively to Jesus.[1] In Mk 11.32 and 12.12, 'crowd' refers to the general population outside of Jesus' opponents.[2]

The minor characters from the crowd make their appearance into the narrative in different ways. Often, these characters emerge from the crowd that has gathered around Jesus and then encounter Jesus as individuals. Others are simply present on the scene apart from the crowd, that is, the specific gathering of people around Jesus. In such cases, the crowd often blocks the individual's access to Jesus. Still others approach Jesus privately. Nevertheless, all of these characters belong to the crowd in the general sense of that term. They are part of the general population that stands outside of Jesus' disciples and opponents.

Little scholarly work has been done on Mark's portrayal of minor characters. This is unusual if for no other reason than that passages

1. In a parallel verse (14.2), the religious leaders do not want to seize and kill Jesus during the feast for fear of an uproar among the people. Here λαός is used with reference to the general population.

2. The most common synonyms in Mark's Gospel for the crowd are used with a similar field of meaning to that of ὄχλος. πολλοί is frequently employed to refer to a specific gathering of people around Jesus (2.2; 6.2, 31, 33; 9.26; 10.48; 11.8; 14.56), but it may also refer to people in general (10.45; 14.24). The undefined subject of a plural verb is often used for a particular gathering of people around Jesus (1.22, 32; 2.3, 4; 5.14, 15, 17; 6.33, 55; 7.32, 37; 8.22; 9.20; 10.13), but it is also used with a more general reference (1.45; 6.56; 7.36).

dealing with minor characters appear at crucial points in Mark's Gospel. At the transition between Jesus' work in Galilee and the beginning of his travel to Jerusalem, Jesus heals the blind man of Bethsaida. At the transition between Jesus' journey to Jerusalem and his arrival in that city, Bartimaeus receives his sight and follows Jesus. At the beginning of Mark's passion narrative, a woman anoints Jesus' head with costly perfume. At the end of Mark's Gospel, after the desertion of the disciples and after the death and resurrection of Jesus, Mary Magdalene, Mary the mother of James and Salome come to the empty tomb.

The function of this chapter is to survey recent research on Mark's presentation of minor characters. The survey will attempt to point out why so little work has been done on this subject, to highlight the difficulties involved in analyzing the topic and to begin clarifying the method and focus of this study.

Redaction-Critical Approaches to Minor Characters in Mark's Gospel

During the past few decades, the method of redaction criticism has dominated scholarly research on the Gospel of Mark.[1] Redaction-

---

1. Writing in 1973, Donahue was able to say, 'The fifteen years since the first edition of Willi Marxsen's *Der Evangelist Markus*, have seen the emergence of *Redaktionsgeschichte* as the dominant methodology in the study of Mark' (J.R. Donahue, *Are You the Christ? The Trial Narrative in the Gospel of Mark* [SBLDS, 10; Missoula, MT: Society of Biblical Literature, 1973], p. 5). Since that time, redaction criticism has continued to dominate the study of Mark's Gospel. Blomberg states that redaction criticism has been 'the most thriving discipline in recent years' within Synoptic studies (C.L. Blomberg, 'Synoptic Studies: Some Recent Methodological Developments and Debates', *Themelios* 12 [1987], p. 40). Black points out that new winds are blowing in Markan research and 'yet the steady breeze of redaction criticism has persisted for some thirty-odd years and continues to propel Markan scholarship' (C.C. Black, 'The Quest of Mark the Redactor: Why has it been Pursued, and what has it Taught Us?', *JSNT* 33 [1988], p. 19). On the continuing dominance of redaction criticism in the study of Mark's Gospel see also the following surveys of scholarly literature on Mark: W.L. Lane, 'The Gospel of Mark in Current Study', *Southwestern Journal of Theology* 21 (1978), p. 7; J.D. Kingsbury, 'The Gospel of Mark in Current Research', *RelSRev* 5 (1979), p. 102; W. Telford, 'Introduction: The Gospel of Mark', in *idem* (ed.), *The Interpretation of Mark* (IRT, 7; Philadelphia: Fortress Press, 1985), p. 6; F.J. Matera, *What are they Saying about Mark?* (New York: Paulist Press, 1987),

critical studies on the Gospels seek to discover the theology of the Evangelists as it is revealed in their editing of traditional material.[1] In addition, redaction criticism attempts to uncover the historical circumstances of the Christian community in which the Gospels arose. Having determined the theological developments which led to the writing of the Gospels, the redaction critic inquires into the historical situation behind these developments.[2]

Later in this study, it will be argued that Mk 10.46-52 is an important turning point in Mark's portrayal of minor characters. Since a number of major redactional studies have been done on this passage, it provides a useful way into examining the characteristic approaches of redaction critics to Mark's presentation of minor characters. Redaction critics have studied Mark's modification of the tradition and his placement of this passage in its present location in order to find Mark's theological perspective on discipleship or Christology.

Theology and Redaction in Mark 10.46-52

The majority of redaction critics conclude that the editorial activity in Mk 10.46-52 reveals Mark's understanding of discipleship.[3] On this view, Mark created the awkward introduction to the pericope in v. 46, in which Jesus enters Jericho and then immediately exits the city.

---

p. 75; C.C. Black, *The Disciples according to Mark: Markan Redaction in Current Debate* (JSNTSup, 27; Sheffield: JSOT Press, 1989), pp. 17, 21, 46-47.

1. For the focus on the Evangelist's theology within redaction-critical studies see especially N. Perrin, *What is Redaction Criticism?* (Guides to Biblical Scholarship; Philadelphia: Fortress Press, 1969), p. 1. See also J. Rohde, *Die redaktionsgeschichtliche Methode: Einführung und Sichtung des Forschungsstandes* (Hamburg: Furche, 1966), pp. 13, 17; R.H. Stein, 'What is *Redaktionsgeschichte*?', *JBL* 88 (1969), p. 46; Donahue, *Are You the Christ?*, p. 5. On the necessity of separating tradition from redaction within this method see also W. Marxsen, *Der Evangelist Markus: Studien zur Redaktionsgeschichte des Evangeliums* (FRLANT, 67; Göttingen: Vandenhoeck & Ruprecht, 1956), pp. 14, 16; Perrin, *Redaction Criticism*, p. 2; Stein, 'What is *Redaktionsgeschichte*?', p. 47.

2. Marxsen, *Der Evangelist Markus*, pp. 12-14; Rohde, *Methode*, pp. 21, 23-24; Perrin, *Redaction Criticism*, p. 39; Donahue, *Are You the Christ?*, p. 48.

3. See especially the following major redaction-critical studies on Mk 10.46-52: E.S. Johnson, 'Mark 10:46-52: Blind Bartimaeus', *CBQ* 40 (1978), pp. 191-204; P.J. Achtemeier, '"And He Followed Him": Miracles and Discipleship in Mk 10:46-52', *Semeia* 11 (1978), pp. 115-45; R. Busemann, *Die Jüngergemeinde nach Markus 10: Eine redaktionsgeschichtliche Untersuchung des 10. Kapitels im Markusevangelium* (BBB, 57; Königstein: Peter Hanstein, 1983), pp. 161-72.

More importantly, Mark added the conclusion to the pericope in order to present Bartimaeus as a true disciple, who follows Jesus in the way. According to these redaction critics, Mark strategically placed this passage at the end of the central section of his Gospel, where Jesus teaches his disciples concerning the cost of discipleship. In this way, Bartimaeus serves as a model of the insight and sacrifice that is necessary for true discipleship.[1]

Other redaction critics emphasize the Christology of Mk 10.46-52.[2] In general, the Christology of the passage is highlighted by arguing that Mark inserted the Son of David title into the Bartimaeus story. On this view, Mark added the Son of David title to Bartimaeus' cry

1. The idea that Mark used the Bartimaeus narrative to present his understanding of discipleship is found in a number of shorter redactional studies on Mk 10.46-52. See K.-G. Reploh, *Markus—Lehrer der Gemeinde: Eine redaktionsgeschichtliche Studie zu den Jüngerperikopen des Markus-Evangeliums* (Stuttgart: Katholisches Bibelwerk, 1969), pp. 222-26; K. Kertelge, *Die Wunder Jesu im Markusevangelium: Eine redaktionsgeschichtliche Untersuchung* (SANT, 23; Munich: Kösel, 1970), pp. 179-82; J. Roloff, *Das Kerygma und der irdische Jesus: Historische Motive in den Jesus-Erzählungen der Evangelien* (Göttingen: Vandenhoeck & Ruprecht, 2nd edn, 1973), pp. 121-26, 270; D.-A. Koch, *Die Bedeutung der Wundererzählungen für die Christologie des Markusevangeliums* (BZNW, supp. 42; Berlin: de Gruyter, 1975), pp. 126-32; E. Best, *Following Jesus: Discipleship in the Gospel of Mark* (JSNTSup, 4; Sheffield: JSOT Press, 1981), pp. 139-45. In addition, a number of commentaries which consistently use redaction criticism find Mark's teaching concerning discipleship in Mk 10.46-52. See D.E. Nineham, *Saint Mark* (Pelican Gospel Commentaries; Baltimore: Penguin Books, 1963), pp. 281-83, 286; E. Schweizer, *Das Evangelium nach Markus* (NTD; Göttingen: Vandenhoeck & Ruprecht, 1967), pp. 127-28; H. Anderson, *The Gospel of Mark* (NCB; London: Oliphants, 1976), pp. 258-59; J. Gnilka, *Das Evangelium nach Markus* (EKKNT; 2 vols.; Zürich: Benzinger Verlag; Neukirchen–Vluyn: Neukirchener Verlag, 1978–79), II, pp. 107-12.

2. See especially C. Burger, *Jesus als Davidssohn: Eine traditionsgeschichtliche Untersuchung* (FRLANT, 98; Göttingen: Vandenhoeck & Ruprecht, 1970), pp. 42-46, 59-63. V.K. Robbins ('The Healing of Blind Bartimaeus [10:46-52] in the Marcan Theology', *JBL* 92 [1973], pp. 224-43) regards both Christology and discipleship as important in Mk 10.46-52, but he emphasizes the Christology of the passage. For a similar approach see L. Schenke, *Die Wundererzählungen des Markusevangeliums* (Stuttgart: Katholisches Bibelwerk, 1974), pp. 350-69. Commentators who use redaction criticism and emphasize the Christology of the Bartimaeus passage include R. Pesch, *Das Markusevangelium II. Teil* (HTKNT; Freiburg: Herder, 1984), pp. 167-75; D. Lührmann, *Das Markusevangelium* (HNT; Tübingen: Mohr [Paul Siebeck], 1987), pp. 181-84.

for help and then created the rebuke of the crowd in order that the blind man might repeat this messianic title in his second cry. Mark clarified the significance of the Son of David title by placing the Bartimaeus narrative immediately before Jesus' entrance into Jerusalem. Through the Bartimaeus story, Mark prepared the way for Jesus to enter Jerusalem as the Son of David (11.10) and to act as the authoritative king in that city.

When analyzing Mk 10.46-52, redaction critics discover Mark's theology, his understanding of discipleship or his view of Christ. However, in focusing on Mark's theology, redaction-critical studies tend to neglect Mark's treatment of blind Bartimaeus. Mk 10.46-52 is interpreted in such a way that the passage is no longer about Bartimaeus and his response to Jesus. There is no attempt to understand how Mark characterized Bartimaeus, the primary actor in the story, or to see how this characterization relates to Mark's portrayal of similar characters who appear in the Gospel before and after Bartimaeus. The blind man becomes a symbol of Jesus' instruction on discipleship or a vehicle for the introduction of a christological title. In seeking to find the theology of Mark, redaction critics have missed an important part of the story.

Theology and Minor Characters in Mark's Gospel
Because of their interest in Mark's theology, redaction critics tend to neglect Mark's portrayal of minor characters.[1] Many aspects of Mark's treatment of minor characters are not explicitly theological. These aspects of Mark's characterization may not be immediately important for understanding Mark's theology, but they may be important for the interpretation of his narrative. Mark's portrayal of minor characters tends to appear insignificant to the critic who is primarily looking for theology.[2] Redaction-critical studies on the Bartimaeus

---

1. Black argues that the center of gravity in redaction criticism remains with the author-theologian. 'To be sure, practitioners of *Redaktionsgeschichte* believed that the method permitted them to intuit the particulars of the redactor's historical and sociological matrix and to interpret a Gospel as a literary product; but the point of entry, as well as the confirmation, for both of these investigations resided with the identification of the redactor's theology' (Black, 'Quest of Mark the Redactor', p. 22). See also Black, *Disciples according to Mark*, pp. 226-27.

2. Fowler argues that seeking only the theology of the Evangelist in the Gospel of Mark causes us to misinterpret the text. 'If one decides before approaching the text that the discovery of the theology of the writer is the goal to be obtained, then

story illustrate this point, since in looking for Mark's understanding of discipleship and Christology, they overlook Mark's presentation of Bartimaeus.

One difficulty with redaction criticism's emphasis on the theology of Mark is that the Gospel of Mark is not a theological essay. Although it contains theological ideas, Mark's Gospel is not a theological treatise, and it should not be treated as such. Therefore, isolating Mark's theology is not the final step in interpreting Mark's Gospel. The Gospel of Mark presents us with a narrative, a narration of a series of events, and if the Gospel of Mark is to be understood, its narrative features must be recognized.[1] This is important because a narrative communicates with a reader in a different manner than does a theological essay. Extracting the theology of the Gospel from its

theology is probably what one will find, whether it is there or not. The temptation is to mold the evidence to fit one's expectations: major and minor theological statements alike are elevated to the heights of theological sublimity; profound theological significance is found in the most trivial, non-theological affirmations; all the while the elements of the text which resist all efforts to be interpreted theologically are purposely ignored because they are irrelevant to the matter at hand' (R.M. Fowler, *Loaves and Fishes: The Function of the Feeding Stories in the Gospel of Mark* [SBLDS, 54; Chico, CA: Scholars Press, 1981], p. 41).

1.   Black argues that 'themes and other such literary characteristics rightly belong in the centre of an interpretation of Mark in a way that "theology" and "theological themes" do not, if for no other reason than that the form of the Second Gospel is not that of a self-consciously theological treatise. Mark is first of all a narrative and, at least on initial approach, should be treated as such' (Black, 'Quest of Mark the Redactor', p. 32). On this same point see also Black, *Disciples according to Mark*, p. 239. On the importance of treating narrative biblical texts precisely as narrative see W.S. Kurz, 'Narrative Approaches to Luke–Acts', *Bib* 68 (1987), p. 195; *idem*, *Reading Luke–Acts: Dynamics of Biblical Narrative* (Louisville, KY: Westminster Press/John Knox, 1993), p. 169. For arguments showing that Mark's Gospel presents a coherent narrative see N.R. Petersen, *Literary Criticism for New Testament Critics* (Guides to Biblical Scholarship; Philadelphia: Fortress Press, 1978), pp. 49-80; *idem*, '"Point of View" in Mark's Narrative', *Semeia* 12 (1978), pp. 97-121. H.W. Frei (*The Eclipse of Biblical Narrative: A Study of Eighteenth and Nineteenth Century Hermeneutics* [New Haven: Yale University Press, 1974]; *idem*, *The Identity of Jesus Christ: The Hermeneutical Bases of Dogmatic Theology* [Philadelphia: Fortress Press, 1975], pp. xiii-xiv; *idem*, 'The "Literal Reading" of Biblical Narrative in the Christian Tradition: Does it Stretch or Will it Break?', in F. McConnell (ed.), *The Bible and the Narrative Tradition* [New York: Oxford University Press, 1986], pp. 62-63) also argues for the need to understand the Gospels as realistic narrative.

narrative setting will cause us to miss the way that the author employs the narrative to move and influence the reader. If interpreters ignore the narrative features of Mark's Gospel, they will not adequately appreciate the potential impact of the story.[1] In fact, removing the theology of the Gospel from its narrative setting may even cause us to misunderstand the theology of the Gospel itself. Theological themes exist within the developing plot of the narrative, and their place within this narrative may affect the way that we understand them. 'Themes which, isolated from their narrative context, appear to be constant may actually shift significantly in meaning through some new development in the plot.'[2] Understanding the narrative of Mark's Gospel is necessary even for understanding the theology of Mark's Gospel.

This study will not look primarily for Mark's theology. It will examine the Gospel of Mark as a narrative and will seek to understand Mark's portrayal of minor characters as a feature of Mark's narrative. Mark's Gospel contains theological ideas, and it may indeed be a worthwhile task to determine the theology of the Evangelist. Nevertheless, if we want to understand Mark's Gospel, we must recognize that it is a narrative, and we must explain its narrative features and the way that the author uses these features to influence a reader.

Redaction and Minor Characters in Mark's Gospel
The redaction critic's attempt to uncover the theology of Mark is related to the task of separating tradition from redaction in the Gospel. After separating tradition from redaction, the redaction critic generally finds Mark's theology in the redactional elements of the text. Unfortunately, the traditional elements are then ignored since they are irrelevant to the issue at hand.[3] It is easy to see how this procedure

---

1.   S.D. Moore, 'Narrative Commentaries on the Bible: Context, Roots, and Prospects', *Forum* 3 (1987), pp. 32-35; D.C. Howell, *Matthew's Inclusive Story: A Study in the Narrative Rhetoric of the First Gospel* (JSNTSup, 42; Sheffield: JSOT Press, 1990), p. 24; R.C. Tannehill, 'Israel in Luke–Acts: A Tragic Story', *JBL* 104 (1985), pp. 70-71; *idem*, *The Narrative Unity of Luke–Acts: A Literary Interpretation. I. The Gospel according to Luke* (Philadelphia: Fortress Press, 1986), p. 8.

2.   R.C. Tannehill, 'The Composition of Acts 3-5: Narrative Development and Echo Effect', in K.H. Richards (ed.), *Society of Biblical Literature Seminar Papers 1984* (Chico, CA: Scholars Press, 1984), p. 217.

3.   D.O. Via, *Kerygma and Comedy in the New Testament: A Structuralist*

would lead the redaction critic to neglect Mark's portrayal of minor characters. Material that deals with minor characters is not redactional enough as well as not theological enough. Since the characterization of these individuals is generally assigned to the traditional material, it does not merit much attention from the redaction critic.

Several problems hamper the task of separating tradition from redaction as a way of discovering Mark's theology. One problem is found in the difficulty of distinguishing tradition from redaction in Mark's Gospel.[1] In order to make such distinctions, it is necessary to speculate on the history of traditions that lie behind the Gospel of Mark. Since the traditions that were available to Mark are not available to us today, distinctions between tradition and redaction cannot be verified completely, and often such divisions are based on insufficient evidence. This does not mean that it is wrong to attempt to separate tradition and redaction, but only that it is easy to overstate the reliability of one's conclusions.

A more serious problem with this procedure is that Mark's message and theological emphasis cannot be confined solely to the redactional elements of the Gospel.[2] 'The question of what is emphasized in a writing is logically separate from the question of the origin of material within it.'[3] Mark may have made changes in his traditional material which reflect only minor concerns on his part. Mark may also have incorporated traditional material without any alteration and then shaped his narrative in order to show that this material is significant within his Gospel. The importance of material in the Gospel is determined ultimately by its function and place in the narrative and not by its source.

Approach to Hermeneutic (Philadelphia: Fortress Press, 1975), p. 72.

1. Black, *Disciples according to Mark*, pp. 238-39; *idem*, 'Quest of Mark the Redactor', pp. 30-31; C.D. Marshall, *Faith as a Theme in Mark's Narrative* (SNTSMS, 64; Cambridge: Cambridge University Press, 1989), pp. 9-12; R.C. Tannehill, 'The Disciples in Mark: The Function of a Narrative Role', *JR* 57 (1977), p. 386; Via, *Kerygma and Comedy*, p. 73.

2. J.A. Darr, *On Character Building: The Reader and the Rhetoric of Characterization in Luke–Acts* (Literary Currents in Biblical Interpretation; Louisville, KY: Westminster Press/John Knox, 1992), p. 89; Fowler, *Loaves and Fishes*, pp. 177-79; Marshall, *Faith*, pp. 12-13; Tannehill, 'Disciples in Mark', p. 386; *idem*, *Luke*, p. 6; W.S. Vorster, 'Mark: Collector, Redactor, Author, Narrator?', *Journal of Theology for Southern Africa* 31 (1980), p. 54.

3. Tannehill, 'Disciples in Mark', p. 386.

Another problem with this procedure is that it focuses our attention on something other than the text of Mark's Gospel.[1] In seeking to distinguish between tradition and redaction, the redaction critic looks at something which lies behind the Gospel, the relation between Mark and his tradition. Likewise, in seeking to uncover the theology of the Evangelist, the redaction critic once again looks at something which stands behind the Gospel, the mind of Mark. Such studies have their place, but they present a problem if they claim to be an interpretation of Mark's text. In the end, redaction criticism focuses on material behind the text, not on the text in its final form.

Scholars have often sought to break down the Gospel of Mark into smaller parts and to examine how these different parts came together.[2] However, if it is valid to tear Mark's Gospel apart, it is also valid to put it back together and study it in its final form, as a whole.[3] Yet, as was stated before, Mark's Gospel as a whole is a narrative, so that studying the Gospel as a whole involves examining it as a narrative. This study of Mark's characterization of the individuals from the crowd will focus on the text of Mark as a whole, and it will therefore deal with Mark's Gospel as a narrative. This study will examine Mark's Gospel in its final form and will not seek to distinguish between tradition and redaction within the Gospel.

1. J.D. Kingsbury, *Matthew as Story* (Philadelphia: Fortress Press, 2nd edn, 1988), p. 2; Marshall, *Faith*, pp. 13-14; Petersen, *Literary Criticism*, pp. 18-19; M.A. Powell, *What is Narrative Criticism?* (Guides to Biblical Scholarship; Minneapolis: Fortress Press, 1990), pp. 7-8.

2. For a helpful discussion on the proper place for the source analysis of a narrative and on the relationship between studying the source and studying the discourse of a writing see M. Sternberg, *The Poetics of Biblical Narrative: Ideological Literature and the Drama of Reading* (Bloomington: Indiana University Press, 1985), pp. 7-23.

3. S.D. Moore (*Literary Criticism and the Gospels: The Theoretical Challenge* [New Haven: Yale University Press, 1989], pp. 4-9) points out that narrative critics emphasize the need to study a Gospel as a whole, although he himself would have difficulties with such a procedure.

Redaction-Critical Approaches to Characterization
in Mark's Gospel

Redaction critics tend to ignore Mark's portrayal of minor characters because of their stress on the importance of the theology and the redactional elements of the Gospel. Yet redaction critics also ignore Mark's portrayal of minor characters because of their approach to characterization. In a recent article, Jack Dean Kingsbury points out that redaction critics study characters with a view to their transparency.[1] Each Gospel was written to the members of the Evangelist's church living at the end of the first century. In light of this fact, redaction critics contend that the Evangelists wrote about the events, words and characters of the past so that they had immediate relevance of some kind for the post-Easter church and its situation. In this way, the material in the Gospels is 'transparent' and gives to us a picture of the Evangelists' churches.[2]

Thus, the characters in the Gospels are portrayed in such a way that they represent individuals or groups who would be recognizable to those within the Evangelists' churches. Kingsbury shows that redaction critics have studied the characters in the Gospel of Matthew in order to view Matthew's community. The characters in Matthew's Gospel are treated in the following way:

> Jesus himself is said to be transparent for the present of the church, for he has about him the aura of the risen Jesus. The Jewish leaders are transparent because they are meant to be representative of the Pharisaic Judaism of the first evangelist's own time. And the disciples, led by Peter, are transparent because they function in the story to school the members of the church in the ways of discipleship.[3]

Redaction critics deal with the characters in Mark's Gospel in the same way. It is not possible to illustrate this approach to characterization with minor characters, since redaction critics have not studied the manner in which Mark portrays them. One reason for this lack of

---

1. J.D. Kingsbury ('Reflections on "the Reader" of Matthew's Gospel', *NTS* 34 [1988], p. 446) limits his remarks to redaction-critical work on the Gospel of Matthew, but his study is relevant to redaction-critical approaches to Mark's Gospel as well.
2. Kingsbury, 'Reflections', pp. 445-46.
3. Kingsbury, 'Reflections', p. 446.

study may be that certain elements of their portrayal resist being treated as representations of the situation in Mark's church. In order to understand how redaction critics deal with characterization, it is necessary to see how they approach other characters in Mark's Gospel. The disciples are a character group in Mark that redaction critics have studied a great deal, and they definitely have studied the disciples with a view to their transparency. Therefore, a redaction-critical approach to characterization in the Gospel of Mark can be illustrated by looking at the way in which redaction critics deal with the disciples in Mark.[1]

Transparency and the Disciples in Mark's Gospel
What stands out about Mark's portrayal of the disciples is its negative tone. The disciples misunderstand and fail repeatedly in Mark's Gospel. Redaction critics have developed two different viewpoints on the function of this negative presentation of the disciples. This harsh portrait is considered to have either a polemical function or a pastoral function.[2] In either case, redaction critics hold that the portrayal of the disciples allows us to view the historical situation of Mark's church.

Theodore J. Weeden and Werner H. Kelber developed extensively the idea that Mark was arguing against certain opponents through his presentation of the disciples. According to Weeden, Mark wrote his Gospel in order to dramatize the christological conflict that was taking place within his own community.[3] Mark staged this conflict in a 'historical' drama in which Jesus serves as a representative for Mark and his viewpoint, while the disciples serve as representatives for Mark's opponents and their heresy. Mark believed that true messiahship is suffering messiahship, while his opponents regarded Jesus as a miracle-working divine man. In his Gospel, Mark totally discredited the disciples, since they hold to the false Christology of Mark's opponents.[4]

1. For an extensive study of redaction-critical analyses of the disciples in Mark's Gospel see Black, *Disciples according to Mark*.
2. This distinction between a polemical function and a pastoral function comes from Telford, *Interpretation*, pp. 23-26.
3. Weeden develops his approach to the disciples in Mark in his book *Mark—Traditions in Conflict*, but his basic viewpoint can also be found in 'The Heresy that Necessitated Mark's Gospel', *ZNW* 59 (1968), pp. 145-58.
4. J.D. Crossan ('Mark and the Relatives of Jesus', *NovT* 15 [1973], pp. 81-

While Weeden feels that Mark was combating a false Christology with eschatological overtones, Kelber holds that Mark was facing a false eschatology with christological overtones.[1] According to Kelber, Mark wrote his Gospel to explain the demise of Jerusalem Christianity during the Roman–Jewish war of 66–70 CE with its destruction of Jerusalem. The Jerusalem Christians brought disaster on themselves because of their false eschatology. They expected the parousia of Jesus in Jerusalem at a time of eschatological crisis. For Kelber, the disciples in Mark's Gospel serve as representatives of what came to be the Jerusalem church. The disciples aid and abet the tragic end of that church by failing to understand the new time and new place for the kingdom.[2]

Not all redaction critics feel that Mark wrote a polemic against the disciples. For example, Ernest Best argues that the disciples represent Mark's whole community.[3] When Mark portrayed the disciples negatively, he was using them as a foil, allowing Jesus to give them instruction. Mark emphasized the failure of the disciples with the intention of helping his own community through the teaching of Jesus. Moreover, Mark's portrayal of the disciples shows forth God's love and strength to those who fail. According to Best, the believers in Mark's community would then receive encouragement, since many of

113) builds on Weeden's thesis concerning Mark's portrayal of the disciples and connects it with Mark's treatment of the relatives of Jesus.

1. Weeden characterizes the difference between his position and that of Kelber in this way in 'The Conflict between Mark and his Opponents over Kingdom Theology', in G. MacRae (ed.), *Society of Biblical Literature Seminar Papers 1973* (Cambridge: Society of Biblical Literature, 1973), II, p. 204. Kelber develops his understanding of Mark's historical situation in W.H. Kelber, *The Kingdom in Mark: A New Place and a New Time* (Philadelphia: Fortress Press, 1974). A summary of his views may be found in *idem*, *Mark's Story of Jesus* (Philadelphia: Fortress Press, 1979), pp. 88-96.

2. It should be noted that Weeden and Kelber were not the first to argue for the polemical view of the disciples. See the following earlier works: J.B. Tyson, 'The Blindness of the Disciples in Mark', *JBL* 80 (1961), pp. 261-68; J. Schreiber, 'Die Christologie des Markus Evangeliums', *ZTK* 58 (1961), pp. 154-83; E. Trocmé, *La Formation de l'Evangile selon Marc* (Paris: Presses Universitaires de France, 1963), pp. 70-109.

3. Best discusses the relationship between Mark's portrayal of the disciples and Mark's historical situation in 'Role of the Disciples'. See also Best, *Following Jesus*, pp. 11-12, 246.

them may have already failed in the midst of persecution. In this way, the negative characterization of the disciples has a pastoral function.[1]

Transparency and Minor Characters in Mark's Gospel
Redaction-critical studies on the disciples in Mark show that this method approaches characterization with a view to transparency. The portrayal of the disciples has immediate relevance for Mark's church because the disciples represent either Mark's opponents or the members of Mark's church. Studying the characterization of the disciples allows us to gain a glimpse into the historical situation of Mark's community.

Examining this approach to characterization uncovers another reason why redaction critics tend to ignore Mark's portrayal of minor characters.[2] Important elements in the characterization of these individuals resist the notion of transparency. The characterization of Bartimaeus is a good example of this. Certain elements in the portrayal of Bartimaeus are important for the story and for comparison of him with similar characters in the narrative, and yet it is highly improbable that these elements are helpful for viewing the historical circumstances of Mark's church. Bartimaeus is a blind beggar. He hears that Jesus is coming. He leaves behind his cloak in coming to Jesus. He is healed of his blindness by Jesus. These aspects of Bartimaeus' characterization are important for Mark's story, but it is unlikely that they are immediately relevant to the historical situation of Mark's church.

---

1. For other redaction-critical studies that view the disciples as representative of the believers in Mark's own community see R.P. Meye, *Jesus and the Twelve: Discipleship and Revelation in Mark's Gospel* (Grand Rapids: Eerdmans, 1968), pp. 222-24; Reploh, *Markus*, pp. 228-30; D.J. Hawkin, 'The Incomprehension of the Disciples in the Marcan Redaction', *JBL* 91 (1972), pp. 491-500; C. Focant, 'L'Incompréhension des disciples dans le Deuxième Evangile', *RB* 82 (1975), pp. 161-85; J.R. Donahue, *The Theology and Setting of Discipleship in the Gospel of Mark* (Milwaukee: Marquette University, 1983).

2. Perhaps the closest that redaction critics come to studying the portrayal of minor characters is by commenting on Mark's characterization of the crowds. The issue of transparency is important also in redaction-critical studies of the crowd in Mark. See, for example, P.S. Minear, 'Audience Criticism and Markan Ecclesiology', in H. Baltensweiler and B. Reike (eds.), *Neues Testament und Geschichte: Historisches Geschehen und Deutung im Neuen Testament* (Zürich: Theologischer Verlag, 1972), pp. 79-89; Hawkin, 'Incomprehension of the Disciples', pp. 497-98.

Making transparency a crucial part of characterization faces certain difficulties. One problem is that the idea of transparency is used in an arbitrary manner rather than a systematic manner.[1] As already noted, certain elements in the portrayal of characters resist being read as representations of Mark's historical situation. This opens the possibility of using the notion of transparency in a selective manner. The choice of which characters and which aspects of their characterization represent Mark's historical situation is not decided finally by the method itself but by the individual redaction critic. The problem expands if the critic is not expected to provide confirmation from outside sources that such historical circumstances actually existed in the early church. 'The determination of exactly which characters, terms, or passages are or are not transparent for the present of the church ultimately proves to be not so much a function of method as of the personal opinion of the interpreter.'[2]

Another problem with the redaction-critical approach is that it oversimplifies the way in which characterization communicates with the reader.[3] A narrative certainly may communicate with the reader in a more complex manner than by simply presenting a symbolic representation of the reader's historical situation. Likewise, characterization may influence a reader in a more complex way than by simply confronting the reader with an allegory of his or her own historical circumstances.[4] Moving directly from Mark's story to Mark's historical circumstances can lead to a misunderstanding of Mark's story and its impact. In other words, making transparency a crucial aspect of characterization 'does not permit one to distinguish sufficiently between the "act of reading or hearing" and the "act of historical reconstruction"'.[5]

In light of these problems, this study will seek to analyze the way in which one set of characters, the minor characters from the crowd,

---

1. Kingsbury, 'Reflections', pp. 454, 460.
2. Kingsbury, 'Reflections', p. 460.
3. Kingsbury, 'Reflections', pp. 457-58.
4. E.S. Malbon, 'Fallible Followers: Women and Men in the Gospel of Mark', *Semeia* 28 (1983), p. 32; *idem*, 'Disciples/Crowds/Whoever', p. 123; J.C. Anderson, 'Matthew: Sermon and Story', in D.J. Lull (ed.), *Society of Biblical Literature Seminar Papers 1988* (Atlanta: Scholars Press, 1988), p. 506; Howell, *Inclusive Story*, pp. 205-208, 230-36; Darr, *Character Building*, pp. 24-25, 90-91.
5. Kingsbury, 'Reflections', p. 458.

function within the story and to explain the way that this characterization influences the reader. This does not mean that it is improper to study Mark's Gospel for the purpose of historical reconstruction. Historical reconstruction is legitimate, but it is not the focus of this study.[1] Instead, I will concentrate on understanding Mark's story. Such an approach should keep this study from ignoring important aspects of Mark's story and from confusing Mark's story with Mark's own historical situation.[2]

Literary-Critical Approaches to Minor
Characters in Mark's Gospel

In recent years, literary-critical studies on Mark's Gospel have sought to follow a holistic approach to the Gospel and to explore the narrative aspects of the text.[3] This has opened the way for an examination of the characters in Mark's narrative and the manner in which Mark's characterization influences the reader.[4] Two literary-critical studies that touch on Mark's portrayal of minor characters are particularly important for this study: 'The Gospel of Mark as Narrative Christology' by Robert C. Tannehill and *Mark as Story* by David Rhoads and Donald Michie.

Robert C. Tannehill

In many ways, Tannehill's article provides the point of departure for this study on minor characters in Mark's Gospel. The article calls attention to the need for a literary study on Mark's treatment of minor characters, but Tannehill does not pursue this study himself, since it is

---

1. On the relationship between historical criticism and literary criticism see Powell, *Narrative Criticism*, pp. 6-10, 96-98; Sternberg, *Poetics*, pp. 7-23.

2. Kingsbury, 'Reflections', pp. 458-59.

3. Two helpful introductions to the present state of literary-critical studies in the New Testament are Moore, *Literary Criticism*, and Powell, *Narrative Criticism*.

4. The following New Testament scholars have written on characterization in New Testament narratives: David R. Bauer, C. Clifton Black, Robert L. Brawley, Fred W. Burnett, Warren Carter, R. Alan Culpepper, John A. Darr, Joanna Dewey, J.A. du Rand, Richard A. Edwards, Stephen E. Fowl, David B. Gowler, Jack Dean Kingsbury, Hans-Josef Klauck, William S. Kurz, Elizabeth Struthers Malbon, Mark Alan Powell, David Rhoads, Jeffrey L. Staley, Mark W.G. Stibbe, Robert C. Tannehill, Mary Ann Tolbert and W.S. Vorster. For further information on their work see the bibliography.

tangential to the main concerns in his article.

According to Tannehill, Mark desired to present Jesus to his readers in such a way that he might clarify the significance of Jesus for their lives. Mark presented Jesus in the form of a story, and because of this, Tannehill wants to take seriously the narrative form of Mark in studying this Gospel's presentation of Jesus.[1] The statements and events recorded in Mark's Gospel should be understood as parts of a unified narrative. Although Mark divided his story into episodes, he also tied the story together with connecting threads of purpose and development. These unifying factors are revealed for the most part through the dominant commissions of the story.[2]

Tannehill finds in the Gospel of Mark a story of the commission that Jesus receives from God and of the way that Jesus takes to fulfill this commission. At the baptism, Jesus is commissioned as God's Son, and in the rest of the Gospel, Jesus fulfills this commission by acting out what it means to be God's Son. Tannehill points out two other dominant commissions. In Mk 1.16-20 Jesus commands certain disciples to follow him. The nature of the commission to follow Jesus is then gradually clarified as the narrative continues. In Mk 3.6 the opponents of Jesus choose a commission for themselves, the destruction of Jesus. These three commissions bind Mark's Gospel together as a single narrative, since they stretch across the Gospel and come to resolution only with the passion story or beyond.[3]

In fulfilling his commission, Jesus assumes certain roles as he interacts with other people. Tannehill studies these role relationships

1. Tannehill, 'Narrative Christology', p. 57.
2. Tannehill, 'Narrative Christology', p. 60. One difficulty with Tannehill's approach in this article is that he speaks of Mark as a unified narrative, but he does not define what he means by 'unified'. S.D. Moore ('Narrative Commentaries', pp. 52-53; *idem*, 'Are the Gospels Unified Narratives?', in K.H. Richards (ed.), *Society of Biblical Literature Seminar Papers 1987* [Atlanta: Scholars Press, 1987], pp. 443-58) points out that Tannehill and other narrative critics who emphasize the unity of the text often smooth over the jarring, ambiguous and perplexing features of the Gospels. For an attempt to confront Moore's complaint see Powell, *Narrative Criticism*, pp. 91-93. In his Acts commentary, Tannehill (*The Narrative Unity of Luke–Acts: A Literary Interpretation*. II. *The Acts of the Apostles* [Minneapolis: Fortress Press, 1990], pp. 6-8) emphasizes the unity of the narrative and shows how the unity is maintained through narrative developments. However, Tannehill does not want to argue that the unity is perfect or focus on unity as his sole concern.
3. Tannehill, 'Narrative Christology', pp. 61-62, 66.

as a way of better understanding Mark's presentation of Jesus and his commission. Four relationships are important, because they involve either developing roles or prominent repeated roles: Jesus' relationship with the disciples, with the opponents, with the supplicants and with the demons. The characters that Tannehill refers to as the supplicants belong to the minor characters from the crowd. Tannehill gives some attention to all four of these relationships, but he emphasizes Jesus' relationship with his disciples and his opponents since these involve significant developments that affect the story as a whole.[1]

Tannehill's comments on the supplicants or minor characters are significant for this study. According to Tannehill, Jesus' relationship with minor characters has a different status than his relationship with the disciples and with the opponents. Each episode that deals with a supplicant is complete in itself, while the material that presents the disciples and the opponents fits into progressive sequences which begin early in the Gospel and continue to its end. The passages on minor characters are not progressive but reiterative. Since these passages do not form a narrative sequence that unifies the story, they are not the focus of Tannehill's study. Nevertheless, as Tannehill points out, re-iteration makes possible a different kind of development. When similar episodes are repeated, points of emphasis and characterization may vary and develop throughout the narrative. An understanding of Jesus' relationship with minor characters may be enriched through the repetition of a basic pattern with variation.[2]

Thus, Tannehill points out the possibility of studying Mark's portrayal of minor characters by paying close attention to the way this presentation varies and develops from one episode to the next. Yet this is a possibility that he does not pursue because of his interest in the aspects of the narrative which unify the story.[3] Tannehill indicates that there are differences in the way that Mark portrays the disciples and opponents and in the way that he treats minor characters from the crowd. In spite of these differences, however, the portrayal of these

1. Tannehill, 'Narrative Christology', p. 63.
2. Tannehill, 'Narrative Christology', pp. 67-68.
3. In his work on the Gospel of Luke, Tannehill (*Luke*, pp. 89-96, 103-39) pursues further the study of repeated scenes. He does this with regard to Luke's repeated presentations of Jesus' contact with those who need healing and with those who are oppressed and excluded.

individuals is still worth studying. As Tannehill points out, Mark is concerned to present Jesus to his readers so that the significance of Jesus for their lives becomes clear. Yet it is impossible to clarify in a complete way Mark's vision of the proper response to Jesus without examining his portrayal of the responses of minor characters to Jesus.[1]

Therefore, this study will pick up where Tannehill's article left off, by tracing the characterization of the different individuals from the crowd in Mark's Gospel. Minor characters from the crowd appear in a sequence of repeating scenes, and this repetition highlights important developments in Mark's portrayal of these characters and their responses to Jesus. Mark's characterization of these individuals is part of his strategy for revealing to the reader the significance of Jesus. This study will examine how Mark's presentation of these characters and their responses to the expectations of Jesus influences the reader's own response to Jesus.

Tannehill emphasizes the differences between Mark's presentation of the disciples and opponents and his presentation of minor characters. Nevertheless, it is worth noting that these differing presentations contain similarities as well. Members of the crowd also receive commissions, because at times Jesus directs his commands to a wider group and not just to the disciples.[2] In this way, it is possible to evaluate the actions of individuals from the crowd by comparing their actions to the demands of Jesus. In addition, the developing portrayal of minor characters spans the whole narrative, since Mark has presented a sequence of repeated scenes that continue up to the passion and beyond. It is true that minor characters appear in one scene and then generally do not appear again in the Gospel. Yet Mark repeatedly presents such scenes and uses them to vary and develop his characterization. Mark begins these episodes early in his Gospel and continues them throughout the narrative as the story moves toward the cross and beyond. In fact, at the end of the Gospel when Mark has finished

1. Howell (*Inclusive Story*, pp. 217, 233-34) makes a similar point with regard to Matthew's Gospel. With regard to Mark's Gospel see Malbon, 'Fallible Followers', p. 30.

2. Tannehill himself ('Narrative Christology', p. 64) notes that Jesus' command to repent and believe in the Gospel (1.15) is general and applies to disciples, crowds and readers. Tannehill ('Narrative Christology', p. 81) also indicates that Jesus gives his instruction in 8.34-38 to the disciples and to others.

presenting the disciples, the opponents and Jesus, certain minor characters are still there (Mk 16.1-8).

David Rhoads and Donald Michie

Since the appearance of Tannehill's article, there has been only a minimal amount of work done on minor characters in Mark's Gospel. The book *Mark as Story* by Rhoads and Michie includes a brief description of Mark's treatment of minor characters.[1] The following summary of their work highlights three insights that help to define the task and focus of my work.

First, Rhoads and Michie point out that the portrayal of minor characters changes or develops through the course of the narrative.[2] For Rhoads and Michie, there is a degree of continuity in the characterization of these individuals throughout the story, but different characteristics are emphasized at different stages of the story. The portrayal of minor characters shifts in response to the emerging standards of Jesus in the narrative. According to Rhoads and Michie, Mark emphasized the faith of different individuals from the crowd in the first half of the Gospel. In the central section of the Gospel, which pertains to the journey of Jesus to Jerusalem, the minor characters from the crowd illustrate losing one's life, renouncing oneself and becoming the least. Mark emphasized the sacrificial service of these characters in the last part of the Gospel where Jesus is in Jerusalem.

Rhoads and Michie are certainly right in noting a development in Mark's treatment of minor characters through the course of the narrative. Moreover, several members of the crowd respond with faith in the first part of the story, while some individuals exemplify service in the last chapters of the Gospel. However, the claim that the minor characters from the crowd in the central section of Mark's Gospel

---

1.   D. Rhoads and D. Michie, *Mark as Story: An Introduction to the Narrative of a Gospel* (Philadelphia: Fortress Press, 1982), pp. 129-34. See also D. Rhoads, 'Narrative Criticism and the Gospel of Mark', *JAAR* 50 (1982), p. 419. J.D. Kingsbury (*Conflict in Mark: Jesus, Authorities, Disciples* [Minneapolis: Fortress Press, 1989], pp. 24-27) has written a short treatment of minor characters in Mark which parallels the work of Rhoads and Michie. Like Rhoads and Michie, Kingsbury shows that in the first half of Mark's Gospel, a number of minor characters exhibit faith. In the second half of Mark's Gospel, minor characters exemplify what it means to serve. Like Rhoads and Michie, Kingsbury shows that minor characters function as contrasting figures to the disciples.

2.   Rhoads and Michie, *Mark as Story*, p. 132.

illustrate losing one's life, renouncing oneself and becoming the least
is certainly inaccurate. On the whole, the developing presentation of
minor characters through the course of the narrative is much more
complicated than the outline of Rhoads and Michie would indicate.
The development of Mark's characterization through the narrative is
an area of study that needs further examination.

A second insight of Rhoads and Michie is that the minor characters
from the crowd serve as foils for the disciples.[1] Often, the actions and
attitudes of these minor characters stand in contrast to the actions and
attitudes of the disciples. Rhoads and Michie argue that at each stage
of the narrative, the minor characters exemplify traits which are
missing in the disciples. Minor characters respond with faith, while
the disciples struggle with disbelief. Minor characters illustrate being
the least, while the disciples strive for status and position. The
individuals from the crowd serve Jesus, while the disciples desert
Jesus.

A careful comparison between the minor characters from the crowd
and the disciples is important for an accurate understanding of both
groups of characters. At times, minor characters serve as contrasts to
the disciples. However, the relationship between minor characters and
the disciples is more complex than Rhoads and Michie envision. This
may be seen in the fact that the portrayal of the disciples is not always
entirely negative and the portrayal of minor characters from the
crowd is not always entirely positive.[2] In fact, at certain points in the
narrative, Mark depicts individuals from the crowd in a more
negative fashion than he does the disciples. The contrast between
minor characters and the disciples is a significant feature in Mark's
narrative, but this contrast is not found in every part of the story.

---

1.   Rhoads and Michie, *Mark as Story*, pp. 130, 132. This is also pointed out by
Tannehill, 'Disciples in Mark', pp. 404-405. See also Marshall, *Faith*, p. 77.

2.   The mixed portrayal of the disciples and the minor characters from the crowd
is a difficulty for Mary Ann Tolbert's analysis of these two character groups (*Sowing
the Gospel: Mark's World in Literary-Historical Perspective* [Minneapolis: Fortress
Press, 1989], pp. 123-24, 148-230). Mark moves between positive and negative
portrayals of the disciples and the minor characters throughout the story. Thus, the
disciples and the minor characters do not always fit easily into one of the four
categories represented by the types of soil found in the parable of the sower (4.1-20).
In his characterization of the disciples and minor characters, Mark is doing something
more complex than simply presenting the disciples as illustrations of the rocky
ground and the healed people as illustrations of the good earth.

Minor characters serve as foils for the disciples primarily in chs. 4–8 and in the passion narrative. To be sure, certain members of the crowd stand in contrast to the disciples, but a further clarification of the relationship between these characters and the disciples is needed in order to develop a more precise understanding of minor characters and their function in Mark's narrative.

A third insight of Rhoads and Michie is that Mark's treatment of minor characters makes an impact on the reader.[1] Rhoads and Michie view Mark's depiction of minor characters as entirely positive. The role of these individuals parallels that of Jesus, since they see the things of God and follow the teachings of Jesus. Thus, Mark only encourages the reader to identify with these minor characters.[2]

Mark used his portrayal of minor characters to influence readers, just as he used the rest of his narrative to influence readers. However, the reader's identification with minor characters is not as simple as Rhoads and Michie indicate. Minor characters are not always portrayed as exemplary figures, which complicates the influence of Mark's characterization on the reader. The manner in which Mark used minor characters to influence the reader is another area of study which demands further attention. The work of Rhoads and Michie, then, highlights the need for a more detailed study on Mark's treatment of minor characters. This study will examine the development of Mark's portrayal of the minor characters from the crowd through the course of the narrative, the relationship between this portrait and Mark's presentation of the disciples and the influence of Mark's characterization on the reader.[3]

The function of this chapter has been to clarify the basic approach of this study to Mark's portrayal of minor characters. The Gospel of Mark will be studied as a whole, in its final form. Since Mark's

1. Rhoads and Michie, *Mark as Story*, p. 130.
2. Rhoads and Michie, *Mark as Story*, pp. 133-34.
3. One other literary-critical study which touches on the characterization of minor characters is Elizabeth Struthers Malbon's article on the comparison between the disciples and the crowds in Mark ('Disciples/Crowds/Whoever'). Malbon wants to show that Mark uses the disciples and the crowd to create a composite image of the followers of Jesus. Malbon's approach is similar to that found in this study, since she includes within her discussion of the crowd a number of exceptional individuals. She also distinguishes between the crowd and the individuals who are singled out from the crowd and shows that the individuals from the crowd are presented in a highly positive manner. See Malbon, 'Disciples/Crowds/Whoever', p. 124.

Gospel as a whole is a narrative, it is crucial to understand the narrative features of the text and the way in which the narrative influences the reader. One aspect of Mark's narrative is his presentation of minor characters. Mark repeatedly introduces scenes in which individuals, who are neither disciples nor opponents, meet with Jesus. Mark brings these individuals into the narrative to show their contact with Jesus, and then generally they do not appear again. This study will explore the way in which Mark develops his characterization of these individuals throughout the Gospel and the manner in which this development influences the reader. In order to prepare for this exploration, the following chapter will deal with the nature of repetition, characterization and the reader.

Chapter 2

ANALOGIES, CHARACTERS AND READERS

The preceding chapter sought to demonstrate the need for a literary study of Mark's presentation of minor characters. Since Mark's Gospel is a narrative, an adequate interpretation of this Gospel involves an analysis of the narrative aspects of the text. This chapter explores the methodological issues involved in a narrative study of Mark's treatment of minor characters.

The thorough examination of narrative features is a recent development in Gospel research. Since the methodology of this narrative approach is less developed than the methodology of older approaches to the Gospels, it is necessary to lay a methodological foundation. Moreover, 'literary criticism' serves as a label for different approaches to the Gospels.[1] Literary criticism is not one simple, well-defined method, because literary critics use a variety of methods and depend on a wide range of studies dealing with narratives in general. Literary critics use studies on narratives in general in order to enhance their understanding of Gospel narrative, but such studies are based on differing theoretical presuppositions. This variety necessitates a clarification of the approach followed in this study.

In this chapter I will seek to explain the methodological approach taken in this narrative study of minor characters in Mark's Gospel.[2]

---

1. For introductions to current approaches to the literary criticism of biblical narrative see J.C. Anderson and S.D. Moore, 'Introduction: The Lives of Mark', in *idem* (eds.), *Mark and Method: New Approaches in Biblical Studies* (Minneapolis: Fortress Press, 1992), pp. 12-16; T. Longman, *Literary Approaches to Biblical Interpretation* (Foundations of Contemporary Interpretation, 3; Grand Rapids: Zondervan, 1987), pp. 19-45; Moore, 'Narrative Commentaries', pp. 39-53; *idem*, *Literary Criticism*; Powell, *Narrative Criticism*, pp. 11-21.

2. The methodology followed in this study may, in general, be categorized as narrative criticism. For introductions to this approach see E.S. Malbon, 'Narrative Criticism: How Does the Story Mean?', in Anderson and Moore (eds.), *Mark and*

I will examine the nature and function of analogous or repeating episodes, and will then investigate the concept of character and Mark's methods of characterization. Finally, I will explore the concept of the reader, the importance of the reading process and the influence of characterization on the reader.

Narrative Analogy and its Function

Mark presents a series of repeating episodes in which an individual comes out from the crowd and comes into contact with Jesus. Three literary critics, Robert Alter, Peter D. Miscall and Meir Sternberg, have explored the use of repeating or analogous stories within the narrative of the Hebrew Bible, and their work sheds light on the use of analogous episodes in Mark's narrative.[1]

Method, pp. 23-49; Powell, *Narrative Criticism*.

    1.   Gérard Genette and Susan Rubin Suleiman attempt to catalogue the kinds of repetition that are possible in any narrative. In dealing with the subject of narrative frequency, Gérard Genette (*Figures III* [Paris: Seuil, 1972], pp. 145-49) lists four possibilities with regard to repetition. He develops his list on the basis of the capacities for repetition in the narrated events of the story and the narrative statements of the text. First, a narrative may narrate once what happened once. Secondly, a narrative may narrate repeatedly what happened repeatedly. Thirdly, a narrative may narrate repeatedly what happened once. Fourthly, a narrative may narrate once what happened repeatedly. The repeating scenes in which Mark deals with minor characters fit into Genette's second category. Mark narrates repeatedly what happened repeatedly. Susan Rubin Suleiman ('Redundancy and the Readable Text', *Poetics Today* 1 [Spring 1980], pp. 122-32) attempts to develop an exhaustive list of the types of repetition that are possible in a narrative. In the process, she discovers 24 categories of repetition. Only four of these categories are relevant to Mark's use of repeating episodes in his depiction of minor characters. First, repetition may involve the same event or same sequence of events happening to more than one character. Secondly, repetition may involve several characters having the same qualities or accomplishing the same qualifying functions. Thirdly, repetition may involve several characters having the same syntagmatic function. Suleiman defines a syntagmatic function as any act which serves to advance the story. Fourthly, repetition may involve several characters having the same actantial function. Suleiman defines an actantial function as a set of actions which determines the general role of a character in the story.

The Nature of Narrative Analogy

According to Alter, the interpreter should note the use of narrative analogy when reading the narrative of the Hebrew Bible.[1] For Alter, a narrative analogy is a recurrent or parallel episode in the biblical story which provides a commentary on or a foil to another episode.[2] Such analogies are important because the biblical writers tend to avoid more explicit means of evaluating characters and actions.[3] As an example, Alter uses parallel episodes in the story of Jacob. In Genesis 27, Jacob receives the firstborn's blessing from his blind father through deception. The biblical writer later provides a commentary on Jacob's action by narrating how Jacob is deceived in the dark by receiving Leah instead of Rachel and then chided about the rights of the firstborn (Gen. 29.21-30).[4]

While noting the importance of narrative analogy in general, Alter is primarily interested in a specific kind of analogy, the 'type-scene'.[5] A coherent reading of biblical narrative requires some awareness of the grid of conventions upon which, and against which, the narrative works. An elaborate set of tacit agreements between the biblical writer and his audience about the ordering of the narrative provides the context in which communication took place. Alter wants to uncover the essential elements of biblical convention in order to understand biblical narrative more precisely. According to Alter, the biblical writers followed literary convention by including certain fixed situations in the careers of biblical heroes and by presenting these episodes according to a set order of motifs. Alter calls these recurrent narrative episodes 'type-scenes'. The biblical writers used a series of recurrent narrative episodes in the careers of biblical heroes in which they followed and manipulated a fixed constellation of predetermined motifs.

Alter's discussion of narrative analogy is useful for the study of Mark's portrayal of minor characters, but his emphasis on type-scenes

---

1.   R. Alter, *The Art of Biblical Narrative* (New York: Basic Books, 1981), pp. 179-80.

2.   R. Alter, 'A Literary Approach to the Bible', *Commentary* 60 (December 1975), p. 73; *idem, Art of Biblical Narrative*, pp. 21, 180.

3.   Alter, *Art of Biblical Narrative*, p. 180.

4.   Alter, *Art of Biblical Narrative*, p. 180.

5.   See Alter, *Art of Biblical Narrative*, pp. 47-51 for a description of Alter's understanding of type-scenes.

is less beneficial. Undoubtedly, Mark used traditional forms and
conventions in writing his Gospel. Nevertheless, it would be difficult
to argue that Mark followed a specific convention that established the
basic motifs to be included in an encounter between Jesus and a minor
character.[1]

Miscall builds on Alter's idea of narrative analogy and seeks to
show how this phenomenon facilitates interpretation.[2] Miscall uses the
term 'narrative analogy' to refer to passages that have enough in
common in terms of plot, characters, settings, theme or terminology
to be considered analogous and which must therefore be analyzed in
conjunction with one another to explain more fully the biblical text
under study.[3] The examination of narrative analogy is valuable,
because the comparative material raises and clarifies issues that might
otherwise be missed. In addition, narrative analogy is a tool that helps
the interpreter to see the text as a whole. Every part of the text is
integral to the whole, and each part modifies the meaning of the
whole. Therefore, a thorough interpretation of a text considers all the
parts of the text, not only on their own but also in relation to each
other. Miscall analyzes the Jacob and Joseph stories as one example of

---

1. In his commentary on Luke–Acts, Tannehill makes use of Alter's discussion
of type-scenes. Tannehill (*Luke*, pp. 18, 170; *idem, Acts*, p. 202) defines a type-
scene as a basic situation which appears several times within a narrative. Each occur-
rence has a similar set of characteristics, but this similarity permits variations and
additions in the development of the scene. Tannehill (*Luke*, pp. 103-105, 170-71)
labels several kinds of repeating scenes in Luke type-scenes. These include scenes in
which Jesus ministers to the oppressed and excluded, scenes in which Jesus eats
with tax collectors and sinners, scenes in which Jesus heals on the Sabbath, scenes
in which Jesus eats in a Pharisee's house and scenes in which a Jewish leader asks
Jesus what he must do to inherit eternal life. In his commentary on Acts, Tannehill
(*Acts*, pp. 201-203, 208, 221-29) isolates public accusation scenes, turning to the
Gentiles scenes and epiphanic commissioning scenes as type-scenes. The episodes
which Tannehill isolates are similar, and they are best understood when examined in
relation to one another. However, they should be regarded as type-scenes only if it is
established that Luke narrated them on the basis of certain literary conventions that he
shared with his audience. It is better to describe these repeating episodes as narrative
analogies.

2. P.D. Miscall, 'The Jacob and Joseph Stories as Analogies', *JSOT* 6 (1978),
pp. 28-40.

3. P.D. Miscall, *The Workings of Old Testament Narrative* (Philadelphia:
Fortress Press, 1983), p. 3; *idem, 1 Samuel: A Literary Reading* (Bloomington:
Indiana University, 1986), p. ix; *idem*, 'Jacob and Joseph', p. 29.

narrative analogy.[1] He notes the similarities between the two stories and shows how the two stories provide commentary on one another.

In his recent work, Miscall emphasizes the idea that narrative analogies add to the richness and openness of the biblical narrative.[2] Parallel texts do not 'clear things up' so that the consistent and definitive meaning of the text is discovered, but rather narrative analogies increase the ambiguity of the text. This emphasis coincides with Miscall's contention that a close reading of a biblical narrative forces the interpreter to recognize the undecidability and indeterminateness of the narrative.

Sternberg also analyzes repetition and analogy in the Hebrew Bible. For Sternberg, 'analogy is an essentially spatial pattern, composed of at least two elements...between which there is at least one point of similarity and one point of dissimilarity'.[3] The similarity allows the reader to link the two elements and the dissimilarity illumines, qualifies or concretizes both elements. Analogy takes place on the level of the plot where the reader finds equivalences and contrasts between events, characters and situations.[4] While analogy is essentially a spatial pattern connecting elements in different parts of the narrative, it is also influenced by the sequence of the text. Because of developments and disclosures in the narrative, an initially straight analogy may turn into a contrast. Moreover, the analogous elements may be disclosed only gradually as a means of influencing the reader into desired attitudes.[5]

Sternberg deals with the subject of analogy in general, but he is primarily interested in a specific type of analogy or repetition which he calls the 'structure of repetition'. In the structure of repetition, the analogous elements are so similar that the second element appears to be simply a complete repetition of the first. The structure of repetition presents a high degree of equivalence in form and meaning and an extreme in redundancy. Sternberg wants to explain why the redundancy is included since initially it does not seem to add anything new

---

1. Miscall, 'Jacob and Joseph', pp. 31-39.
2. Miscall, *Workings*, p. 3; *idem*, *1 Samuel*, p. ix.
3. Sternberg, *Poetics*, p. 365.
4. Sternberg, *Poetics*, p. 366.
5. Sternberg, *Poetics*, p. 480. On the importance of the sequence of the text in studying repetition see also J.C. Anderson, 'Double and Triple Stories, the Implied Reader, and Redundancy in Matthew', *Semeia* 31 (1985), pp. 72-73.

to the text.[1] For the most part, Sternberg's discussion on the structure
of repetition is not helpful for the study of repeating episodes in
Mark's Gospel, since these episodes are by no means redundant. The
scenes in which Mark presents individuals from the crowd include
both similarities and differences.

By way of summary, then, we can say that narrative analogy refers
to two or more texts in a narrative that show similarity in plot,
character, setting, theme or terminology. Through this similarity, the
narrator implies a connection and encourages the reader to compare
the texts as a way of better understanding each passage. In addition,
narrative analogy involves dissimilarity, since a parallel text is not an
exact repetition. A comparison of analogous episodes in a narrative
may reveal important differences which lead to a clearer understanding of each episode. The examination of narrative analogy grows
out of a concern for viewing the text as a whole, whereby the reader
examines each part of the narrative and studies the relationship
between the parts. How are the parts of the narrative related to one
another and what impact does this relationship have on the
understanding of the individual parts? The study of narrative analogy
is one attempt to answer this question. In Sternberg's terms, narrative
analogy is 'an essentially spatial pattern'.[2] In recognizing narrative
analogy, the reader connects passages from different parts of the
narrative and examines them in conjunction with one another.
Although it is a spatial pattern, narrative analogy is influenced by the
sequence of the story.[3] Developments in the overall plot and the order
in which the repeated events occur will influence the way in which
analogies are viewed. A later passage may draw together elements of
earlier passages which until that point seemed unrelated. Since a series
of analogous episodes will be influenced by the sequence of the
narrative, it will be important to examine the order of the narrative
analogies and their place in the overall plot.

---

1.   On the structure of repetition see Sternberg, *Poetics*, pp. 367-440.
2.   Sternberg, *Poetics*, p. 365. Sternberg (*Poetics*, p. 480) also refers to analogy
as a 'suprasequential form'.
3.   The importance of the sequence of the text in the reading process will be dealt
with later in this chapter.

The Use of Narrative Analogy in Mark
One contention in this study is that Mark narrated a series of
analogous episodes in the passages that present minor characters.
Although the analogous character of these episodes has been noted in
previous scholarship, the nature and function of these analogous
scenes have never been fully explored. Mark set up repeating scenes in
which minor characters have contact with Jesus. Since these different
passages are analogous, they should be analyzed in conjunction with
one another, and such an analysis should help to clarify the meaning
of each episode.

1. *Similarity and Analogy in Mark*
The similarity between the passages that deal with minor characters
mark them as narrative analogies. The passages are alike in that they
present similar characters, individual members of the crowd. These
characters are not disciples who have been specifically called and
commissioned by Jesus, nor are they opponents who reject the
teaching of Jesus and seek to destroy him, but rather they are part of
the crowd in the broad sense of that term. They are drawn from the
general population, from the many people who are neither disciples
nor opponents of Jesus. These characters make their appearance in the
narrative when they approach Jesus, but then, for the most part, they
disappear again from the narrative. Mark presents these minor
characters as those who come to Jesus for help or as those who
exemplify the teaching of Jesus. Mark repeatedly introduces minor
characters into his narrative, and the similar ways in which Mark
presents these individuals encourages the reader to regard passages
dealing with minor characters as analogous.[1]

Passages dealing with minor characters show a similarity in plot as
well as in characterization. A needy person comes to Jesus in faith.
Jesus solves the individual's difficulty with a miracle, after which the
person leaves and does not appear again in the narrative. This basic
plot appears repeatedly, reminding the reader to compare the passages
that follow this pattern. However, the basic plot within passages that

---

1.   In a similar way, Malbon ('Disciples/Crowds/Whoever', p. 124) examines
the individuals who are singled out from the crowd and shows that Mark presents
them in a positive manner. Marshall (*Faith*, pp. 75-77) deals with the individuals
who come to Jesus seeking help together with other minor characters who respond
positively to Jesus as a more or less unified character group.

present minor characters changes after the healing of blind Bartimaeus. In the narrative after Bartimaeus, Mark shows minor characters in some way living up to the expectations of Jesus. Bartimaeus himself is a transitional figure. Like minor characters in the preceding narrative, he is a needy person who is healed by Jesus because of his faith, and like minor characters in the subsequent narrative, he lives up to the expectations of Jesus, since he follows Jesus in the way. Part of the task of this study is to explain the nature of this development and its influence on the reader.

Passages that deal with minor characters also contain numerous thematic and lexical connections. These similarities in theme and terminology will be presented in the following chapters of this study as the individual passages are examined. The similarities in characterization, plot, theme and wording between the passages presenting minor characters point to the fact that these episodes are analogous to one another.

2. *Structure and Analogy in Mark*

There are also structural reasons for connecting passages on minor characters.[1] Throughout his Gospel, Mark arranges his material in such a way that he highlights the similarities between stories that present minor characters.[2] As Sternberg states, narrative analogy is a spatial pattern, and an examination of the patterning of material in the Gospel shows that Mark used care in his spatial arrangement of the episodes on minor characters.

Mark 2.1–3.6. Mk 2.1–3.6 contains two passages dealing with minor characters, the healing of the paralytic (2.1-12) and the healing of the man with the withered hand (3.1-6). These two stories contain a number of similarities, and the overall structure of Mk 2.1–3.6

1.   For a catalogue of possible structural relationships between literary units in the Gospels see D.R. Bauer, *The Structure of Matthew's Gospel: A Study in Literary Design* (JSNTSup, 31; Sheffield: Almond Press, 1988), pp. 13-19.

2.   For summaries of past approaches to the organization of Mark's Gospel see Trocmé, *Formation*, pp. 57-66; R. Pesch, *Naherwartungen: Tradition und Redaktion in Mk 13* (Düsseldorf: Patmos, 1968), pp. 48-53; J.M. Robinson, 'The Literary Composition of Mark', in M. Sabbe (ed.), *L'Evangile selon Marc: Tradition et rédaction* (Leuven: Leuven University Press, 2nd edn, 1988), pp. 11-13; F.G. Lang, 'Kompositionsanalyse des Markusevangeliums', *ZTK* 74 (1977), pp. 1-24.

enhances these analogous features. Mark organizes his material in this section in such a way that these two healing miracles function as parallel stories.

In all, Mk 2.1–3.6 presents five controversy stories: the healing of the paralytic (2.1-12), the question about eating with tax collectors and sinners (2.13-17), the question about fasting (2.18-22), the question about picking grain on the Sabbath (2.23-28) and the healing of the man with a withered hand (3.1-6). The theme of Jesus' conflict with the religious leaders pervades the section. Mark sets off these controversy stories as a literary unit by framing the section with similar statements concerning the popularity of Jesus. Immediately before the section, Mark states that Jesus was no longer able to appear openly in a city. Instead, Jesus stayed outside in the deserted places and people came to him from everywhere (1.45). Immediately after the controversy stories, Mark repeats this idea, by stating that Jesus withdrew to the sea and many people came to him from everywhere (3.7-8).[1]

In her analysis of the literary structure of Mk 2.1–3.6, Joanna Dewey has argued that Mark carefully arranged a chiastic structure with these controversy stories.[2] In this chiastic pattern, Mk 2.1-12 and 3.1-6 are parallel stories, because they contain similar healings, and Mk 2.13-17 and 2.23-28 are parallel, since they contain conflicts over the subject of eating. Mk 2.18-22, standing at the center of the chiasm, deals with the subject of fasting.

In analyzing this chiastic pattern, Dewey treats the two passages on the individuals from the crowd, Mk 2.1-12 and 3.1-6, as analogous episodes. Dewey is able to support her argument through the numerous connections between these two passages.[3] The stories begin with almost identical introductions. Mk 2.1 begins with καὶ εἰσελθὼν πάλιν εἰς, while the initial words of Mk 3.1 are καὶ εἰσῆλθεν πάλιν εἰς. According to Dewey, both stories use a mixed and

---

1.   J. Dewey ('The Literary Structure of the Controversy Stories in Mk 2:1-3:6', *JBL* 92 [1973], pp. 394-95; *idem, Markan Public Debate: Literary Technique, Concentric Structure, and Theology in Mk 2:1-3:6* [SBLDS, 48; Chico, CA: Scholars Press, 1980], p. 17) argues that Mk 2.1–3.6 should be regarded as a coherent literary unit.

2.   Dewey, 'Literary Structure', pp. 394-99; *idem, Public Debate*, pp. 109-16. See also A. Stock, 'Chiastic Awareness and Education in Antiquity', *BTB* 14 (1984), pp. 23, 26.

3.   Dewey, 'Literary Structure', pp. 395-96; *idem, Public Debate*, pp. 111-12.

relatively uncommon form, a controversy apophthegm inserted into a healing miracle. In each case, the controversy apophthegm is set off from the healing miracle by means of Jesus' twofold address to the healed man. In the first healing, the conflict section is framed by the words λέγει τῷ παραλυτικῷ (2.5, 10), and in the second healing, the controversy is framed by the words λέγει τῷ ἀνθρώπῳ (3.3, 5). Both healing stories use the word ἐγείρω. Mark uses ἐγείρω three times in the story of the healing of the paralytic (2.9, 11, 12), while in Mk 3.3, Jesus commands the man with a withered hand using the odd expression ἔγειρε εἰς τὸ μέσον. This brings the verb ἐγείρω into the healing miracle even though the healing itself does not raise the man up. The opponents of Jesus do not state their objection openly in either passage. In the first healing, Jesus confronts his opponents because of what they were reasoning in their hearts (καρδίαις, 2.6). In the second healing, Jesus responds with anger and grief at the hardness of their hearts (καρδίας, 3.5). In both situations, Jesus replies to the silent objection with a question. 'What is easier, to say to the paralytic, "Your sins are forgiven", or to say "Arise and take up your pallet and walk?"' (2.9). 'Is it lawful on the Sabbath to do good or to do wrong, to save a life or to kill?' (3.4). Jesus heals the paralytic and the man with the withered hand through his word alone (2.11-12; 3.5). Therefore, in light of these similarities, Dewey is able to support the parallel between Mk 2.1-12 and 3.1-6 in defense of her chiastic outline of Mk 2.1–3.6.

In fact, Dewey argues convincingly for the chiastic structure of the entire section of controversy stories. This chiastic pattern, in turn, underlines the analogous nature of Mk 2.1-12 and 3.1-6. The healing of the paralytic and the healing of the man with the withered hand function as narrative analogies not only because of the similarities between the two passages, but also because of their placement in the overall structure of Mk 2.1–3.6.

Mark 4.1–8.21. In Mk 3.9, the disciples prepare a boat for Jesus while he is ministering to a large crowd along the seashore. If the crowd becomes too large, Jesus will be able to enter into the boat and maintain a safe distance from the crowd. This detail concerning the boat is then dropped only to be revived again in Mk 4.1. There, Jesus is teaching the crowd alongside the sea and the size of the crowd causes Jesus to get into a boat and to teach from the boat as it floats on the sea. Prior to 4.1, Mark shows Jesus alongside the sea (1.16; 2.13; 3.7), but never in a boat on the sea. However, from Mk 4.1 until 8.22, Jesus is in and out of the boat traveling back and forth across the Sea of Galilee. In Mk 6.45, Jesus initiates one of these sea crossings by forcing his disciples to go ahead of him to the other side, to Bethsaida. Jesus meets them by walking on the sea, but a wind has blown the vessel off course so that they arrive at Gennesaret rather than Bethsaida. Eventually, in Mk 8.22, Jesus and his disciples arrive at Bethsaida by boat, and from that point on in the narrative the boat motif disappears.[1] Thus, through the repeated use of the boat, chs. 4–8 are distinguished from the preceding and following sections of the narrative.[2]

Within 4.1–8.21, Mark includes four passages that present minor characters: the deliverance of the Gerasene demoniac (5.1-20), the intercalated stories of Jairus and the hemorrhaging woman (5.21-43), the deliverance of the Syrophoenician woman's daughter (7.24-30) and the healing of the deaf man (7.31-37). Mark arranges these passages into two pairs.[3] He juxtaposes an exorcism and intertwined healing stories in ch. 5, and then places an exorcism next to a healing in ch. 7. In this way, Mark groups together similar stories dealing with minor characters.

In addition, the first of these miracle stories (5.1-20) and the last healing miracle in the section (7.31-37) are situated in similar settings. In 7.31, Mark takes Jesus through a rather complicated and unusual travel route in order to locate the healing of the deaf man in a setting that is reminiscent of the setting for the healing of the Gerasene demoniac. In 7.31, Jesus leaves the region of Tyre and goes through Sidon to the Sea (θάλασσαν, 7.31; cf. θαλάσσης, 5.1) of Galilee through the region (ὁρίων, 7.31; cf. ὁρίων, 5.17) of Decapolis (Δεκαπόλεως, 7.31; cf. Δεκαπόλει, 5.20). In Mark's Gospel,

---

1. Lührmann, *Markusevangelium*, p. 139; F.J. Matera, 'The Incomprehension of the Disciples and Peter's Confession (6,14-8,30)', *Bib* 70 (1989), pp. 167-68.

2. See especially N.R. Petersen, 'The Composition of Mk 4:1-8:26', *HTR* 73 (1980), pp. 194-96. On the idea that the boat motif binds together the individual stories in Mk 4–8 see also Kelber, *Story of Jesus*, p. 30; Lührmann, *Markusevangelium*, p. 93.

3. Malbon, 'Fallible Followers', pp. 36-37. On the similarities between these miracle stories see also E.S. Malbon, 'Echoes and Foreshadowings in Mark 4-8: Reading and Rereading', *JBL* 112 (1993), pp. 221-22.

Decapolis is mentioned only in 5.20 and 7.31. Thus, both the deliverance of the Gerasene demoniac and the healing of the deaf man take place by the Sea of Galilee near the region of Decapolis.

Moreover, Mark's initial description of the Syrophoenician woman is reminiscent of his presentation of Jairus and the hemorrhaging woman. In this way, Mark highlights the analogy between the miracles in 5.21-43 and the miracle in 7.24-30. Mark introduces the Syrophoenician woman as a woman who has heard about Jesus (ἀκούσασα γυνὴ περὶ αὐτοῦ, 7.25), thus echoing his initial description of the hemorrhaging woman as a woman who has heard about Jesus (γυνὴ...ἀκούσασα περὶ τοῦ Ἰησοῦ, 5.25-27). Like Jairus, the Syrophoenician woman makes an entreaty on behalf of a needy daughter (θυγάτριον, 7.25; cf. θυγάτριον, 5.23). In Mark's Gospel, the diminutive θυγάτριον is used only in 5.23 and 7.25. The Syrophoenician woman falls at Jesus' feet (προσέπεσεν πρὸς τοὺς πόδας αὐτοῦ, 7.25) which is reminiscent of the response of Jairus (πίπτει πρὸς τοὺς πόδας αὐτοῦ, 5.22) as well as the action of the hemorrhaging woman (προσέπεσεν αὐτῷ, 5.33). These connections serve to underline the similarity with which Jairus, the hemorrhaging woman and the Syrophoenician woman respond to Jesus.

Thus, Mark shows care in arranging the episodes on minor characters in this major section of the Gospel. Besides grouping these analogous passages on minor characters into two pairs of stories, Mark also uses a similar setting to tie together the first and the last and a similar characterization to connect the second and the third of these passages.

Mark 8.22–10.52. As has often been observed, Mark appears to have paid close attention to the structure of the central section in his Gospel.[1] In this section, Mark arranges his material around three

---

1.   The study of the structure of Mk 8.22–10.52 has been emphasized in the writings of Eduard Schweizer and Norman Perrin. See E. Schweizer, *Das Evangelium nach Markus* (NTD; Göttingen: Vandenhoeck & Ruprecht, 4th edn, 1975), p. 214; *idem*, 'Toward a Christology of Mark?', in J. Jervell and W.A. Meeks (eds.), *God's Christ and His People* (Oslo: Universitetsforlaget, 1977), p. 32; *idem*, 'The Portrayal of the Life of Faith in the Gospel of Mark', *Int* 32 (1978), pp. 388-89; *idem*, 'Die theologische Leistung des Markus', in R. Pesch (ed.), *Das Markus-Evangelium* (Darmstadt: Wissenschaftliche Buchgesellschaft, 1979), pp. 178, 183-84; N. Perrin, 'The Christology of Mark: A Study in Methodology', *JR* 51 (1971), p. 179; *idem*, 'Towards an Interpretation of the Gospel of Mark', in H.D. Betz (ed.), *Christology and a Modern Pilgrimage: A*

passion predictions by Jesus. In Mk 8.27-30, Jesus asks his disciples about his identity and Peter responds by stating that Jesus is the messiah. At this point, Jesus begins to teach the disciples that the Son of Man must suffer, be rejected, be killed and rise again. This is the first of the three predictions in Mark 8–10 concerning the passion and resurrection of the Son of Man (8.31). Similar predictions appear in Mk 9.31 and 10.33-34. Each prediction is followed by the mis-understanding of the disciples (8.32-33; 9.32, 38; 10.35-41), and Jesus responds to this misunderstanding by teaching the disciples about the nature of true discipleship (8.34–9.1; 9.33-37, 39-50; 10.42-45). This repeated pattern of prediction/misunderstanding/teaching about discipleship provides the basic structure for Mk 8.22–10.52.[1]

Mark's special care for the arrangement of his material in 8.22–10.52 extends to his placement of the episodes on minor characters. Mark includes a passage dealing with a minor character prior to each passion prediction. Before the confession of Peter and the first passion prediction, Jesus heals the blind man of Bethsaida (8.22-26). Prior to the second prediction, Jesus converses with the man whose son has an unclean spirit (9.14-29). Before the third prediction, Jesus deals with the rich man concerning eternal life (10.17-31). In this central section, Mark places passages on minor characters into similar positions in the overall structure of the section.

One further passage on a minor character appears at the end of this central section of Mark's Gospel. Jesus responds to the misunder-standing of the disciples with instructions on the nature of discipleship for the third time in Mk 10.42-45. The next passage after this instruc-tion presents the healing of blind Bartimaeus, so that Mk 8.22–10.52 ends with Jesus healing a blind man. This central section of Mark begins with the only other healing of a blind man in the Gospel, the healing of the blind man of Bethsaida. Consequently, Mk 8.22–10.52

Discussion with Norman Perrin (Missoula, MT: Scholars Press, 1974), pp. 3-9; *idem, The New Testament: An Introduction* (New York: Harcourt Brace Jovanovich, 1974), pp. 155-58.

1.   V.K. Robbins ('Summons and Outline in Mark: The Three-Step Progression', *NovT* 23 [1981], pp. 97-114; *idem, Jesus the Teacher: A Socio-Rhetorical Interpretation of Mark* [Philadelphia: Fortress Press, 1984], pp. 19-51) argues that a similar three-step pattern may be found throughout the Gospel of Mark wherever Jesus calls disciples. In each instance, the final step in the pattern features Jesus summoning disciples. According to Robbins, these three-step progressions form interludes in the narrative that establish the basic outline for Mark's Gospel.

opens and closes with two similar stories in which Jesus gives sight to
the blind.

Of the four passages that deal with minor characters in Mk 8.22–
10.52, the first and the last passages are similar in that they both deal
with the healing of a blind man. Similarities also exist between the
second and third passages that present minor characters (9.14-29;
10.17-31). After Jesus returns from the mount of transfiguration, the
crowd runs (προστρέχοντες) to Jesus and one (εἷς) from the crowd
presents Jesus with a problem concerning his son (9.15-17). In
Mk 10.17, one (εἷς) runs (προσδραμών) to Jesus and presents him
with a problem concerning eternal life. The men in both of these
stories address Jesus as 'Teacher' (διδάσκαλε, 9.17; 10.17, 20).
Neither of the men responds in an entirely positive manner toward
Jesus, since the man whose son has an unclean spirit expresses doubt as
to whether or not Jesus is able to help (9.22-23), and the rich man
leaves with grief when he learns that Jesus wants him to sell all that he
has and give to the poor (10.21-22). In both stories, Jesus uses the
events as a way of instructing his disciples (9.28-29; 10.23-31). Both
passages deal with the issue of what is possible. All things are possible
to the one who believes (πάντα δυνατὰ τῷ πιστεύοντι, 9.23). All
things are possible with God (πάντα γὰρ δυνατὰ παρὰ τῷ θεῷ,
10.27). The similarity between these two passages strengthens the
analogous relationship between them.

The structure of Mk 8.22–10.52 serves to highlight the similarities
between passages on minor characters. Stories dealing with minor
characters appear before each of the three passion predictions in
Mk 8.22–10.52, and this central section of Mark begins and ends with
Jesus giving sight to blind men.

Mark 11.1–13.37. In chs. 11–13, Mark organizes his material around
three journeys of Jesus to the temple.[1] After the triumphal entry, Jesus
comes to the temple, surveys the situation and leaves for Bethany with
his disciples (11.11). On the next day, Jesus casts out of the temple
those who were buying and selling and then does not allow anyone to
carry a vessel through the temple (11.15-17). When Jesus arrives at
the temple on the third day, he engages in a series of controversies

1.   On the overall outline of Mk 11–13 see Dewey, *Public Debate*, p. 56; Kelber,
Story of Jesus, p. 57; S.H. Smith, 'The Literary Structure of Mk 11:1-12:40', *NovT*
31 (1989), pp. 104-24.

with the religious leaders (11.27–12.44). Upon leaving the temple, Jesus predicts the destruction of the temple (13.1-2) which leads to the apocalyptic discourse that Jesus gives as he sits on the Mount of Olives opposite the temple (13.3-37).

This section of Mark on the relationship between Jesus and the temple includes two passages that present minor characters. They appear in the midst of the controversy stories that take place on Jesus' third day in the temple. When Jesus arrives at the temple, he is met by the chief priests, scribes and elders who demand from Jesus an explanation for his cleansing of the temple. Jesus refuses to answer their question directly, but proceeds with a parable in which he claims authority as God's beloved Son. Following the parable, Jesus engages in a series of three debates, first on taxes (12.13-17), then on the resurrection (12.18-27) and finally on the greatest commandment (12.28-34). In the first two debates, Jesus speaks with religious leaders who are hostile toward him and his teaching. In the third debate, Jesus answers the question of an individual, a scribe, who is receptive to Jesus and swayed by his teaching. Following the three debates, Mark records three teaching sections in which Jesus does not respond to questions, but rather takes the initiative in giving instruction. Jesus teaches on the identity of David's son (12.35-37), the hypocrisy of the scribes (12.38-40) and the gift of the widow (12.41-44). In the first two sections, Jesus reacts against the teaching and lifestyle of a hostile group, the scribes. In the third teaching passage, Jesus commends the action of an individual, a poor widow, who gives all that she has. Mark 12 is composed of a parable, three debates and three teachings.[1] Jesus commends an individual in the third debate and the third teaching passage, with the result that passages on minor characters appear in similar positions.

The connection between the scribe of 12.28-34 and the widow of Mk 12.41-44 is strengthened by the juxtaposition of scribes and widows in the verses between these two passages.[2] In Mk 12.35-40,

---

1. Perrin offers a similar outline of Mk 12 in *New Testament*, pp. 158-59. See also Smith, 'Literary Structure', pp. 119-21.

2. Donahue (*Are You the Christ?*, p. 116) argues that Mark constructs this section by means of sequential appearances of adversaries and catchwords. Mark places together three controversies in 12.28-40 since they each deal with the scribes. The denunciation of the scribes in 12.38-40 and the commendation of the widow in 12.41-44 are connected by the catchword χήρα.

Jesus questions the teaching of the scribes and denounces their behavior. Jesus condemns the scribes in part because they devour the homes of widows. Jesus' teaching in Mk 12.35-40 connects scribes and widows and also provides a basis for contrast. The individual scribe shows interest in the first commandment, while the scribes in general desire the first seats in the synagogue and the first places in the banquets (12.28, 39). The possessions of the widows are mercilessly devoured by the scribes, but the individual widow freely gives all that she owns (12.40, 44). The connection between scribes and widows in this intervening material encourages the reader to compare the understanding scribe and the giving widow.

Mark 14.1–16.8. The first incident in Mark's passion narrative, the anointing of Jesus in Bethany, not only introduces the passion narrative but also serves to link the passion narrative with the preceding section. Before and after the apocalyptic discourse, Jesus commends the gift of a woman. The story of the poor widow and the story of the woman who anoints Jesus have much in common.[1] The poor widow gives all that she has, and her costly giving stands in contrast to the giving of others who share out of their abundance. The woman who anoints Jesus pours on his head an expensive perfume, and her costly giving stands in contrast to the complaint of others who do not recognize the importance of the presence of Jesus. Jesus commends the actions of both women, and in each case he begins his commendation with the words ἀμὴν λέγω ὑμῖν (12.43; 14.9). The first story presents a poor (πτωχή) widow who does well, while the second story shows that the poor (πτωχούς) may be helped at any time. In both stories, the actions of the women stand in contrast to the actions of Jesus' opponents in the immediate context. The scribes act with pretense and desire public recognition, while in secret they devour the possessions of the poor (12.38-40). The poor widow does her good in secret. Only Jesus notices. The story of the anointing of Jesus is interposed between the plot of the chief priests and scribes to kill Jesus and

---

1. Dewey (*Public Debate*, p. 154) compares the two stories and argues that these two similar stories form a frame around the apocalyptic discourse. See also S.C. Barton, 'Mark as Narrative: The Story of the Anointing Woman (Mk 14.3-9)', *ExpTim* 102 (1991), pp. 231-32; E.S. Malbon, 'The Poor Widow and her Poor Rich Readers', *CBQ* 53 (1991), pp. 598-99; *idem*, 'Fallible Followers', p. 39.

the offer of Judas to deliver Jesus to them (14.1-2, 10-11). While the opponents of Jesus seek to kill him, the woman shows kindness to Jesus by acting in advance to anoint his body for burial. The giving of the poor widow and the giving of the woman at Bethany show progression as well as similarity. The poor widow gives her whole life (βίος), while the woman at Bethany anoints Jesus for burial. Their actions foreshadow events which will take place in the passion narrative. Thus Mark places these two analogous episodes on either side of the apocalyptic discourse.[1]

The anointing at Bethany ties the passion narrative to the previous section of Mark's Gospel, but it also plays a role in the structure of the passion narrative. Mark's passion narrative begins and ends with women seeking to anoint Jesus for burial (14.3-9; 16.1-8).[2] The woman at Bethany anoints Jesus' body before his burial, while Mary Magdalene, Mary the mother of James and Salome seek to anoint Jesus after his burial. In this way Mark places analogous events on either side of the passion narrative. He also introduces analogous passages on minor characters on either side of the crucifixion account. On the way to the crucifixion Simon of Cyrene serves Jesus by taking up his cross (15.21), and after the death of Jesus Joseph of Arimathea serves Jesus by taking his body down from the cross and laying it in a tomb (15.42-47). Both of these men act in ways that have been associated with discipleship earlier in Mark's Gospel (cf. 6.29; 8.34). There is only one other mention of a minor character in the passion narrative. At the high point of the crucifixion account, the centurion sees Jesus breathe his last and says, 'Truly, this man was the Son of God' (15.39).

Throughout his Gospel, Mark appears to arrange carefully the episodes on minor characters in order to strengthen the idea that these passages serve as narrative analogies. The structure of the Gospel highlights the similarities between stories that present individual

---

1. In addition, the word ὅλος is used in both passages. In Mk 12.44 Jesus states that the widow gave her whole (ὅλον) life, while in Mk 14.9 he states that the woman will be remembered in the whole (ὅλον) world because of her gift. Also, ἔχω is used in a similar manner in both passages. In Mk 12.44 Jesus states that the poor widow cast in all that she had (ὅσα εἶχεν ἔβαλεν), while in Mk 14.8 he states that the woman did what she could (ὃ ἔσχεν ἐποίησεν).

2. Barton, 'Mark as Narrative', p. 232; A.T. Lincoln, 'The Promise and the Failure: Mk 16:7, 8', *JBL* 108 (1989), p. 288; Trocmé, *Formation*, p. 66.

members of the crowd. Since these episodes are analogous, they should be examined in conjunction with one another.

The Function of Narrative Analogy

In his Gospel, Mark relates a series of repeating scenes in which individuals come out from the crowd to have contact with Jesus. While these episodes contain differences, they also show repeated similarities. Why would Mark include repetitive material in his Gospel? This question raises the issue of the function of narrative analogy.[1] Within a narrative, repetition may serve a number of purposes.

One function of repetition in a narrative is to emphasize matters that are central to the proper understanding of the story.[2] Through repetition, Mark is able to underline the ideas that he regards as important. For example, he repeatedly displays certain characteristics in minor characters as a way of emphasizing the significance of such qualities. In Mk 1.14-15 the Evangelist summarizes the message of Jesus with the words, 'The time has been fulfilled and the kingdom of God has drawn near; repent and believe in the gospel'. According to Mark, believing is a crucial aspect of a proper response to the proclamation of Jesus. Mark is able to emphasize the importance of

---

1.   On the function of repetition in narratives outside the New Testament see Alter, *Art of Biblical Narrative*, pp. 88-113; Genette, *Figures III*, pp. 145-82; B.F. Kawin, *Telling it Again and Again: Repetition in Literature and Film* (Ithaca, NY: Cornell University Press, 1972); R. Scholes, *Elements of Fiction* (New York: Oxford University Press, 1968), pp. 35-40; Sternberg, *Poetics*, pp. 365-440; Suleiman, 'Redundancy', pp. 132-39; S. Wittag, 'Formulaic Style and the Problem of Redundancy', *Centrum* 1 (1973), pp. 123-36. On the function of repetition in New Testament narratives see Anderson, 'Redundancy in Matthew', pp. 71-73, 82-85; F.W. Burnett, 'Prolegomenon to Reading Matthew's Eschatological Discourse: Redundancy and the Education of the Reader in Matthew', *Semeia* 31 (1985), pp. 91-109; R.A. Culpepper, *Anatomy of the Fourth Gospel: A Study in Literary Design* (FFNT; Philadelphia: Fortress Press, 1983), pp. 73-75; Rhoads and Michie, *Mark as Story*, pp. 46-47; R.C. Tannehill, *The Sword of His Mouth* (SBLSS, 1; Philadelphia: Fortress Press, 1975), pp. 39-45; *idem*, *Acts*, pp. 49-50, 74-77; *idem*, 'Composition', pp. 217-40; *idem*, *Luke*, pp. 93-94, 103-105, 170-71.

2.   Alter, *Art of Biblical Narrative*, p. 97; Anderson, 'Redundancy in Matthew', p. 72; Bauer, *Structure*, p. 13; R.M. Fowler, *Let the Reader Understand: Reader-Response Criticism and the Gospel of Mark* (Minneapolis: Fortress Press, 1991), p. 140; Powell, *Narrative Criticism*, pp. 39-40; Rhoads and Michie, *Mark as Story*, p. 46; Tannehill, *Acts*, pp. 50, 75; *idem*, 'Composition', pp. 229, 238; *idem*, *Sword*, pp. 40-41, 43.

faith by repeatedly portraying minor characters as responding to Jesus with faith.

Repetition also highlights variations.[1] Repeating episodes contain both similarities and differences, since repetition without variation is impossible.[2] Repetition emphasizes similarities and accentuates differences. In this way, the narration of similar situations with variations adds resonance to the story.[3] Placing different characters in similar situations allows the narrator to explore possible responses. Through his repeated depiction of minor characters and their reactions to Jesus, Mark is able to define in a greater way his understanding of the proper response to Jesus.

In addition, significant differences in repeating episodes may signal new developments in character and plot.[4] Repetition allows the narrator to create a pattern but then to alter the pattern as a way of signaling the development of a new design. In the passages that present minor characters, Mark uses variations in order to indicate developments in his portrayal of these individuals. He will present a series of minor characters according to a similar configuration of characteristics, but then he will alter this configuration in order to establish a new pattern of traits. Thus, certain minor characters become transitional figures. They possess characteristics which make them similar to minor characters in preceding scenes, but they also have traits which make them different. Mark takes up these new traits and begins to repeat them in his portrayal of minor characters in the following scenes. These developments in characterization are marked through the use of repetition with variation. Perhaps the most decisive development in Mark's portrayal of minor characters takes place in the characterization of Bartimaeus, although significant differences also appear in Mark's treatment of the women who follow Jesus to the cross and to the tomb (15.40-41; 16.1-8).

---

1. Anderson, 'Redundancy in Matthew', pp. 72, 85; Tannehill, *Acts*, pp. 50, 76; *idem*, 'Composition', pp. 229, 239; *idem*, *Sword*, p. 44.

2. G. Genette, 'L'autre du même', *Corps Ecrit* 15 (1985), pp. 11-13; *idem*, *Figures III*, pp. 145-46.

3. Rhoads and Michie, *Mark as Story*, p. 47; Tannehill, *Acts*, pp. 49-50, 76-77; *idem*, 'Composition', pp. 229, 240; *idem*, *Luke*, pp. 94, 105, 170-71.

4. Alter, *Art of Biblical Narrative*, pp. 97-98, 100; Tannehill, 'Composition', p. 239.

Repetition also creates expectations.[1] Through repetition, a narrator may establish a pattern and, with the pattern, the expectation that the pattern will continue. Similar characters, in similar situations, are expected to respond in similar ways, but these expectations may or may not be fulfilled in the narrative. Mark repeatedly presents minor characters as people who are not silent. Jesus commands the leper to say nothing to anyone about his healing, but the leper speaks freely and spreads the word concerning Jesus (1.44-45). Jesus commands the Gerasene demoniac to report to his people what the Lord did for him, and he goes out and proclaims the great things that Jesus did for him (5.19-20). Jesus insists that no one should talk about his healing of the deaf man, but the people freely proclaim the news. The more that Jesus demands silence, the more the people speak about his miraculous power (7.36). Many people tell Bartimaeus to be silent, but he cries out all the more for the mercy of Jesus (10.48). Through repetition, Mark creates the expectation that minor characters will speak freely when they are confronted by the miraculous power of Jesus. This expectation may or may not be confirmed as the narrative progresses.

Mark, then, narrates a series of analogous episodes dealing with minor characters. Passages which present these individuals show important similarities in character, plot, theme and wording, and, moreover, the structure of Mark's Gospel highlights the connections between these passages. Since these episodes dealing with minor characters serve as narrative analogies, they should be analyzed in conjunction with one another. Mark uses these repeating scenes to emphasize central themes, highlight variations, signal developments and create expectations.

Character and Characterization

It is beyond the scope of this study to present a complete exegesis of these analogous passages in which individual members of the crowd come into contact with Jesus. The focus of this study is on one aspect of the narrative in these passages, the characterization of these individuals from the crowd.[2] This focus necessitates an examination of the

---

1. Anderson, 'Redundancy in Matthew', pp. 84-85; Tannehill, *Acts*, pp. 75-76; *idem*, 'Composition', pp. 217, 239; *idem*, *Sword*, pp. 43-44.

2. On the importance of character portrayal in literary analysis and composition in the Hellenistic period see Weeden, *Traditions in Conflict*, pp. 12-19;

methodological issues surrounding the nature of character and the means by which characters are portrayed in narratives. What is character? How are characters inferred from a narrative text? What methods of characterization does Mark use in his narrative?

The Concept of Character

Understanding the people in Mark's Gospel is different than understanding living people.[1] The people in Mark's Gospel exist within a narrative, and a narrator conveys the information about them. What is known about these people is controlled by a narrator who influences both the extent of the information and the manner of its presentation. Differences exist between characters in a narrative and living people because of the mediating role of the narrator.[2]

A narrator shapes the reader's understanding of characters in a number of ways. To begin with, a narrator controls the amount of information that is available to the reader concerning a character.[3] A

Malbon, 'Jewish Leaders', pp. 259-61.

1.   A number of critics emphasize the idea that understanding characters in narratives differs from understanding people in our everyday experience. See Culpepper, *Anatomy*, p. 105; Darr, *Character Building*, p. 47; E.M. Forster, *Aspects of the Novel* (New York: Harcourt Brace, 1927), pp. 69-99; B. Hochman, *Character in Literature* (Ithaca, NY: Cornell University Press, 1985), pp. 59-85; M. Price, *Forms of Life: Character and Moral Imagination in the Novel* (New Haven: Yale University Press, 1983), pp. 44-45; *idem*, 'The Other Self: Thoughts about Character in the Novel', in M. Mack and I. Gregor (eds.), *Imagined Worlds* (London: Methuen, 1968), pp. 288-89, 292-93; Scholes, *Elements*, pp. 17-19; R. Schwartz, 'Free Will and Character Autonomy in the Bible', *Notre Dame English Journal* 15 (Winter 1983), p. 51; M. Sternberg, *Expositional Modes and Temporal Ordering in Fiction* (Baltimore: Johns Hopkins University Press, 1978), pp. 96-97; W.S. Vorster, 'Characterization of Peter in the Gospel of Mark', *Neot* 21 (1987), p. 61; R. Wilson, 'On Character: A Reply to Martin Price', *Critical Inquiry* 2 (1975), pp. 194-95; *idem*, 'The Bright Chimera: Character as a Literary Term', *Critical Inquiry* 5 (1979), p. 748. Scholes clearly states his position on this matter: 'The greatest mistake we can make in dealing with characters in fiction is to insist on their "reality". No character in a book is a real person. Not even if he is in a history book and is called Ulysses S. Grant. Characters in fiction are *like* real people. They are also unlike them' (Scholes, *Elements*, p. 17).

2.   On the validity of referring to people in biblical narratives as characters see Culpepper, *Anatomy*, pp. 105-106; Longman, *Literary Approaches*, p. 88.

3.   Hochman, *Character*, p. 61; Vorster, 'Characterization', p. 61; Wilson, 'On Character', p. 195.

great deal more can be known about a living person than about a
character in a narrative, because in a narrative only a selective part of
a character's personality and story is presented. In Mark's Gospel a
limited amount of data is given concerning minor characters. Jesus is
the most fully depicted figure in Mark's Gospel, but the information
about him is also limited. This limitation of information increases the
significance of the material that is available to the reader concerning a
character.[1] Characters provide less evidence than living people, but
the evidence is more significant, because it is selected and organized
by the narrator. The information discovered about living people is
generally unplanned, accidental and random. The limited information
in Mark's Gospel concerning characters is important, because it is
carefully chosen and planned.

The narrator not only controls the extent of the data on a character,
but also chooses the order in which the information is presented.[2] In
studying characters in a narrative, it is necessary to analyze the order
of the presentation and the effect of that arrangement on the reader's
understanding of a character. For example, Mark chooses to delay a
clear statement concerning the necessity of Jesus' death until ch. 8 of
his Gospel. A more natural presentation would provide the reader
with this crucial and relevant information about Jesus' mission at the
initial introduction of Jesus.[3] Since Mark delays this information, it is
worth analyzing the effect of this delay on the overall portrayal of
Jesus in the Gospel.

A narrator is able to increase the depth and clarity of the information available to the reader concerning a character.[4] The personalities
of living people are often opaque, complicated and confusing. A narrative, however, may provide a deep and clear understanding of a
character by revealing aspects of the individual which would normally
be hidden from observation. A narrative may relate a character's
hidden motives, inner thoughts and secret actions. For example,
Mk 3.1-6 provides data concerning the thoughts and actions of
characters that a first-hand observer would miss. When Jesus comes to
a synagogue where there is a man with a withered hand, Jesus' opponents watch him in order to see if he will heal the man on the Sabbath.

1. Hochman, *Character*, p. 61; Wilson, 'On Character', p. 195.
2. Sternberg, *Expositional Modes*, pp. 96-97.
3. See Sternberg, *Expositional Modes*, p. 98.
4. Forster, *Aspects*, pp. 69-99.

Mark displays the motives of these opponents, for he indicates that they desired to accuse Jesus of breaking the Sabbath. Mark also reveals the inner thoughts of Jesus by pointing out that Jesus observed the opponents with anger and that he was grieved at the hardness of their hearts. After presenting Jesus' healing of the man's hand, Mark shows the secret actions of the opponents. The Pharisees leave and discuss with the Herodians how they might destroy Jesus. Mark provides information about hidden thoughts and actions in order to convey a clear understanding of Jesus and his opponents.

Mark's Gospel is a narrative, a narration of a series of events, and the narrative form of the Gospel influences the reader's understanding of the characters within the Gospel. The unique circumstances involved in understanding people in a narrative necessitate an examination of the manner in which narratives work to portray characters. One influential approach to character in narrative is that of Seymour Chatman.[1] Chatman constructs his viewpoint on character in reaction to a structuralist approach which, in general, treats characters as participants rather than as beings.[2] Since structuralists emphasize the controlling nature of the plot, they regard characters as functions of the plot. Therefore, they analyze only what characters do in a story and make no attempt to reconstruct who the characters are. On this model, the actions of the characters rather than their traits or qualities are important in a narrative. Thus, structuralists are interested in the roles that characters play in the overall plot of the story.[3] Moreover, structuralists argue that the roles that characters take in a plot are limited and typical.[4] Narratives follow an underlying structure which

1. S. Chatman, 'On the Formalist-Structuralist Theory of Character', *Journal of Literary Semantics* 1 (1972), pp. 57-79; *idem, Story and Discourse: Narrative Structure in Fiction and Film* (Ithaca, NY: Cornell University Press, 1978), pp. 107-38. For a survey of approaches to character among literary critics in the twentieth century see Hochman, *Character*, pp. 13-40.

2. J. Culler, *Structuralist Poetics: Structuralism, Linguistics, and the Study of Literature* (Ithaca, NY: Cornell University Press, 1975), pp. 230-32; Chatman, 'Formalist-Structuralist Theory', p. 57; *idem, Story*, pp. 111-16.

3. Certain New Testament critics have been influenced by this structuralist approach and have analyzed the characters in the New Testament narratives according to the roles that they play in the story. See Tannehill, 'Disciples in Mark', p. 388; *idem*, 'Narrative Christology', pp. 58-60, 63; *idem, Luke*, pp. 1, 5; Culpepper, *Anatomy*, pp. 102-103.

4. Culler, *Structuralist*, p. 235; Chatman, 'Formalist-Structuralist Theory',

provides only a limited number of roles for the characters of the narrative, so that any particular character will fit into one of a limited number of slots.

In response to the structuralist viewpoint, Chatman argues that both character and plot are logically necessary to any narrative, and where the chief interest lies is a matter of the changing tastes of authors and critics.[1] Since stories require both events and beings, characters should be treated as autonomous beings and not merely plot functions. Moreover, Chatman wants to preserve an open theory of character. He has no desire to classify characters into a limited number of roles or functions.[2] For Chatman, characters are autonomous beings which are reconstructed by the reader from the evidence announced or implicit in the text. The reader reconstructs what characters are like. Thus, Chatman wants to analyze not only the actions of characters but also the traits or qualities of characters. Chatman defines character, then, as a 'paradigm of traits'.[3] A trait is any distinguishable way in which one individual differs from another. For the purpose of analyzing a narrative, a trait is an adjective which labels a personal quality of a character that persists over a part or the whole of the story.[4] Chatman regards traits as relatively stable or abiding personal qualities, but he also recognizes that a character's traits may change in the course of a story. Traits may emerge earlier or later in a narrative and may disappear or be replaced in the course of the story.[5]

This study follows Chatman's approach to character in narrative. Characters in Mark's Gospel are analyzed according to their qualities as well as their actions. Different minor characters are examined in order to reconstruct the narrator's view of what they are like by inferring the traits of these individuals from the crowd from the manner in which they are portrayed in Mark's Gospel.

p. 57; *idem*, *Story*, p. 111.
1. Chatman, 'Formalist-Structuralist Theory', p. 78; *idem*, *Story*, p. 113.
2. Chatman, *Story*, pp. 119-20.
3. Chatman, *Story*, p. 126.
4. Chatman, *Story*, pp. 121, 125. See also J. Garvey, 'Characterization in Narrative', *Poetics* 7 (1978), pp. 72-73.
5. Chatman, *Story*, p. 126.

The Nature of Characterization

Shlomith Rimmon-Kenan builds on Chatman's work by analyzing the process by which a reader reconstructs a character from the details given in a narrative text.[1] Rimmon-Kenan bases her understanding of character and characterization on the essential components of narrative. For Rimmon-Kenan, a narrative is the narration of a succession of events.[2] This definition leads to a clarification of the basic components of a narrative: the events, their verbal representation and the act of telling or writing. Rimmon-Kenan labels these three aspects story, text and narration.[3] 'Story' refers to the narrated events abstracted from their place in the text and then reconstructed in their chronological order and to the characters who participate in these events. 'Text' designates a spoken or written discourse which relates the story. In this discourse, the events do not necessarily appear in chronological order and all the traits of the characters do not necessarily appear at the first introduction of the characters. Moreover, in the discourse, all the contents of the story are filtered through a particular perspective. 'Narration' refers to the act of producing the spoken or written discourse. For Rimmon-Kenan, character is part of the story and characterization belongs to the text.

Characters exist in the story. They are constructs put together by the reader from the various indicators dispersed throughout the text.[4] Although characters in a narrative are different than living people in

1. S. Rimmon-Kenan, *Narrative Fiction: Contemporary Poetics* (London: Methuen, 1983), pp. 29-42, 59-70. The main interest of Rimmon-Kenan's book is in narrative fiction, but she points out that some of the procedures used in analyzing narrative fiction may also be applied to narratives conventionally defined as non-fiction. For a discussion of this point see Rimmon-Kenan, *Narrative Fiction*, p. 3.

2. Rimmon-Kenan, *Narrative Fiction*, p. 2.

3. Rimmon-Kenan, *Narrative Fiction*, p. 3. In making this threefold distinction, Rimmon-Kenan is relying primarily on Genette's classification of narrative into *histoire*, *récit* and *narration*. See Genette, *Figures III*, p. 72. The distinction between story and text dates back to the Russian Formalists who distinguished between the *fabula* and *sjužet*. See V. Erlich, *Russian Formalism: History-Doctrine* (The Hague: Mouton, 3rd edn, 1969), p. 240. Chatman (*Story*, pp. 9, 19) uses the terms 'story' and 'discourse' in order to distinguish between the content of the story and the means by which the story is told.

4. Rimmon-Kenan, *Narrative Fiction*, pp. 33, 36; Chatman, *Story*, p. 125; U. Margolin, 'Characterization in Narrative: Some Theoretical Prolegomena', *Neophilologus* 67 (1983), pp. 1, 9; *idem*, 'The Doer and the Deed: Action as a Basis for Characterization in Narrative', *Poetics Today* 7 (1986), pp. 205-206.

everyday experience, they are modeled after the reader's conception of people, and so they are person-like. In reconstructing a character, the reader makes inferences drawn from the information given in the text, and what is inferred is a set of traits. In addition, Rimmon-Kenan points out that the reader's reconstruction of a character is influenced by the sequence of the text.[1] In the course of the narrative, the reader may come upon an element in the text which does not fit with his or her understanding of a particular character. In this case, the reader's construct may be mistaken—a mistake which may have been encouraged by the text—or the character may have changed. Thus, a proper understanding of character must take into account the possibility of the character's development.

While characters exist in the story, characterization exists in the text.[2] A character can be described as a network of traits, but these traits may or may not appear explicitly in the text. The construct of a character is produced by assembling various character indicators distributed in the text and, when necessary, inferring the traits from them. Rimmon-Kenan labels the textual indicators of traits 'characterization'. A text may define a character directly by naming the trait with an adjective or abstract noun, but a text may also present a trait indirectly by displaying and exemplifying it in various ways. The reader is then left with the task of inferring the quality from the indirect presentation. Any element in the text may serve as an indicator of a trait, and indications of traits may serve other purposes in the narrative as well.

Thus, characterization refers to the elements in a narrative text which state or present the traits of a particular character. This study is on the characterization of minor characters in Mark's Gospel, and will therefore analyze the indications that Mark uses to present these individuals. It is an attempt to clarify the elements in Mark's narrative that define or present the traits of minor characters.

The Means of Characterization in Mark

Mark uses a number of literary devices to characterize the people in his Gospel, and the following list identifies the most important of these. Certain literary critics have sought to provide comprehensive

1. Rimmon-Kenan, *Narrative Fiction*, pp. 38-39.
2. Rimmon-Kenan, *Narrative Fiction*, pp. 59-60.

lists of the literary devices that may be used to express character-ization in narrative. The following list, however, deals specifically with Mark's narrative and provides examples from the Gospel of Mark. The list begins with the most explicit and moves on to the most covert means of characterization. At times, Mark specifically states the qualities of his characters, and at other times he leaves the reader to make inferences about what these people are like. In Mark's Gospel, characterization takes place through the following means.

1. The narrator may directly state the traits of a character.[1] Since the narrator of Mark's Gospel is reliable, this information given by the narrator is both certain and explicit.[2] Although Mark does not often state the qualities of people in the form of an adjective, he does use this means of characterization. Mark tells the reader that the demonic spirits were unclean (ἀκάθαρτος, 1.23, 26; 3.11; 5.2, 13; 6.7; 7.25; 9.25), that John the Baptist was righteous (δίκαιον) and holy (ἅγιον, 6.20), that Herod was deeply grieved (περίλυπος) at the request of Herodias's daughter (6.26), that Peter, James and John were terrified (ἔκφοβοι) at the transfiguration of Jesus (9.6) and that the widow who gave two coins was poor (πτωχή, 12.42).[3]

2. The narrator may express an evaluation of what a character is like without directly stating a trait.[4] In other words, the narrator may use a grammatical construction other than an adjective in order to communicate what the character is like. In such cases, the narrator's description may serve to advance the plot as well as to characterize a person. Once again, in this case, the narrator's viewpoint is reliable, but the description is less explicit. By stating that Jesus was teaching as one who had authority and not as the scribes (1.22), Mark characterizes Jesus as authoritative. Mark portrays Jesus as angry

---

1. See S. Bar-Efrat, *Narrative Art in the Bible* (JSOTSup, 70; Sheffield: Almond Press, 1989), pp. 53-54; A. Berlin, *Poetics and Interpretation of Biblical Narrative* (Bible and Literature Series, 9; Sheffield: Almond Press, 1983), pp. 34-36; D.B. Gowler, *Host, Guest, Enemy, and Friend: Portraits of the Pharisees in Luke and Acts* (Emory Studies in Early Christianity; New York: Peter Lang, 1991), pp. 55-59; Rimmon-Kenan, *Narrative Fiction*, pp. 59-60; Sternberg, *Poetics*, p. 476.

2. On the reliability of the narrator in Mark's Gospel see Fowler, *Let the Reader Understand*, pp. 61-64; Malbon, 'Narrative Criticism', p. 28; Powell, *Narrative Criticism*, p. 26.

3. See also Mk 9.26, 14.52 and 15.43.

4. Sternberg, *Poetics*, p. 476; Alter, *Art of Biblical Narrative*, p. 117.

when he states that Jesus looked at his opponents with anger, because he was grieved at the hardness of their hearts (3.5). Mark indicates that the chief priests were envious, in that they delivered Jesus up on account of their envy (15.10). Throughout the narrative, Mark uses verbs with an intransitive sense that express the traits of characters. The crowd is amazed (ἐξίστασθαι, 2.12), the people of Nazareth are offended (ἐσκανδαλίζοντο, 6.3), the disciples' hearts are hardened (πεπωρωμένη, 6.52), Jesus is distressed (ἐκθαμβεῖσθαι, 14.33), and the women at the tomb are both distressed (ἐξεθαμβήθησαν, 16.5) and afraid (ἐφοβοῦντο, 16.8). When a character is first introduced into the narrative, Mark often gives a brief description of the person. In general, the description conveys information about the character without directly stating the character's traits. For example, when Mark introduces Joseph of Arimathea, he calls him a prominent member of the council who was waiting for the kingdom of God (15.43).[1]

3. A character may directly state the traits of another character.[2] This means of characterization is less explicit because of the source of the information. The characters in Mark's narrative may or may not be reliable, and the reader is forced to weigh the value of the different claims. Since Mark presents Jesus as authoritative, Jesus' characterization of others is trustworthy. Jesus accurately depicts the disciples as without understanding (ἀσύνετοι, 7.18) and the people of his generation as unbelieving (ἄπιστος, 9.19). Because the opponents of Jesus are not reliable in Mark's Gospel, the reader cannot immediately accept their characterization of others. The chief priests and elders and scribes are wrong in condemning Jesus as guilty (ἔνοχον) and worthy of death (14.64). Nevertheless, the opponents of Jesus may characterize others accurately. When the Pharisees and Herodians tell Jesus that he is truthful (ἀληθής, 12.14), their statement is correct, but their praise is used to deceive and trap Jesus.[3]

4. A character may express an evaluation of what another character is like without directly stating the person's traits.[4] In other

---

1. See also Mk 1.1, 4-6; 5.2-5, 25-26; 7.25-26; 10.46; 12.18; 15.7, 40-41.
2. Alter, *Art of Biblical Narrative*, p. 117; Bar-Efrat, *Narrative Art*, pp. 53-56; Gowler, *Portraits*, pp. 59-61; Margolin, 'Characterization', p. 8; Sternberg, *Poetics*, p. 476.
3. See also Mk 1.7, 11; 4.40; 8.38; 9.7, 34; 10.17; 12.34, 43; 13.13; 14.38, 70.
4. Bar-Efrat, *Narrative Art*, pp. 56-58; Sternberg, *Poetics*, p. 476.

words, characters may use a grammatical construction other than an adjective in order to communicate their understanding of another person. Since the statements of characters vary in their truthfulness, the reader must analyze both the reliability of the speaker and the speaker's characterization. Jesus accurately describes the Pharisees and the scribes as hypocrites (7.6) and offers an example of their hypocritical behavior (7.8-13). When opponents evaluate Jesus, their evaluation is often wrong. For the scribes, Jesus is one who blasphemes (2.7). For his family, Jesus has lost his mind (3.21). For the scribes from Jerusalem, Jesus is possessed by an unclean spirit (3.22, 30). For the people of Nazareth, Jesus is only a carpenter and not worthy of honor (6.2-4).

5. A character may express an evaluation of another character through the use of a drastic action that speaks for itself.[1] Characters may communicate their understanding of others through deeds rather than through words. Jesus does not label the actions of those who buy, sell and serve in the temple as inappropriate and dishonest. Instead, he expresses his evaluation by casting out those who are involved in commerce in the temple, overturning the tables of the moneychangers and refusing to allow anyone to carry a vessel through the temple (11.15-16). When Jesus states that Jairus's daughter is not dead but sleeping, those who are mourning her death laugh at Jesus (5.40). Their action reveals that they regard Jesus as foolish. The soldiers mock Jesus, beat him and spit at him (15.16-20). With their words, they call Jesus King of the Jews, but with their deeds, they show that they regard Jesus as a powerless fool who deserves cruelty rather than respect.

6. A narrator may show the traits of a character by presenting the character's inward thoughts.[2] This means of characterization is less explicit, because, instead of directly stating what a character is like, the narrator shows the reader the person's thoughts and leaves the reader to make inferences concerning the person's traits. At times, Mark reveals the thoughts of his characters in order that the reader

---

1. Sternberg, *Poetics*, pp. 476-77.

2. Alter, *Art of Biblical Narrative*, p. 117; Bar-Efrat, *Narrative Art*, pp. 58-59, 63-64; Berlin, *Poetics*, pp. 37-38; Gowler, *Portraits*, p. 62; Margolin, 'Characterization', p. 8; Rimmon-Kenan, *Narrative Fiction*, p. 63; Sternberg, *Poetics*, pp. 477-78. See also the discussion of inside views in Fowler, *Let the Reader Understand*, pp. 120-26.

may have an accurate picture of their attitudes, feelings and intentions. These inward thoughts may not be perceptible in the outward actions and words of the characters. Outwardly, some of the scribes are silent, but inwardly they accuse Jesus of blasphemy for claiming to forgive sins (2.6-7). This inward look shows the reader their true attitude. Mark tells the reader that Jesus felt love for the rich man when he gave the man the difficult command to sell all that he possessed and give to the poor (10.21). The reader is left to make inferences about a character when Mark reports a character's thoughts. In a similar way, the reader must make inferences with some of the following means of characterization, with Mark's presentation of a character's actions, speech and appearance.

7. The narrator may show the traits of a character by presenting the character's actions.[1] Mark's characterization frequently takes place through the display of people's actions. He does not include long descriptions of his characters, but rather he shows what they do and allows the reader to make inferences concerning their traits. For example, instead of stating that Peter was deeply sorrowful, Mark shows Peter weeping (14.72). A narrator may imply character traits through habitual actions or through a single act.[2] For example, the disciples in Mark's Gospel repeatedly respond with incomprehension, while one act of betrayal marks Judas as a betrayer (3.19; 14.10-11, 18-21, 42-45).

8. The narrator may show the traits of a character by presenting the character's speech.[3] Mark not only presents the actions of his characters, but he also reports their words. Mark tells the reader that Jesus taught with authority (1.22), and he also includes the authoritative words of Jesus. On the other hand, the words of the disciples show their lack of understanding. For example, Jesus indicates to his disciples that he wants to feed a great crowd of people, and the

---

1. Alter, *Art of Biblical Narrative*, p. 116; Bar-Efrat, *Narrative Art*, pp. 77-86; Berlin, *Poetics*, p. 38; Gowler, *Portraits*, pp. 63-65; Margolin, 'Characterization', p. 8; *idem*, 'Doer', pp. 208-25; Rimmon-Kenan, *Narrative Fiction*, p. 61.

2. Rimmon-Kenan, *Narrative Fiction*, p. 61.

3. Alter, *Art of Biblical Narrative*, p. 117; Bar-Efrat, *Narrative Art*, pp. 64-77; Berlin, *Poetics*, p. 38; Gowler, *Portraits*, pp. 62-63; Margolin, 'Characterization', p. 8; Rimmon-Kenan, *Narrative Fiction*, p. 63. See also M.A. Powell, 'Direct and Indirect Phraseology in the Gospel of Matthew', in E.H. Lovering (ed.), *Society of Biblical Literature Seminar Papers 1991* (Atlanta: Scholars Press, 1991), pp. 405-17.

disciples answer him by saying, 'How will anyone be able to feed these people with bread here in the wilderness?' (8.4). This question shows a stubborn lack of understanding, because Jesus has already fed a crowd of over five thousand. The words of Jesus' opponents reveal their deceit. Mark reports the deceitful questioning of the Pharisees and the Herodians who want to trap Jesus. They flatter Jesus as one who teaches the way of God in truth and pretend to desire Jesus' teaching on the payment of tax to Caesar (12.13-15), but Jesus recognizes their hypocrisy and refuses to fall into their trap.

9. The narrator may show the traits of a character by presenting the character's appearance.[1] Mark uses this means of characterization infrequently, so that his portraits of the external appearance of people contain mostly empty canvas. One exception is Mark's portrayal of John the Baptist, who is shown clothed with camel hair and wearing a leather belt around his waist (1.6).[2] Thus, Mark characterizes John the Baptist as one who is similar to the prophet Elijah (2 Kgs 1.8).

10. The narrator may highlight the traits of a character through the use of analogy.[3] When two different characters are presented in similar circumstances, the similarities or differences in their responses emphasize the distinctive traits of both. This means of characterization is less explicit than the presentation of a character's actions and words, because it requires the reader to make inferences concerning the actions and words of two characters rather than one character.

Mark often presents analogous scenes which highlight the qualities of different characters. For example, Mark intertwines his account of the trial of Jesus with his account of the testing of Peter. In Mk 14.53, Jesus is led away to the high priest and the Sanhedrin. In the next verse, Mark relates how Peter followed Jesus at a distance right into the courtyard of the high priest where he sat with the servants and warmed himself by the fire. In vv. 55-65, Mark deals with the trial of Jesus before the Sanhedrin, and in vv. 66-72 he presents an analogous scene, the testing of Peter. Mark connects these two similar events and, by so doing, he is able to contrast the distinctive traits of Jesus

---

1. Alter, *Art of Biblical Narrative*, p. 116; Bar-Efrat, *Narrative Art*, pp. 48-53; Gowler, *Portraits*, pp. 65-67; Margolin, 'Characterization', p. 8; Rimmon-Kenan, *Narrative Fiction*, p. 65.

2. See also Mk 3.1; 5.15; 9.3, 18; 12.38; 14.51-52; 15.17; 16.5.

3. Berlin, *Poetics*, p. 40; Gowler, *Portraits*, p. 73; Margolin, 'Characterization', p. 8; Rimmon-Kenan, *Narrative Fiction*, pp. 67-69; Sternberg, *Poetics*, pp. 479-80.

and Peter. Jesus faces false accusations and inconsistent testimonies, but he responds with silence. Peter faces a true accusation and consistent testimonies, but he responds with denials. When the high priest questions Jesus, he answers with the truth even though this response will lead to his condemnation. The servant girl of the high priest confronts Peter, but Peter answers with a lie. At the end of his trial, Jesus is mocked and ridiculed for presenting himself as a prophet. At the end of his testing, Peter remembers with sorrow that the prophecy of Jesus concerning his failure had come true. A comparison of the responses of Jesus and Peter highlights their contrasting characteristics. Jesus is truthful and courageous, innocent and yet condemned, while Peter is dishonest and cowardly, guilty and yet not condemned.

As argued earlier in this chapter, Mark's use of analogy affects the characterization of minor characters, since he places minor characters into analogous situations. A comparison of the passages that deal with these characters will highlight the traits of these individuals.

11. The narrator may influence the reconstruction of a character's traits through the order of presentation.[1] This means of characterization is less explicit than the presentation of a character's actions and words, because it requires the reader to make inferences concerning the character's actions and words and also concerning the order of their appearance in the narrative. First impressions are important in life, but they are more important in narratives, because in narratives they are controlled by the narrator. For example, the reader's reconstruction of what Jesus is like is influenced by Mark's initial introduction of Jesus as the messiah, the Son of God (1.1). The order of the narrator's presentation is especially important when it involves a displacement in the chronological or logical order of the story. For example, Mark delays his presentation of John the Baptist's death, taking it out of its proper chronological place in the story (6.17-29). It is worth analyzing how this delay in presentation affects the characterization of John and also the characterization of Jesus, since John is the one who prepares the way of Jesus. Mark presents minor characters in a series of analogous scenes, the order of which is important

---

1. Sternberg, *Poetics*, pp. 478-79. See also Darr, *Character Building*, pp. 42-43; M. Sternberg, 'Time and Reader', in E. Spolsky (ed.), *The Uses of Adversity: Failure and Accommodation in Reader Response* (Lewisburg, PA: Bucknell University Press, 1990), pp. 82-83.

because it affects the reader's understanding of what these individuals are like.

Mark uses various means of characterization to communicate the traits of the people in his narrative, including his minor characters. Through a variety of devices, Mark conveys the traits of these individuals with a view to influencing the reader's response.

The Implied Reader and Characterization

An author writes a text in order to communicate with readers, and Mark's Gospel is no exception to this. In seeking to understand this act of communication, New Testament scholarship has focused primarily on the author, along with his historical situation, and on the text. However, there is a growing interest in the reader and the reader's place in the interpretation of New Testament narratives.[1] In analyzing the role of the reader, New Testament scholars have depended on reader-oriented approaches drawn from nonbiblical literary criticism.[2]

---

1. The following are some of the biblical scholars who have used a reader-oriented approach to New Testament narratives: Janice Capel Anderson, Jouette M. Bassler, Mary Ann Beavis, J.E. Botha, Fred W. Burnett, John A. Darr, Joanna Dewey, Richard A. Edwards, Robert M. Fowler, John Paul Heil, David B. Howell, Jack Dean Kingsbury, Hans-Josef Klauck, William S. Kurz, Elizabeth Struthers Malbon, Norman R. Petersen, Gary A. Phillips, Susan M. Praeder, Bernard Brandon Scott, Jeffrey L. Staley and Robert C. Tannehill. See the bibliography for further information on their work.

2. There are a number of introductions to reader-response criticism. The most helpful of these is S.R. Suleiman, 'Introduction: Varieties of Audience-Oriented Criticism', in S.R. Suleiman and I. Crosman (eds.), *The Reader in the Text: Essays on Audience and Interpretation* (Princeton: Princeton University Press, 1980), pp. 3-45. See also J.P. Tompkins, 'An Introduction to Reader-Response Criticism', in *idem* (ed.), *Reader-Response Criticism: From Formalism to Post-Structuralism* (Baltimore: Johns Hopkins University, 1980), pp. ix-xxvi, and E. Freund, *The Return of the Reader: Reader-Response Criticism* (London: Methuen, 1987). J. Culler (*On Deconstruction: Theory and Criticism after Structuralism* [Ithaca, NY: Cornell University, 1982], pp. 31-83) surveys reader-response criticism as a background for deconstructive criticism. R.C. Holub (*Reception Theory: A Critical Introduction* [London: Methuen, 1984]) provides an introduction to reader-oriented approaches to literary criticism within Germany. A number of theoretical studies have been written by New Testament scholars dealing with the relationship between reader-response criticism and New Testament studies. The most helpful of these are Moore, *Literary Criticism*, pp. 71-107, and R.M. Fowler, 'Who is "the Reader" in

The recent emphasis on the reader highlights the fact that texts exist within the context of an act of communication. Meir Sternberg expresses the importance of understanding narratives in the context of communication when he states that a narrative is 'a means to a communicative end, a transaction between the narrator and the audience on whom he wishes to produce a certain effect by way of certain strategies'.[1] The task of the interpreter is then 'to explain the *what's* and the *how's* in terms of the *why's* of communication'.[2] Sternberg warns that biblical literary criticism has tended 'to read biblical texts out of communicative context, with little regard for what they set out to achieve'.[3] An examination of the communication context is important for establishing the presence of literary patterns in the text. Thus, Sternberg states,

> Even the listing of so-called forms and devices and configurations... is no substitute for the proper business of reading. Since a sense of coherence entails a sense of purpose, it is not enough to trace a pattern; it must also

Reader-Response Criticism?', *Semeia* 31 (1985), pp. 5-23. See also S. Brown, 'Reader Response: Demythologizing the Text', *NTS* 34 (1988), pp. 232-37; R.M. Fowler, 'Reader-Response Criticism: Figuring Mark's Reader', in Anderson and Moore (eds.), *Mark and Method*, pp. 50-83; *idem, Let the Reader Understand*; B.C. Lategan, 'Current Issues in the Hermeneutical Debate', *Neot* 18 (1984), pp. 1-17; E.V. McKnight, *Postmodern Use of the Bible: The Emergence of Reader-Oriented Criticism* (Decatur, GA: Abingdon, 1988); *idem, The Bible and the Reader: An Introduction to Literary Criticism* (Philadelphia: Fortress Press, 1985); S.D. Moore, 'Stories of Reading: Doing Gospel Criticism as/with a "Reader"', in D.J. Lull (ed.), *Society of Biblical Literature Seminar Papers 1988* (Atlanta: Scholars Press, 1988), pp. 141-59; N.R. Petersen, 'The Reader in the Gospel', *Neot* 18 (1984), pp. 38-51; S.E. Porter, 'Why hasn't Reader-Response Criticism Caught On in New Testament Studies?', *Journal of Literature and Theology* 4 (1990), pp. 278-92; M.A. Powell, 'Types of Readers and their Relevance for Biblical Hermeneutics', *Trinity Seminary Review* 12 (1990), pp. 67-76; *idem, Narrative Criticism*, pp. 16-21; J.L. Resseguie, 'Reader Response Criticism and the Synoptic Gospels', *JAAR* 52 (1984), pp. 307-24; W. Schenk, 'Die Rollen der Leser oder der Mythos des Lesers?', *LB* 60 (1988), pp. 61-81; A.C. Thiselton 'Reader Response Hermeneutics, Action Models, and the Parables of Jesus', in R. Lundin, A.C. Thiselton and C. Walhout (eds.), *The Responsibility of Hermeneutics* (Grand Rapids: Eerdmans, 1985), pp. 79-113; W.S. Vorster, 'The Reader in the Text: Narrative Material', *Semeia* 48 (1989), pp. 21-39.

   1.   Sternberg, *Poetics*, p. 1.
   2.   Sternberg, *Poetics*, p. 1.
   3.   Sternberg, *Poetics*, p. 2.

be validated and justified in terms of communicative design. After all, the very question of whether that pattern exists in the text—whether it has any relevance and any claim to perceptibility—turns on the question of what it does in the text.[1]

Our concern here is to establish the presence of a literary pattern in Mark's presentation of minor characters. As Sternberg insists, establishing a literary pattern involves showing how that pattern functions as part of the communication between author and readers, in this case between Mark and his readers. Therefore, it is necessary to deal with the issues surrounding the reader of Mark's Gospel and the way Mark uses characterization to communicate with the reader.

The function of this section is to answer certain questions regarding the reader of Mark's Gospel. Who is the reader of Mark's Gospel? Why should we analyze the reader and Mark's communication with the reader? How does Mark's characterization of people influence the reader?

The Implied Reader of Mark's Gospel

In Mark 13 Jesus gives an apocalyptic discourse to his disciples on the Mount of Olives. In the midst of this discourse, Mark interrupts the account and speaks directly to his reader, telling the reader to understand (Mk 13.14). Thus, a concern for the reader was certainly not foreign to Mark. Increasingly, literary critics have also shown an interest in the reader of Mark's Gospel. They want to analyze the nature of the reader of Mark's Gospel in order to explain how Mark uses the text to influence the reader. Who is the reader of Mark's narrative? How should the reader be described? Perhaps the best way to begin answering this question concerning the identity of the reader is to analyze the author of Mark's Gospel, since the relationship between the reader and the text is similar to that between the author and the text.

Literary critics regularly make a distinction between the real author and the implied author of a text.[2] The real author of Mark's Gospel is

---

1. Sternberg, *Poetics*, p. 2.

2. The distinctions which are made in this section are primarily built on the work of W.C. Booth (*The Rhetoric of Fiction* [Chicago: University of Chicago Press, 2nd edn, 1983], pp. 67-77, 137-44, 420-31). Booth was one of the first literary critics to deal with the concepts of the implied author and the implied reader and with their place in analyzing the rhetoric of narrative. Other literary critics (S. Chatman,

the historical, flesh-and-blood person who wrote the Gospel at a particular time and place. In writing a narrative, a real author creates a second self, a literary version of himself or herself, so that when we read a narrative we do not encounter directly the real author but the implied author, the author who is implied by the text. In the process of reading, the reader is then able to reconstruct the implied author and his or her values. The implied author may be understood as the maker of the narrative. The implied author selects the material which is included in the narrative, establishes the values which operate in the story, orders the presentation of the events in the narrative and devises the rhetorical features found in the text. The implied author, along with his or her values, beliefs and norms, may be reconstructed through an examination of the choices made in the writing of the narrative.

Literary critics also frequently make a distinction between the implied author and the narrator. The implied author is the maker of the narrative, while the narrator is the one who speaks to the reader and tells the story. In Mark's Gospel, the implied author and the narrator, for all practical purposes, merge into one figure. There is no real distance between the choices and values of the maker of Mark's narrative and those of the teller of Mark's narrative.[1]

Coming to Terms: The Rhetoric of Narrative in Fiction and Film [Ithaca, NY: Cornell University Press, 1990], pp. 74-108; *idem, Story*, pp. 147-51; Rimmon-Kenan, *Narrative Fiction*, pp. 86-89, 117-19; Sternberg, *Expositional Modes*, pp. 254-55, 261; *idem, Poetics*, pp. 74-75) show a dependence on Booth for their understanding of the implied author and the implied reader. Booth himself had a precursor in W. Gibson ('Authors, Speakers, Readers, and Mock Readers', *College English* 11 [1950], pp. 265-69). Gibson made a distinction between the real author and the speaker of a narrative and between the real reader and the mock reader.

1. Booth (*Rhetoric*, p. 73) considers the narrator to be seldom if ever identical with the implied author. Sternberg (*Expositional Modes*, p. 255) feels that in certain narratives the narrator and implied author virtually merge into each other, so that they may be regarded as interchangeable. Sternberg (*Poetics*, p. 75) holds that this merging of the implied author and the narrator may be seen in the narrative of the Hebrew Bible. Kingsbury (*Matthew as Story*, p. 31) notes that in Matthew's Gospel, the narrator is reliable and in full accord with the ideas, values and beliefs of the implied author. Thus, he does not distinguish rigorously between the narrator and implied author in Matthew. Fowler (*Let the Reader Understand*, pp. 33, 77-78) regards the narrator of Mark's Gospel as virtually indistinguishable from the implied author of the Gospel. Malbon ('Narrative Criticism', p. 28) states that most narrative critics see little or no difference between the implied author and the narrator in first

Literary critics also make a distinction between the real reader and the implied reader. This differentiation is parallel to that made between the real author and the implied author. The real reader is any living, flesh-and-blood person who takes up the text of Mark's Gospel and reads it. A real reader of Mark's Gospel may have been an individual living in the first century, or may be a person living in the twentieth century.[1]

The implied author has a counterpart in the implied reader. Just as real authors create an image of themselves when writing a narrative, they also operate with an image of the text's reader. A text not only implies a picture of its author, but also a picture of its reader. In other words, the implied reader is the reader presupposed by the author when writing the text, the reader who fulfills the purposes for which the implied author wrote the narrative. The implied reader reads the narrative, follows the sequence of the implied author's presentation of the story, responds appropriately to the rhetorical features of the text which call for a response and accepts the values and beliefs of the implied author. The interpreter may reconstruct the role of the implied reader by examining the rhetorical features of the text and the way in which these features encourage the reader to accept the beliefs of the author. Characterization is one rhetorical tool that an author may use to influence the reader. Real readers may take on the role of the implied reader when they read a text, and in doing so, they will fulfill the purposes of the implied author. Real readers may also overlook or refuse to accept the role of the implied reader. If a real reader completely refuses to accept the implied reader's role, he or she will simply set the book down or throw the book away.

The concept of the implied reader makes it possible to interpret a narrative within the context of an act of communication. The interpreter may examine how an author who is implied in the text uses the narrative to communicate with and influence the reader, that is, the reader who is implied in the text. This approach to the reader opens the possibility of asking questions about the rhetorical effect of a

century Gospels. See also Malbon, 'Echoes and Foreshadowings', p. 212. No attempt will be made in this study to distinguish between the implied author and the narrator of Mark's Gospel. Also, the term 'Mark' will frequently be used with reference to the implied author or narrator of the Gospel.

1. A real 'reader' of the first century may have been a hearer of the text rather than a reader of the text, as is pointed out in Moore, *Literary Criticism*, pp. 84-88.

narrative. How does the implied author present the story in order to influence the implied reader? This approach to the reader also allows for discussion on the potential effect of the narrative on real readers. Real readers, to some extent, may take on the role of the implied reader, with the result that they may fulfill the implied author's purposes for the narrative and come to take on the values and beliefs of the implied author.

Who then is the reader of Mark's Gospel? In this study, the 'reader' is, unless otherwise noted, the implied reader, the reader implied by the text. This is the reader who reads the narrative in the order of its presentation, who is influenced by the rhetorical features of the text and who comes to accept the beliefs and commitments of the implied author.

Reader-oriented approaches to literary criticism are by no means uniform, and not all literary critics would accept the preceding explanation concerning the reader. The preceding definition of the reader differs from that of certain reader-response critics who have exerted an influence on reader-oriented approaches to New Testament narrative. These critics give a greater place for real readers to create meaning in the act of reading.

One such critic is Wolfgang Iser.[1] For Iser, meaning is the product of the interaction between the text and the reader. Meaning is not in the text, nor do texts by themselves convey meaning. Interpretation is misguided if it sets out to express the meaning of the text or to make the text comprehensible to the reader.[2] Instead, meaning in literary texts is created in the act of reading, because it is the product of the interaction between the text and the reader and not a quality hidden in the text. Literary texts initiate performances of meaning by the reader rather than actually formulating meaning themselves.[3] Meaning is

---

1. For a helpful introduction to Iser's approach, see Holub, *Reception Theory*, pp. 82-106. Iser's most important early work on critical theory is 'Indeterminacy and the Reader's Response in Prose Fiction', in J. Hillis Miller (ed.), *Aspects of Narrative* (New York: Columbia University Press, 1971), pp. 1-45. Examples of Iser's approach to literary texts are found in *The Implied Reader: Patterns of Communication in Prose Fiction from Bunyan to Beckett* (Baltimore: Johns Hopkins University Press, 1974). Iser's major theoretical work is *The Act of Reading: A Theory of Aesthetic Response* (Baltimore: Johns Hopkins University Press, 1978).

2. Iser, 'Indeterminacy and the Reader's Response', pp. 1-5; *idem*, *Act of Reading*, pp. 3-19, 22.

3. Iser, 'Indeterminacy and the Reader's Response', p. 4; *idem*, *Act of Reading*, p. 27.

not 'an object to be defined, but an effect to be experienced'.[1] Thus, according to Iser, texts only have meaning when they are read, so that the reader's activity must become the central concern of interpretation.

For Iser, who is this reader? The reader who creates meaning is the implied reader. However, Iser defines the implied reader in a different way than the definition given above. According to Iser, the implied reader is 'both the prestructuring of the potential meaning by the text, and the reader's actualization of this potential through the reading process'.[2] Iser wants to include in his definition both the potential effect of the text and the creative work of the reader. The implied reader includes both 'the reader's role as a textual structure, and the reader's role as a structured act'.[3] At times, Iser emphasizes the controlling nature of the text. Thus, he states that 'the concept of the implied reader is therefore a textual structure anticipating the presence of a recipient'.[4] At other times, Iser emphasizes the contribution of the reader. The reader responds to the text with creative acts of comprehension which, although they may have been set in motion by the text, defy control by the text. The text provides a set of governing rules, but the literary object is produced by the reader's imagination.[5] The implied reader, according to Iser, is then a construct which seeks to hold together both the textual features which call for a response and the types of moves that a reader will perform when reading a text.

The switch that activates the reader's imagination and contribution is the indeterminate nature of literary texts. The gaps or indeterminacies of the text call forth the response of the reader.[6] Since a narrative text can never fully explain its story, it will necessarily include gaps, omissions and missing connections of thought. In other words, texts have both written and unwritten parts. The incomplete nature of

1. Iser, *Act of Reading*, p. 10.

2. Iser, *Implied Reader*, p. xii.

3. Iser, *Act of Reading*, p. 35.

4. Iser, *Act of Reading*, p. 34. See also Iser's statement that the implied reader is 'a network of response-inviting structures, which impel the reader to grasp the text' (*Act of Reading*, p. 34).

5. Iser, *Act of Reading*, pp. 36-38, 107-108.

6. Iser, 'Indeterminacy and the Reader's Response', pp. 12, 43; *idem, Act of Reading*, pp. 167, 169.

a text is not a defect but rather a virtue, since the gaps invite the participation of the reader's imagination.[1] Iser uses the illustration of two people gazing at the night sky. They may see the same collection of stars, but one sees the image of a plough, while the other makes out a dipper. The text contains the fixed stars, but the connections between the stars are missing. Thus, texts call forth the reader's participation to supply the missing connections. Different individuals may vary in how they fill in the gaps, but in any case, the text will exert influence on the reader's imagination.[2] The gaps in the text invite the reader to participate by filling in what is left unsaid in the text, and in this way the reader contributes to the production of meaning in the act of reading.

In the end, who is in control, the text or the reader? Does the text govern the reader in the production of meaning or does the reader exercise authority over the text? Iser tends to be ambiguous in answering this question.[3] At times, he seems to give this control to the text, and at other times he grants the control to the reader. Iser never fully clarifies his position on this issue. In this study, control is given to the text over the reader, that is, over the implied reader. The reader who is implied in the text is governed by the text and is a feature of the text. The text may or may not control real readers, since real readers have a choice in whether or not they will take on the role of the implied reader.[4]

1. Iser, 'Indeterminacy and the Reader's Response', pp. 11, 13; *idem, Implied Reader*, pp. 280-82; Iser, *Act of Reading*, pp. 167-69.

2. Iser, *Implied Reader*, p. 282. Iser also deals with the subject of gaps in 'Interaction between Text and Reader', in S.R. Suleiman and I. Crosman (eds.), *The Reader in the Text* (Princeton: Princeton University Press, 1980), pp. 106-19.

3. On this point see Holub, *Reception Theory*, p. 85; Suleiman, 'Audience-Oriented Criticism', pp. 23-24.

4. For evaluations of Iser's approach to the reader see Holub, *Reception Theory*, pp. 96-106; J.L. Staley, *The Print's First Kiss: A Rhetorical Investigation of the Implied Reader in the Fourth Gospel* (SBLDS, 82; Atlanta: Scholars Press, 1988), pp. 32-33; Suleiman, 'Audience-Oriented Criticism', pp. 23-26. Iser answers criticisms concerning his view of indeterminacy in 'The Indeterminacy of the Text: A Critical Reply', *Comparative Criticism: A Yearbook* 2 (1980), pp. 27-47. Iser answers objections related to subjectivism and the affective fallacy in *Act of Reading*, pp. 23-27. Stanley Fish evaluates Iser's position in 'Why No One's Afraid of Wolfgang Iser', *Diacritics* 11 (Spring 1981), pp. 2-13. See also Iser's reply in 'Talk Like Whales: A Reply to Stanley Fish', *Diacritics* 11 (Fall 1981), pp. 82-87.

One reader-response critic who has sought to give control to the reader in a more rigorous manner is Stanley Fish.[1] Fish's position is complicated to describe, since it has changed over time with the result that his earlier position is significantly different from his later approach.[2] Fish's concern in his early position is to reject the notion that a text is a self-sufficient repository of meaning.[3] Such a notion ignores the reader and the fact that reading is something that a person does.[4] A text is not an object, a thing-in-itself, but rather an event which happens when a reader reads a text. For Fish, this event and not any information which may be taken away from the event is what constitutes the meaning of the text. Thus when approaching a text, the critic should not ask the question, 'What does this text, sentence, or phrase mean?' but rather 'What does this text, sentence, or phrase do?'[5] The reader's response is not a response to the meaning of the text, but rather it is the medium by which meaning comes into being. Therefore, the reader's progressive responses to the text cannot be ignored without missing the whole point.[6] Fish wants to take the attention away from the text and move it to the reader and the reader's temporal experience of the text. His practice then is to analyze the developing responses of the reader as they succeed one another in time.[7]

Fish anticipates the objection that tying meaning to the reader's

1. For an introduction to Fish's approach and an investigation of how his work could influence New Testament studies see S.D. Moore, 'Negative Hermeneutics, Insubstantial Texts: Stanley Fish and the Biblical Interpreter', *JAAR* 54 (1986), pp. 707-19. On the relationship of Fish's thought to that of other literary critics see S. Mailloux, 'Reader-Response Criticism?', *Genre* 10 (1977), pp. 413-31.

2. Examples of Fish's earlier approach may be found in *Surprised by Sin: The Reader in Paradise Lost* (New York: St Martin's Press, 1967); *idem, Self-Consuming Artifacts: The Experience of Seventeenth-Century Literature* (Berkeley: University of California Press, 1972). Fish explains the theory behind his earlier practice in the essay, 'Literature in the Reader: Affective Stylistics', which is included on pp. 21-67 of his book *Is there a Text in this Class? The Authority of Interpretive Communities* (Cambridge, MA: Harvard University Press, 1980). Fish gives an account of his earlier position in the introduction to *Is there a Text in this Class?*, pp. 1-7.

3. Fish, *Is there a Text in this Class?*, p. 2.

4. Fish, *Is there a Text in this Class?*, p. 22.

5. Fish, *Is there a Text in this Class?*, pp. 25, 32.

6. Fish, *Is there a Text in this Class?*, p. 3.

7. Fish, *Is there a Text in this Class?*, pp. 4, 42.

experience of the text will lead to interpretive anarchy, with as many experiences of a text as there are readers of a text. Focusing on the reader's experience would mean giving up the possibility of saying anything that would be of general interest.[1] Fish meets this objection by stating that all readers share a basic linguistic competence. This competence allows for an understanding that will, in some sense, be uniform. At least it is possible to repress what is subjective and idiosyncratic in one's reading in favor of a response that everyone uniformly shares as they read a specific text. For Fish, this controlled subjectivity is adequate, since objectivity in interpretation is simply an illusion.[2]

If there is uniformity in response, then why do readers disagree and hold contrary interpretations about the meaning of the same text? Fish insists that the problem is not with the initial response in the act of reading but with the response to that response. Disagreement takes place in the act of interpretation, not in the act of reading. Literary critics have obscured their uniform experience of a text by their later interpretive reflections.[3]

In the end, Fish rejects this earlier approach, because he feels that it grants too much control to the text. In his earlier position, Fish sought to enhance the importance of the reader and to diminish the objectivity of the text, but in order to claim some general validity for his method he insisted that the text imposed constraints on the reader. Thus, since the text was able to call forth uniform responses from readers, it became more powerful rather than less powerful. The reader still needed to be freed from the tyranny of the text.[4]

In his later approach, Fish removes the constraints of the text on the reader, and this leads him in a new direction.[5] Fish now argues that the text does not control the reader's experience, because the text itself does not exist independently of the reader's experience or prior to the

1. Fish, *Is there a Text in this Class?*, p. 4.
2. Fish, *Is there a Text in this Class?*, pp. 4-5, 44-49.
3. Fish, *Is there a Text in this Class?*, pp. 5-6, 51-52.
4. Fish, *Is there a Text in this Class?*, pp. 6-7.
5. Fish's later approach is best explained in his essay, 'Interpreting the *Variorum*', which may be found in *Is there a Text in this Class?*, pp. 147-73. See also Fish's discussion of this essay in his introduction to *Is there a Text in this Class?*, pp. 12-17. Fish emphasizes his later approach again in his collection of essays *Doing What Comes Naturally: Change, Rhetoric, and the Practice of Theory in Literary and Legal Studies* (Durham, NC: Duke University Press, 1989).

reader's interpretation. The text itself and the literary features and patterns we choose to notice in the text come into existence in the interpretive act. Interpretation does not arise from the givens of a text, but rather interpretation makes the text. Therefore, meaning is not extracted from a text, but rather it is produced by the reader in the act of interpretation.[1]

How, then, could two different readers ever agree about the interpretation of the same text? In Fish's model, how is it possible to account for agreement and stability in the interpretation of texts? Are we not back to interpretive anarchy? In order to answer this objection, Fish develops his notion of interpretive communities. According to Fish, readers do not have the authority or ability to make texts mean whatever they want them to mean, because both texts and readers stand under the authority of interpretive communities. A reader is not an independent agent, but rather a member of an interpretive community which limits his or her interpretive strategies and choices. Interpretive communities are made up of those who share convictions about the proper interpretive strategies for reading and writing texts. These interpretive strategies exist prior to any particular reading and determine the nature of that reading. In the end, interpretive communities rather than texts or readers produce meanings.[2] Thus, literary criticism does not involve demonstrating the true understanding of the meaning of a text. Instead, criticism involves persuading others to see things from the perspective of one's own interpretive community.[3]

According to Fish, who is in control? Is the text or the reader in control in the process of interpretation? Fish's inclination is to give control to the reader. Nevertheless, he finds it difficult to maintain consistently the authority of the reader over the text and still distance himself from complete subjectivism in interpretation. His solution is to put interpretive communities in complete control. Both the text and the reader lose control, and in fact they tend to lose their independent existence. The lesson appears to be that it is difficult if not impossible to free the reader from the constraints of the text without enslaving the reader to some other master.[4]

1. Fish, *Is there a Text in this Class?*, pp. 12-13, 161-67, 172.
2. Fish, *Is there a Text in this Class?*, pp. 13-15, 171-73.
3. Fish, *Is there a Text in this Class?*, pp. 15-17.
4. A number of critiques of Fish's position have been written. See especially

The Value of a Reader-Oriented Approach

Why should an interpreter bother with theoretical discussions concerning the reader of Mark's Gospel? Why should the interpreter not simply examine the author of the Gospel, along with his historical situation, and the text itself? What may be gained from an examination of the reader implied by the text?

One important benefit of a reader-oriented approach is that it emphasizes the rhetorical function of narratives.[1] Narratives in general and Mark's Gospel in particular have been written in order to influence their readers. The Gospel of Mark is not simply a more or less adequate source for the historical reconstruction of the events that lie behind the text. Mark's Gospel does not simply present a well-formed story. Mark uses his Gospel to convey a narrative that is meant to move its readers. Mark has constructed the narrative and its literary techniques—including characterization—in order to influence the reader. Missing the rhetorical nature of Mark's Gospel will lead the interpreter to overlook the purpose of many aspects of Mark's presentation of the story of Jesus. Moreover, if interpreters neglect the rhetoric of Mark's narrative, they will miss what may potentially happen when a real reader actually reads Mark's Gospel.

A recognition of the rhetorical nature of narratives allows the interpreter to ask a new question when dealing with the text.

M.H. Abrams, 'How to Do Things with Texts', *Partisan Review* 46 (1979), pp. 565-88. See also J.T. Bagwell, 'Who's Afraid of Stanley Fish', *Poetics Today* 4 (1983), pp. 127-33; W.C. Booth, 'A New Strategy for Establishing a Truly Democratic Criticism', *Daedalus* 112 (1983), pp. 175-92; Holub, *Reception Theory*, pp. 150-52; S. Rendell, 'Fish vs. Fish', *Diacritics* 12 (Winter 1982), pp. 49-57; R. Scholes, *Textual Power: Literary Theory and the Teaching of English* (New Haven: Yale University Press, 1985), pp. 149-65. Two objections are persistently raised against Fish's position. First, Fish argues that the text does not exist in itself, but exists only in the act of interpretation. However, when interpreters interpret, what are they interpreting? Fish (*Is there a Text in this Class?*, p. 165) states that he has no answer to that question, but he insists that no one else does either. Secondly, Fish holds that there is no such thing as an independent text. Instead, the reader makes the text when he or she reads. In this case, it is unclear why Fish keeps writing texts. Fish's act of writing to communicate his ideas argues against the ideas themselves.

1. Booth, *Rhetoric*, pp. 89-116; M. Sternberg, 'Time and Space in Biblical (Hi)story Telling: The Grand Chronology', in R. Schwartz (ed.), *The Bible and the Text: The Bible and Literary Theory* (Oxford: Basil Blackwell, 1990), pp. 89, 91; *idem*, *Poetics*, pp. 1-2; Suleiman, 'Audience-Oriented Criticism', p. 9.

Interpreters generally come to Mark's Gospel and ask, 'What does this text mean?' Yet interpreters should also ask, 'What does this text do?'[1] Authors write narratives in order to communicate a message or story, but they also write narratives in order to influence their readers. Thus, the interpreter may ask about what an author meant to do to the reader through the narrative. How was Mark trying to move the reader through the literary techniques of his Gospel? Asking this question allows the interpreter to analyze not only the meaning of the text but also the potential impact of the text.

A second benefit of a reader-oriented approach is that it highlights the temporal nature of reading and the sequential flow of the narrative.[2] Readers read, and the activity of reading is a process that takes place over time. Reading involves following the sequence of the text,

1. See Resseguie, 'Reader Response Criticism', pp. 307, 322. The reader-response critic who has consistently asked this question about what a text does is Stanley Fish (*Is there a Text in this Class?*, pp. 3, 22, 25-27). Fish (*Is there a Text in this Class?*, pp. 3, 25, 28, 32) argues that a recognition of the idea that texts do something to the reader, that texts create an event in the reader, eliminates the contention that texts convey meaning. What a text does is what it means. Fish never explains why a text cannot both convey a meaning and influence a reader.

2. The temporal nature of reading is emphasized in a number of reader-oriented works. See especially Fish, *Surprised by Sin*, pp. 23, 31; *idem, Is there a Text in this Class?*, pp. 2-4, 27, 42, 44; Iser, *Act of Reading*, pp. 108-109; *idem, Implied Reader*, p. 280; S. Mailloux, 'Learning to Read: Interpretation and Reader-Response Criticism', *Studies in the Literary Imagination* 12 (Spring 1979), pp. 96, 100; M. Perry, 'Literary Dynamics: How the Order of a Text Creates its Meanings', *Poetics Today* 1 (Autumn 1979), pp. 35-64, 311-61; Sternberg, *Expositional Modes*, pp. 34, 96-97; *idem*, 'Time and Reader', pp. 50-51, 77-78, 85. A number of critics within New Testament studies also emphasize the temporal aspect of reading. See especially R.A. Edwards, *Matthew's Story of Jesus* (Philadelphia: Fortress Press, 1985), p. 9; *idem*, 'Narrative Implications of Gar in Matthew', *CBQ* 52 (1990), p. 641; *idem*, 'Reading Matthew: The Gospel as Narrative', *Listening* 24 (1989), p. 252; *idem*, 'Uncertain Faith: Matthew's Portrait of the Disciples', in F. Segovia (ed.), *Discipleship in the New Testament* (Philadelphia: Fortress Press, 1985), p. 48; Fowler, *Let the Reader Understand*, pp. 3, 42-46; *idem*, 'Reader-Response Criticism', pp. 56-57; *idem*, 'Who is "the Reader"', pp. 18-21; Howell, *Inclusive Story*, pp. 43-44, 243-45; Resseguie, 'Reader Response Criticism', pp. 316-21; Staley, *Print's First Kiss*, pp. 8-9, 19-20. Robbins (*Jesus the Teacher*, pp. 9-10) does not follow a reader-oriented approach in his socio-rhetorical study of Mark's Gospel. However, one aspect of his study parallels the concerns of reader-oriented critics for examining the sequential flow of the narrative, since he studies the progressive forms in Mark's Gospel.

since language necessarily yields information in a linear fashion. The time-bound nature of reading is not simply an unfortunate consequence of the limitations of language. On the contrary, an author may use the fact that a text is perceived sequentially in order to produce important rhetorical effects on the reader. The ordering of the elements in a narrative is one of the chief literary techniques that an author may use in order to influence the reader's perception of the story.

A narrative is not a spatial object that may be viewed as a whole at any one moment. Rather a narrative presents its story in a sequential manner.[1] A narrative has a beginning, middle and end. In a narrative, the author takes the reader through a presentation of the story step by step, and the story may have twists and turns along the way. It is possible to come to the end of the narrative and ask questions about the cumulative effect of the story, but an approach which examines only the story as a whole will miss all the twists and turns of the narrative. Such an approach will miss the path that the author has chosen for the reader along with the rhetorical motivations for that path.

The Gospels have often been treated as a static set of theological themes or literary motifs. Evidence for a theme or motif is taken from throughout the Gospel with little concern for the place of this evidence in the development and movement of the plot. Such an approach neglects the path which the Gospel writer has prepared for the reader. It neglects the way that the Gospel writer uses the development of the narrative to influence the reader's view of the theological and literary concerns of the Gospel.[2]

An author may control the reader's experience of a story by controlling the order of the elements of the story. Given the influence of the sequence of the text, the interpreter should ask questions concerning a narrative's order of presentation. Why is this piece of information presented at this precise point in the narrative? Why is this event related first and another event later? Why is this event

---

1. Staley points out that the temporal nature of a narrative is not simply part of the reader's experience. Narratives themselves are temporal. 'It is true that the temporal flow of narrative in textual mediums is activated by reading, but it does not necessarily follow that this perception of narrative temporality is merely a fiction created by the reader. Unlike other objects of sense perception, narratives have beginnings, middles, and ends. Narratives are temporal' (Staley, *Print's First Kiss*, p. 33).

2. On this point, see Tannehill, 'Composition', p. 217.

narrated out of its chronological order? Why is this person introduced at this point of the narrative? Why is this characteristic of a person presented first while information concerning another trait is presented later? How is the author using the sequence of the narrative to influence the way that the reader understands the events, people and values of the narrative? Does the author have a rhetorical motivation for the order of presentation?

These questions are worth asking concerning Mark's presentation of minor characters. The contention of this study is that the order in which Mark introduces different minor characters and their placement within the flow of the plot serves a rhetorical purpose. A careful examination of Mark's order of presenting minor characters shows that he is encouraging a proper response to Jesus while causing the reader to reflect on improper responses to Jesus. This study does not seek to examine Mark's overall view, cumulative view of minor characters, but rather seeks to trace the sequential flow of Mark's presentation of these individuals and to explore the effect of this ordered presentation on the reader.

In his analysis of reader-oriented studies, Stephen Moore raises an objection to approaches which pay close attention to the sequential flow of the Gospel narratives. The objection involves the prior knowledge of the readers. Moore points out that much of the Gospel material is traditional and that Mark as well as the other Gospel writers would have envisioned mainly Christian audiences. Given this set of circumstances, the sequence of Mark's narrative is largely irrelevant. The audience envisioned by Mark would have already known important elements in the later parts of the story and would have drawn on their knowledge of the story of Jesus to interpret the earlier portions of Mark's narrative.[1] The sequence of the text may then have played

---

1. Moore, *Literary Criticism*, p. 91. M.A. Beavis ('The Trial before the Sanhedrin [Mark 14:53-65]: Reader Response and Greco-Roman Readers', *CBQ* 49 [1987], pp. 581-82, 592-96; *idem, Mark's Audience: The Literary and Social Setting of Mk 4.11-12* [JSNTSup, 33; Sheffield: JSOT Press, 1989], pp. 16-17, 124-26) raises a similar objection. According to Beavis, Mark would have envisioned a situation in which a reader would have read the Gospel aloud before an assembly. The reader would have thoroughly studied the text in advance. When reading the text to the assembly, the reader would have stopped to explain the meaning of the text and would have answered questions from the audience. In giving explanations and answers, the reader would have drawn on an understanding of the entire text. Thus, elements from the end of the Gospel may well have been introduced in the reading of

only a small part in the reception of Mark's Gospel by the original audience. A more important aspect of the original reception would have involved the preacquaintance of Mark's audience with the story of Jesus.[1] 'This aspect is no doubt better accounted for by traditional exegetical methods, in which strict sequentiality plays little part.'[2]

This objection fails to recognize a crucial distinction, the distinction between story and discourse.[3] As noted earlier in this chapter, 'story' refers to the narrated events of the story abstracted from their place in the text and to the characters who participate in these events. 'Discourse' designates the written narrative which relates the story. The content of the narrative is the story, and the means by which this story is expressed is the discourse. In other words, the story is the 'what' of the narrative, while the discourse is the 'how' of the narrative. Mark's Gospel is a discourse or a text which narrates the story of Jesus. Mark's Gospel is one version of the story of Jesus.

The focus of a reader-oriented approach is on the discourse. Robert Fowler states that

> The great bulk of modern criticism of biblical narrative, whether primarily historical or literary in aim, has focused primarily upon the story level of biblical narrative and the events or ideas to which it is thought to refer, whereas reader-response criticism invites us to shift our attention primarily to the experience of encountering the discourse level of biblical narrative in the act of reading...Reader-response criticism is a salutary way

the early portions of the text. In light of these historical circumstances, scholars may ignore the sequence of the text and read later elements of the story back into earlier passages when analyzing the responses of the original audience.

1. Moore, *Literary Criticism*, p. 93.

2. Moore, *Literary Criticism*, p. 93. Other critics (Sternberg, *Poetics*, pp. 260-62; Perry, 'Literary Dynamics', pp. 356-57) have dealt with the issue of the prior knowledge of the reader and have come to very different conclusions. Powell (*Narrative Criticism*, pp. 20, 97; *idem*, 'Types of Readers', p. 72) points out that the implied reader does know some things that are not stated in the text. The text itself makes certain assumptions about what the reader knows. For example, the text of the Gospels assumes that the reader knows how much a denarius is worth and what a centurion does. This assumed knowledge of the reader should be taken into account when analyzing the effect of the narrative on the reader. Darr (*Character Building*, pp. 20-29) also discusses the background information that the reader must possess in order to read a Gospel competently.

3. This distinction has already been discussed under the preceding section on characterization. The terminology used here is that of Seymour Chatman. For Chatman's views on 'story' and 'discourse', see Chatman, *Story*, pp. 9, 19.

to learn how to focus critical scrutiny upon the discourse level, as
opposed to the story level, of biblical narrative.[1]

The fact that a reader-oriented approach focuses on the discourse
rather than on the story has important implications for the issue of the
reader's prior knowledge. Mark's original audience no doubt was
acquainted with the story of Jesus. Yet while they knew the story of
Jesus, they would not have known the discourse of Mark's Gospel, nor
should we assume that their knowledge of the story of Jesus would
keep them from listening carefully to the discourse of Mark's Gospel.
Focusing on the discourse of the Gospel simply involves allowing
Mark to tell the story of Jesus in the manner he has chosen to do so. A
knowledge of the story need not preclude careful attention to the
discourse.

Certainly, the discourse of Mark's Gospel is of primary importance
for analyzing the effect of the narrative upon the implied reader.
Mark chose to relate the story of Jesus in a particular manner and to
arrange his material in a specific order. Mark's choices as they are
reflected in the text imply a reader who will accept those choices and
who will allow those decisions to affect his or her response to the
story. A reader-oriented approach emphasizes the discourse of the
narrative in order to show how the literary techniques and literary
patterns of the narrative will influence the implied reader. The order
of presentation in the narrative is one of the literary means that an
author may use in order to shape the response of the reader to the
story. Thus, the sequence of the material as it is found in the discourse
of Mark's Gospel is important for analyzing the effect of the narrative
upon the implied reader of Mark's Gospel.[2]

1. R.M. Fowler, 'The Rhetoric of Direction and Indirection in the Gospel of
Mark', *Semeia* 48 (1989), p. 116.
2. Moore (*Literary Criticism*, pp. 41-45, 64-68) is quite aware of the distinction
between story and discourse, and he discusses it thoroughly in his book. In the end,
Moore rejects the distinction, since in following a post-structuralist approach he
rejects the idea that a text conveys content. In Mark, as in any narrative, we find discourse, but no story. We have form, but no content. The Gospels are all discourse
and nothing but discourse. However, if Moore rejects the idea that there is a story of
Jesus which can be distinguished from the discourse of Mark, then how can he
maintain that Mark's original audience possessed a knowledge of the story of Jesus
prior to its reception of the Gospels? It is difficult to maintain at the same time that
there is no story of Jesus and that Mark's audience knew the story of Jesus.

The Implied Reader and Mark's Characterization

What is the relationship between the reader of Mark's Gospel and the people who are portrayed in the Gospel? How does Mark's characterization of people influence the reader? Questions concerning the influence of Mark's characterization on the reader have been answered to a great extent in an article by Robert C. Tannehill on the role of the disciples in Mark's Gospel.[1]

Tannehill deals with Mark's presentation of the disciples as part of the implicit dialogue between the author and the reader.[2] In other words, when Tannehill looks at Mark's portrayal of the disciples, he is asking the question of how Mark uses his treatment of the disciples to communicate with his reader. How does Mark want to influence his reader through his description of the disciples and their relationship with Jesus?

According to Tannehill, Mark communicates and recommends his values and norms to the reader by narrating the story of the disciples and by expressing his evaluation of them. In Mark's Gospel, Jesus functions as a reliable and authoritative guide to the author's evaluation of people and events. The values and demands of the author may be found in the values and demands of Jesus. The reader will judge the words and actions of the disciples on the basis of how they measure up to the judgment of Jesus. Thus, Mark primarily expresses his evaluation of the disciples through his narration of the shifting relationship between Jesus and the disciples. The process of evaluating the disciples according to the values of the narrative leads the reader to self-evaluation and to an examination of the proper response to Jesus.[3]

Tannehill argues that Mark begins his Gospel with a positive portrayal of the disciples. The first event that Mark narrates after Jesus begins to preach involves the call of four disciples (1.16-20). When Jesus commands Simon and Andrew and then James and John to follow him, they immediately leave everything and follow. In 3.13-19, Jesus selects twelve disciples for a special relationship and responsibility. Their primary responsibility is to be with Jesus, but in addition, Jesus will send them out to share in his work of preaching and casting out demons. This appointment of the twelve is closely associated with the mission of the disciples in 6.7-13, where the

1.   Tannehill, 'Disciples in Mark'.
2.   Tannehill, 'Disciples in Mark', pp. 386, 389-90.
3.   Tannehill, 'Disciples in Mark', pp. 390-92.

disciples are actually sent out to preach and to display their authority over demons and sickness. In these three scenes, Mark portrays the disciples as having a special relationship with Jesus and a role similar to Jesus.[1]

According to Tannehill, Mark's initial positive presentation of the disciples encourages the reader to identify with the disciples, to regard them as individuals who represent the reader's own concerns and situation. Since the first readers of Mark's Gospel were Christians, they would have related most easily and immediately to the characters in the story who follow Jesus and his commands. The disciples are the primary continuing characters who seem, at least at first, to follow Jesus. Thus, the first readers of Mark's Gospel would have identified with the disciples. According to Tannehill, Mark anticipated this response and composed his story with an initially positive presentation of the disciples in order to strengthen the tendency of the first readers to associate themselves with the disciples. Tannehill argues that Mark will use this initial identification with the disciples to speak indirectly to the reader through the disciples' story.[2]

As early as ch. 4, Mark hints at negative developments in the story of the disciples.[3] In 4.13, Jesus appears to be critical of the lack of understanding on the part of the disciples. Then at the end of ch. 4 Mark narrates the first of three boat scenes that show Jesus interacting with his disciples. The portrayal of the disciples in these boat scenes becomes increasingly negative. In the first boat scene, Jesus criticizes the disciples for their cowardice and lack of faith (4.35-41). In the second, the disciples respond with fear and astonishment when they see Jesus walking on the water (6.45-52). The narrator attributes their reaction to a lack of understanding and hardened hearts. In the third boat scene (8.14-21), Jesus accuses the disciples of the same blindness,

---

1. Tannehill, 'Disciples in Mark', pp. 396-97.

2. Tannehill, 'Disciples in Mark', pp. 392-94, 398. J. Dewey ('Point of View and the Disciples in Mark', in K.H. Richards [ed.], *Society of Biblical Literature Seminar Papers 1982* [Chico, CA: Scholars Press, 1982], pp. 97-99, 103-106) points out that there is a sense in which the reader identifies in some ways with Jesus and in other ways with the disciples. The reader identifies with Jesus in terms of values or ideology and with the disciples in regard to situation.

3. G. Fay ('Introduction to Incomprehension: The Literary Structure of Mk 4.1-34', *CBQ* 51 [1989], pp. 65-81) shows that the literary structure of Mk 4.1-34 highlights the incomprehension of the disciples.

deafness and lack of understanding which he had earlier attributed to the outsiders in 4.11-12.[1]

According to Tannehill, the nature of the disciples' problem is further clarified in Mk 8.31–10.45. In this section of Mark's Gospel the passion predictions of Jesus are followed by resistance or by behavior contrary to that of Jesus on the part of the disciples (8.32-33; 9.33-34; 10.35-41). Jesus calls on the disciples to recognize that following him involves a willingness to suffer and a renunciation of the desire for status and domination (8.34-38; 9.35-37; 10.42-45).[2]

Tannehill argues that the negative development in the story of the disciples requires the reader to distance himself or herself from the disciples and their behavior. Yet this dissociation from the disciples is not easy for the reader. The initial identification of the reader renders the dissociation more difficult and it adds a sense of seriousness to the move away from the disciples. Distancing oneself from the disciples is also not easy, because it involves accepting the values, demands and judgments of Jesus. The difficulty of following Jesus reminds the reader that he or she is still like the disciples in many ways.[3]

Tannehill points out that the misunderstanding of the disciples leads to failure. The behavior of the disciples results in disaster in ch. 14. The disciples' failure is seen clearly in the betrayal of Judas (14.43-46), the flight of the other disciples (14.50) and the denials of Peter (14.66-72). The desertion and denial of the disciples stands in sharp contrast to the command of Jesus to take up the cross and follow him.[4] In one sense, the story of the disciples is over, since the disciples do not appear again in Mark's Gospel, but the narrative holds open the future of the disciples. In 14.28 and 16.7, first Jesus and then the young man at the tomb announce a meeting between the risen Jesus and the disciples which may lead to the restoration of the disciples. Mark's Gospel holds open the possibility that the disciples who deserted Jesus may once again become his followers.[5]

According to Tannehill, the tension between the reader's identification with and dissociation from the disciples, along with the recognition of the disastrous failure of the disciples, should lead the reader

1. Tannehill, 'Disciples in Mark', pp. 398-99.
2. Tannehill, 'Disciples in Mark', pp. 400-401.
3. Tannehill, 'Disciples in Mark', pp. 393-95, 401-402.
4. Tannehill, 'Disciples in Mark', pp. 402-403.
5. Tannehill, 'Disciples in Mark', pp. 403-404.

to self-evaluation. Mark uses his presentation of the disciples to awaken his readers to their own failures as disciples and to call them to repentance. Mark leads the reader into the comfortable assumption that Jesus, the disciples and the reader are all in agreement. However, as the story goes on to reveal fundamental points of conflict between Jesus and his followers, the reader is left with a choice between the differing ways of Jesus and his disciples. The narrative moves the reader toward the path of faithfully following Jesus.[1]

Tannehill's analysis of the role of the disciples highlights the ways in which Mark uses characterization to influence the reader. Mark presents people in such a way that he also expresses his evaluation of them. Most often, Mark expresses this evaluation by showing how people measure up to the teaching and example of Jesus. By portraying certain characters in a positive manner, Mark encourages the reader to identify with these characters.[2] The reader will regard these people as worthy examples to imitate and their actions as part of a proper response to the demands of Jesus. When portraying characters negatively, Mark calls on the reader to dissociate from the characters.[3] If certain characters fail to live up to the teaching and ways of

---

1. Tannehill, 'Disciples in Mark', pp. 393, 395.

2. Mailloux ('Learning to Read', pp. 103-104) explains some of the moves that reader-response critics make when dealing with the characterization of a narrative. Reader-response critics will point out the places where the reader is encouraged to identify with characters. On this same point see also Resseguie, 'Reader Response Criticism', p. 312. Powell (*Narrative Criticism*, pp. 25, 56-57) uses the term 'empathy' for the reader's identification with a character. He distinguishes between realistic empathy, where the reader identifies with a character who is similar to the reader, and idealistic empathy, where the reader identifies with a character who represents what the reader would like to be. For example, in Matthew's Gospel, the reader's identification with Jesus is idealistic, while the reader's identification with the disciples is realistic.

3. According to Mailloux ('Learning to Read', p. 104), reader-response critics will point out places at which the reader must detach himself or herself from characters. This detachment leads the reader to stand in judgment against the characters. On this point, see also Resseguie, 'Reader Response Criticism', p. 312. Powell (*Narrative Criticism*, p. 57) uses the term 'antipathy' for the reader's detachment from a character. Powell also uses the term 'sympathy' to describe a further relationship between the reader and a character. The reader may care about, have sympathy for, a character who nonetheless is portrayed in a negative manner by the narrator. The narrator may create the reader's sympathy by attributing such sympathy to another character with whom the reader has come to identify.

Jesus, the reader will reject their actions as unworthy of imitation and will instead choose to follow the values of the author. In addition, Mark may portray characters in the story in a positive manner and then, following this positive portrayal, present the same characters in a negative light. Mark is calling on the reader both to identify with the characters and to dissociate from them. In this case, the reader will need to make judgments about the inadequacy of the characters' responses to Jesus. Yet in light of the reader's prior identification with the characters, the reader will also need to judge the inadequacy of his or her own response to Jesus. The tension between identification and dissociation should lead the reader to self-evaluation.[1]

Tannehill's work on the disciples reveals the moves that the implied reader will make in responding to Mark's characterization. Nevertheless, it is inadequate to focus only on the disciples in analyzing the response of the reader to the characters in Mark's narrative.[2] Mark includes other followers of Jesus. Minor characters are often portrayed in a positive manner, in a manner which commends itself to the reader. The remaining chapters of this study trace Mark's treatment of minor characters and the influence of his presentation on the implied reader.

---

1.   According to Mailloux ('Learning to Read', pp. 104-105), reader-response critics maintain that the reader's evaluation of characters may lead to the reader's self-evaluation. The reader will judge the character in the text and himself or herself in everyday life. For a similar point see also Resseguie, 'Reader Response Criticism', p. 312. Weeden (*Traditions in Conflict*, pp. 12-19) points out that first-century readers were taught during their education to interpret the message of a text by examining the way in which the text portrays characters. Students were taught to examine characters, so that they might emulate the lives of the virtuous and disdain the lives of the corrupt. Thus, an approach to the Gospels which pays close attention to the characters and the use of characterization to influence the reader is a historically relevant procedure. On this issue see also Malbon, 'Jewish Leaders', pp. 259-61. The historical relevance of pointing out the influence of characterization on the reader may also be seen in W.S. Kurz, 'Narrative Models for Imitation in Luke–Acts', in D.L. Balch, E. Ferguson and W.A. Meeks (eds.), *Greek, Romans, and Christians* (Minneapolis: Fortress Press, 1990), pp. 171-89. Kurz surveys a wide spectrum of Hellenistic narratives and shows that such narratives frequently portray characters as models for imitation. He argues that the author of Luke–Acts was quite familiar with the paradigmatic function of narrative and that he shaped some of his narratives concerning Jesus and his followers so that they might serve as models for the behavior of his readers.

2.   Tannehill ('Disciples in Mark', p. 405) also notes that the disciples' story is not the sole interest of the author of Mark's Gospel.

Chapter 3

MINOR CHARACTERS PRIOR TO THE BARTIMAEUS NARRATIVE

Jesus is clearly the central figure in Mark's Gospel. At least in part, Mark wrote his narrative in order to move the reader toward a fitting response to Jesus. In other words, Mark's narrative has a rhetorical function. Mark's largely negative portrayal of the disciples is one of the significant means that he uses to instruct the reader concerning the demands of following Jesus. Nevertheless, an analysis of Mark's rhetorical strategy cannot be limited to an analysis of his treatment of the disciples, since he also uses his presentation of minor characters to move the reader toward a proper response to Jesus. Mark includes a series of analogous scenes throughout his narrative which feature individual members of the crowd, neither disciples nor opponents of Jesus but part of the general population. Mark uses these analogous scenes and their strategic placement throughout the course of the narrative in order to have a rhetorical effect on the reader. Through his treatment of minor characters, Mark moves the reader toward faith or trust in Jesus along with an understanding of his person. However, Mark also seeks to move the reader toward an acceptance of the demands and values of Jesus. Particularly crucial in the overall development of the characterization of these individuals from the crowd is Mark's portrayal of Bartimaeus (10.46-52). At that point in the narrative, Mark encourages the reader to respond with faith in Jesus, but also with a faithful following of Jesus. After the Bartimaeus story, Mark continues to move the reader to follow Jesus through the positive example of a number of minor characters and also through the negative example of the women at the tomb who respond with disobedience and failure. Mark uses his overall narrative to call the reader to follow Jesus, and his presentation of minor characters reinforces this call by moving the demands and expectations of Jesus into the reader's own situation and time. The contention of this study, then, is that Mark's portrayal of minor characters is meant to influence the reader, moving the reader toward faith and faithful following, and that Mark's characterization of Bartimaeus (10.46-52) plays a crucial role within this rhetorical strategy.

The function of the following chapters is to trace Mark's presentation of minor characters through the course of the narrative. These chapters will pay close attention to the thematic and lexical connections between the analogous scenes featuring minor characters and to the placement of these scenes in the sequence of the narrative. Not every aspect of these analogous passages will be examined in detail, since the focus of this survey is on Mark's treatment of minor characters. The following chapters will seek to isolate the traits of these individuals and the means that Mark uses to communicate those traits. Mark presents minor characters in such a way that he also expresses his evaluation of them. This evaluation is communicated primarily through the standards of judgment found in the teaching and actions of Jesus. A comparison between Mark's portrayal of minor characters and the words and deeds of Jesus helps the reader to evaluate the responses of these characters. Through such evaluations, the reader is guided toward a fitting response to Jesus and his demands. In looking at Mark's presentation of minor characters, then, I will be looking at the ways in which this presentation influences the reader. This chapter will examine Mark's treatment of minor characters who appear in the narrative prior to the Bartimaeus story, Chapter 4 the characterization of Bartimaeus in Mk 10.46-52 and Chapter 5 the presentation of minor characters in the narrative following the Bartimaeus story.

Minor Characters in Mark 1.1–3.35

Mk 1.1-15 serves as the introduction to Mark's narrative.[1] The function of a narrative introduction is to provide the reader with the

---

1. For the idea that the introduction to the Gospel extends to v. 15 see Anderson, *Mark*, pp. 63-65; M.E. Boring, 'Mark 1:1-15 and the Beginning of the Gospel', *Semeia* 52 (1990), pp. 53-59; Gnilka, *Markus*, I, pp. 39-40; R.A. Guelich, 'The Beginning of the Gospel: Mark 1:1-15', *BR* 27 (1982), pp. 5-15; *idem, Mark 1-8:26* (WBC; Dallas: Word Books, 1989), p. 4; L.E. Keck, 'The Introduction to Mark's Gospel', *NTS* 12 (1966), pp. 352-70; Lührmann, *Markusevangelium*, pp. 32-33; C.S. Mann, *Mark* (AB, 27; Garden City, NY: Doubleday, 1986), p. 193; R. Pesch, *Das Markusevangelium I. Teil* (HTKNT; Freiburg: Herder, 4th edn, 1984), pp. 71-73.

necessary background for a proper understanding of the narrative.[1] This background information is generally dealt with in a summary fashion as a preparation for the beginning of the story proper. Then, the first scene of the story proper is normally given a fuller treatment in order to mark the end of the background and the beginning of the story itself.[2] Throughout 1.1-15, Mark presents background information in a summary fashion, as for example in 1.14-15 where he summarizes the proclamation of Jesus in Galilee. Mark introduces his summary of Jesus' message with the present participles κηρύσσων and λέγων, indicating that Jesus was repeatedly speaking this message.[3] Thus, the introduction to Mark's narrative extends through 1.15, and 1.16-20 serves as the first scene in the narrative proper.

Primarily, Mark uses the introduction to orientate the reader to Jesus, the central figure in the narrative. The introduction bestows on Jesus a unique and lofty authority.[4] Mark initially presents Jesus as messiah and Son of God (1.1).[5] Mark does not immediately elaborate

1. Sternberg, *Expositional Modes*, p. 1.
2. Sternberg, *Expositional Modes*, pp. 19-21.
3. E.d.W. Burton, *Syntax of the Moods and Tenses in New Testament Greek* (Chicago: University of Chicago Press, 3rd edn, 1898), p. 54; A.T. Robertson, *A Grammar of the Greek New Testament in the Light of Historical Research* (Nashville: Broadman, 1934), p. 891; C.F.D. Moule, *An Idiom Book of New Testament Greek* (Cambridge: Cambridge University Press, 2nd edn, 1971), p. 99. See also Marshall, *Faith*, p. 38.
4. Literary critics talk about the authority of Jesus within the narrative in different ways. Several literary critics (Petersen, 'Point of View', pp. 101-102, 107-108; Dewey, 'Point of View', p. 97; J.D. Kingsbury, *The Christology of Mark's Gospel* [Philadelphia: Fortress Press, 1983], pp. 47-49) express the authority of Jesus in terms of 'point of view' or 'ideological point of view'. Mark aligns his ideological point of view with the point of view of Jesus which in turn is aligned with the point of view of God. In this way, the point of view of Jesus becomes normative for the narrative. Other literary critics (Tannehill, 'Disciples in Mark', p. 391; Fowler, *Loaves and Fishes*, pp. 168-69; *idem, Let the Reader Understand*, pp. 61, 127; Rhoads and Michie, *Mark as Story*, p. 40; Marshall, *Faith*, pp. 35-36) refer to Jesus as a 'reliable character'. Jesus is a reliable character who communicates the implied author's norms and values to the reader. The reader is expected to judge the words and actions of different characters through the words and actions of Jesus.
5. Manuscript support for the inclusion of the words υἱοῦ θεοῦ is early and widespread, and so υἱοῦ θεοῦ should probably be regarded as original. See B.M. Metzger, *A Textual Commentary on the Greek New Testament* (Stuttgart: United Bible Societies, 1971), p. 73.

on the full significance of these titles, but rather he uses the remainder of the narrative to show what it means for Jesus to be the messiah, Son of God.[1]

Nevertheless, the titles 'messiah' and 'Son of God' mark Jesus as an agent of God. The coming of Jesus is connected with the message of the prophets (1.2-3), but he himself is greater than the prophets, greater even than John the Baptist (1.4-8). Jesus is beloved by God, empowered by the Spirit and victorious over Satan (1.9-13). Thus, when Jesus comes into Galilee proclaiming a message, Mark has prepared the way for this message to be accepted by the reader as 'the gospel of God' (1.14). Mark has endorsed Jesus as an authoritative communicator of God's message. Jesus proclaims the values and demands of God, and, through the extremely positive presentation of Jesus in the introduction, Mark shows that he also shares these values and expectations. Jesus functions as a reliable character who communicates and exemplifies the values of God as well as those of the implied author.

The initial summary of Jesus' message is significant for the reader's evaluation of the characters in the narrative. Jesus, the authoritative communicator of the gospel of God, demands repentance and faith in light of the nearness of God's kingdom (1.14-15). This initial summary provides the reader with standards for judging the responses of the characters. The reader will judge in a positive way those characters who acknowledge and accept the authority of Jesus and who respond to the message of Jesus with repentance and faith.

After the introduction of 1.1-15, Mark narrates the initial ministry of Jesus in the region of Galilee. He uses the early chapters of the Gospel to introduce different character groups and to show their reactions to Jesus. In a rough pattern of rotation, Mark shows Jesus interacting with the disciples, the crowd, the demons and the religious authorities.[2] At times, he narrates scenes that show Jesus interacting with more than one group of characters.[3] After the completion of the narrative introduction, the first scene in the story proper portrays Jesus calling four disciples (1.16-20). Mark follows this discipleship

---

1. Kelber, *Story of Jesus*, p. 17; Kingsbury, *Christology*, p. 56; *idem, Conflict in Mark*, p. 32; F.J. Matera, 'The Prologue as the Interpretive Key to Mark's Gospel', *JSNT* 34 (1988), p. 4.
2. Tannehill, 'Narrative Christology', p. 68.
3. Tannehill, 'Narrative Christology', p. 69.

scene with a description of a typical day in Jesus' ministry (1.21-34). Here, Mark introduces minor characters for the first time. These minor characters make their first appearance in a mixed episode, that is, in an episode in which Jesus is dealing with more than one character group.

One Day in Capernaum (1.21-34)

After the call of the four disciples (1.16-20), Mark narrates the activity of Jesus during one day in Capernaum (1.21-34).[1] Mk 1.21-34 is held together as a unit by both time and location. In v. 21, Jesus comes to Capernaum, and on the Sabbath he enters into the synagogue and teaches. From the synagogue, Jesus goes immediately to the home of Simon and Andrew, which is apparently still in the city of Capernaum, since in the evening the whole city gathers at the door of the house seeking Jesus. The activity of Mk 1.21-34 takes place in Capernaum within the confines of one day, and then both the time and the setting change in v. 35.[2] Early in the morning of the next day, Jesus departs to a deserted place in order to pray. Mark pictures Jesus out in the deserted places again in v. 45, with the result that Jesus departs from Capernaum in v. 35 and does not return again until Mk 2.1. Verse 35 also shows a shift in Jesus' activity. Jesus ministers to the people of Capernaum in 1.21-34, but in v. 35 he withdraws from these people. Jesus distances himself from the crowds that he has created. Therefore, Mk 1.21-34 functions as a unit that presents a typical day of Jesus' ministry, and Mk 1.35 indicates the beginning of a new scene.

In this passage covering one day in Capernaum, Mark introduces Jesus' ministry to minor characters, but in the process he also includes

1.   On the idea that Mark presents 1.21-34 as a unit see especially Pesch, *Markusevangelium I. Teil*, pp. 116-17. See also Guelich, *Mark*, p. 55; W.L. Lane, *The Gospel according to Mark* (NICNT; Grand Rapids: Eerdmans, 1974), pp. 70-71. Ernst Lohmeyer (*Das Evangelium des Markus* [Kritisch-exegetischer Kommentar über das Neue Testament; Göttingen: Vandenhoeck & Ruprecht, 17th edn, 1967], pp. 34, 40) treats 1.21-31 as a unified report on one day in Capernaum and then includes the summary of 1.32-34 within the larger section of 1.32-45 which he entitles 'Outside Capernaum'. Lohmeyer's positioning of 1.32-34 outside of Capernaum is unusual since the events of 1.32-34 take place within Capernaum. Apparently, Lohmeyer's purpose for including 1.32-34 with the following verses is to maintain an outline which is based entirely on series of three related pericopes.

2.   Pesch, *Markusevangelium I. Teil*, pp. 137.

material on the crowd, the scribes, the demons and the disciples. In the context of Jesus' authoritative teaching in the synagogue, Mark notes the presence of a man with an unclean spirit. Mark shows little interest in the man himself, choosing instead to narrate the interaction between Jesus and the unclean spirit.[1] Jesus silences the unclean spirit and commands the spirit to come out of the man. After causing the man to convulse (σπαράξαν)[2] and crying out with a loud voice, the unclean spirit comes out of the man in obedience to Jesus. In this way, the presence of the possessed man in the synagogue serves as a opportunity for Jesus to illustrate the authority of his teaching (1.27). In Mk 1.16-20, Jesus calls four fishermen to follow him and they follow. In 1.23-27, Mark introduces a new type of contact with Jesus. The possessed man is not called on to follow Jesus, but rather he is simply helped by Jesus. The man is needy, since he is dominated, controlled and attacked by an unclean spirit, but he is also delivered by Jesus, who has authority over demonic beings.

Mark follows his depiction of a needy man with a description of a needy woman (1.29-31). In the home of Simon and Andrew, the four followers of Jesus speak to him concerning Simon's mother-in-law, who is sick and suffering with a fever. Jesus takes the woman's hand and raises her up, causing the fever to leave the woman. In light of her restored health, the woman serves Jesus and his followers. At this point in the narrative, the service of the woman seems to function simply as evidence that she is completely healed of her affliction.[3] Mark's characterization of Simon's mother-in-law is brief. He uses the incident to reveal the trust of Jesus' four followers and the authority of Jesus over sickness. The woman is portrayed as needy and suffering, but helped and restored to health by Jesus.

---

1. As Guelich (*Mark*, p. 59) points out, the possessed man plays no active part in the narrative apart from his appearance in v. 23.

2. σπαράσσω is used metaphorically to express an attack against a person. See LSJ, p. 1624. When σπαράσσω is used for the attack of a demon against a possessed person, it has the meaning of 'convulse'. See BAGD, p. 760; LSJ, p. 1624.

3. Gnilka, *Markus*, I, p. 84; Guelich, *Mark*, p. 63; R.H. Gundry, *Mark: A Commentary on his Apology for the Cross* (Grand Rapids: Eerdmans, 1993), p. 91; M.D. Hooker, *The Gospel according to Saint Mark* (BNTC; Peabody, MA: Hendrickson, 1991), p. 70; Lane, *Mark*, p. 78; Lührmann, *Markusevangelium*, p. 52; Nineham, *Mark*, p. 81; Pesch, *Markusevangelium I. Teil*, p. 131; V. Taylor, *The Gospel according to Mark* (New York: St. Martin's Press, 2nd edn, 1966), p. 180.

In the evening of this day in Capernaum, the people of the city bring to Jesus all those who are sick and demon possessed (1.32). Jesus heals those who are sick with various diseases and casts out the demons from those who are possessed (1.34). This summary of Jesus' activity in the evening fulfills several functions in the narrative. First, the summary of Mk 1.32-34 shows that Jesus' deliverance of the possessed man in the synagogue and his healing of Simon's mother-in-law are not unique events. Instead, Jesus' response to these two individuals is typical of his ministry to many.[1] Jesus repeatedly responds to needy individuals with care and help. Secondly, this summary connects Jesus' ministry of healing the sick with his deliverance of those who are possessed. In Mark's Gospel, those who are sick and those who are possessed are characterized in a similar fashion.[2] The juxtaposition of the healing of a possessed man and the healing of a sick woman followed by a generalizing summary in which Jesus both heals the sick and delivers the possessed encourages the perception that sickness and demon possession are similar difficulties which both call for authoritative action by Jesus. Thirdly, the summary of 1.32-34 creates in the reader an expectation that Jesus will continue to come into contact with those who need healing and that Jesus has the authority and the will to help them.

The Leper (1.40-45)

In line with the expectation of the reader, Mark almost immediately narrates the healing of a leper (1.40-45). This man, who is simply identified as a leper, comes to Jesus asking him for help. The man's leprosy shows his physical need, and his kneeling before Jesus reveals

---

1. Hooker, *Mark*, p. 71; F.J. Matera, '"He Saved Others; He Cannot Save Himself": A Literary-Critical Perspective on the Markan Miracles', *Int* 47 (1993), p. 17; Pesch, *Markusevangelium I. Teil*, pp. 128, 132-33.

2. For a similar point see Tannehill, 'Narrative Christology', pp. 66-67. Mark's summary of Jesus' ministry in 3.7-12 also makes this connection between Jesus' authority over sickness and his authority over unclean spirits. The similarity between healing the sick and healing the possessed is expressed in passages where people come to Jesus to make a request on behalf of another. Jesus receives such requests with regard to the sick (1.29-31; 2.1-12; 5.21-24, 35-43; 7.31-37; 8.22-26) and with regard to the possessed (7.24-30; 9.14-29). In addition, demon possession is presented in Mark's Gospel as causing physical suffering (5.5; 9.17-18, 20-22, 25-27).

his reverence and respect for Jesus' authority.[1] The leper expresses his
entreaty with the words, 'If you will, you are able to cleanse me'
(1.40). This statement emphasizes the leper's confidence in the ability
of Jesus to heal, and it is not intended to cast doubt on the willingness
of Jesus to cleanse.[2] In this way, the leper shows his recognition of the
authority of Jesus over sickness. Jesus responds to the leper with compassion.[3] Thus, the reader is directed to recognize that this man and
other suppliants like him are worthy of the compassion of Jesus and
the sympathy of the reader.[4] Jesus expresses his willingness and gives

1.   The words καὶ γονυπετῶν are omitted by the uncials B, D, W, Γ, 0104, and
a few Itala manuscripts. The words may have been omitted accidentally through
homoeoteleuton. Yet the evidence against the inclusion of καὶ γονυπετῶν is fairly
strong and not much exegetical weight should be placed on the words for an understanding of the passage or Mark's characterization of the leper. For a discussion of
the evidence see Metzger, *Textual Commentary*, p. 76. On the significance of
bowing in miracle stories see G. Theissen, *Urchristliche Wundergeschichten: Ein
Beitrag zur formgeschichtlichen Erforschung der synoptischen Evangelien* (SNT, 8;
Gütersloh: Gütersloher Verlagshaus/Gerd Mohn, 1974), p. 63.
2.   C.E.B. Cranfield, *The Gospel according to Saint Mark* (CGTC; Cambridge:
Cambridge University Press, 4th edn, 1972), p. 91; Guelich, *Mark*, 73; Taylor,
Mark, p. 187.
3.   A number of commentators (Cranfield, *Mark*, p. 92; Gnilka, *Markus*, I,
pp. 92-93; Guelich, *Mark*, p. 74; Hooker, *Mark*, pp. 79-80; Lane, *Mark*, p. 86;
Mann, *Mark*, p. 219; Nineham, *Mark*, pp. 86-87; Pesch, *Markusevangelium I. Teil*,
pp. 141, 144; Schweizer, *Markus*, p. 31; Taylor, *Mark*, p. 187) take ὀργισθείς as
the original reading rather than σπλαγχνισθείς. The reading ὀργισθείς is supported
by the Western manuscript D and a few early Itala manuscripts. These commentators
generally argue that Jesus' anger is directed against the illness which represents the
distortion of God's creation by the forces of evil. However, the reading
σπλαγχνισθείς has early and widespread manuscript support and should be
regarded as the original reading. The reading ὀργισθείς may have been introduced in
order to make the reaction of Jesus in v. 41 compatible with his reaction in v. 43. On
this point see L.W. Hurtado, *Mark* (Good News Commentary; San Francisco:
Harper & Row, 1983), p. 20; Lührmann, *Markusevangelium*, p. 54; Metzger,
Textual Commentary, pp. 76-77. Lohmeyer (*Markus*, pp. 44-45) is ambiguous as to
which is the correct reading. He regards 1.40-45 as a compilation of two versions of
the same story: the first version ends with the silence command of Jesus and the
other ends with the command to report to the priest. Lohmeyer regards this compilation theory as important for the textual problem. One version of the story used
ὀργισθείς, while the other used σπλαγχνισθείς. The differences in the oral tradition
were maintained in the manuscript tradition even after the writing of the Gospel.
4.   Powell, *Narrative Criticism*, p. 57.

a word of command to the leper to be cleansed (1.41). Immediately, the leprosy leaves the man, and he is made clean (1.42).

Thus far, the leper's interaction with Jesus follows the pattern that was established in Mk 1.21-34. Jesus comes into contact with a needy person. Here the contact comes about because of the initiative of the man himself, who recognizes the authority of Jesus to cleanse him. The leper expresses his confidence in Jesus, and Jesus responds to this needy person with compassion and help. The result is the immediate and complete healing of the individual.

Beginning in v. 43, Mark includes certain features in his narration that go beyond the pattern established in 1.21-34. After cleansing the leper, Jesus treats him in a harsh manner. He sends the man away and sternly warns him not to speak about this healing to anyone.[1] Instead, the healed leper is to show himself to the priests and to make the proper offering as a testimony against them (1.44). This testimony has the meaning of incriminating evidence, presumably against the priests.[2] The healing of the leper serves as evidence for the authority of Jesus, an authority which the unbelieving religious leaders will refuse to accept. In direct disobedience to Jesus' command, the healed leper goes out and begins to spread around the word concerning Jesus (1.45).[3] The disobedience of the healed man explains the harsh words of Jesus in v. 43. Jesus was able to foresee the likely disregard of his command by the leper and sought to impress upon the man the

1. Previously in Mark's Gospel the word ἐκβάλλω has been used for Jesus' action of casting out demons (1.34, 39), so that the word conveys an antagonism toward the demons. However, ἐκβάλλω is also used of the Spirit's action of compelling Jesus to go out into the desert in order to be tested by Satan. In 1.43 Mark uses ἐξέβαλεν to show that Jesus is strongly compelling the man to leave. ἐμβριμάομαι is also a strong word which implies an attitude of anger and displeasure on the part of the speaker. See MM, p. 206. In 1.43 ἐμβριμησάμενος can be translated 'warn sternly', or 'admonish urgently'. See BAGD, p. 254; LSJ, p. 540.

2. E.K. Broadhead, 'Mk 1,44: The Witness of the Leper', *ZNW* 83 (1992), pp. 257-65; Guelich, *Mark*, p. 77; Lane, *Mark*, p. 88; Lührmann, *Markusevangelium*, p. 55; H. Strathmann, 'μάρτυς, μαρτυρέω, μαρτυρία, μαρτύριον', *TDNT*, IV, pp. 502-503. Elsewhere in Mark's Gospel, μαρτύριον is used in contexts where someone is giving a testimony against those who reject the message of Jesus (6.11; 13.9). In contrast, μαρτυρία and μάρτυς are used in Mark's Gospel for the false testimony brought against Jesus (14.55, 56, 59, 63).

3. The article ὁ in v. 45 refers to the leper and not to Jesus. See J. Swetman, 'Some Remarks on the Meaning of ὁ δὲ ἐξελθών in Mark 1,45', *Bib* 68 (1987), pp. 245-49.

seriousness of the injunction.[1] The likely disobedience of the healed leper moves Jesus from compassion to severity.

The result of the man's disobedience is that people start coming to Jesus from everywhere, and Jesus therefore becomes more restricted in his travels. In Mk 1.35 Jesus withdraws from the crowds that have been created by his miracles in Capernaum, in order that he might find a deserted place in which to pray. When Simon and the other disciples find Jesus to inform him that the people of Capernaum are seeking him, Jesus leaves the area around that city and travels to other towns to proclaim his message (1.36-38). In Mk 1.45 Jesus is once again out in the deserted places, but because of the disobedience of the leper the deserted places are no longer a refuge. In response to the miraculous power of Jesus, people come to him from everywhere. In Mark's Gospel, the people crowd Jesus and restrict his activity.[2] Jesus is not able to withdraw from the crowd to the deserted places for prayer, nor is he able to enter other cities in order to proclaim his message. Although he is able ($\delta\acute{u}\nu\alpha\sigma\alpha\iota$) to cleanse the leper (1.40), Jesus is not able ($\delta\acute{u}\nu\alpha\sigma\theta\alpha\iota$) to enter a city openly because of the leper's disobedience (1.45). When he finally returns to the city of Capernaum after a number of days, once again many people gather together at the door of the house where he is staying (2.1-2). The proclamation of the healed leper creates crowds that keep Jesus from important aspects of his mission.

The leper is characterized in ways that make him similar to the people who are healed in Mk 1.21-34. He is needy, insightful, trusting and healed. In contrast to the people who are healed in Mk 1.21-34, the leper is also disobedient, since he disregards Jesus' command to silence. Thus, the characterization of the leper includes both positive and negative traits.

The Paralytic (2.1-12)

The next two passages that deal with minor characters occur within the larger section of 2.1–3.6, in which Mark details the growing conflict between Jesus and the religious authorities. Mark presents the paralytic at the beginning of this section (2.1-12) and the man with the withered hand at the end (3.1-6). In a sense, Mark's portrayal of

---

1. Cranfield, *Mark*, p. 94; Gnilka, *Markus*, I, p. 93; Hurtado, *Mark*, p. 20; Lane, *Mark*, p. 87; Lührmann, *Markusevangelium*, pp. 54-55.
2. Malbon, 'Disciples/Crowds/Whoever', p. 120.

minor characters in this section is subservient to his narration of the growing antagonism of the religious authorities against Jesus. The needs of minor characters provide the setting in which Jesus and his opponents disagree. Thus, the passages that present minor characters in this section serve other purposes in the narrative beyond the characterization of these individuals.

The opening of the story concerning the paralytic is reminiscent of the summary of Jesus' healing ministry in Mk 1.32-34. Once again, Jesus is in a house in Capernaum, and many people are gathered (ἐπισυνηγμένη, 1.33; συνήχθησαν, 2.2) at the door (θύραν, 1.33; 2.2). In this second gathering, the size of the crowd increases so that there is no longer any room even at the door. In Mk 2.3, a paralytic is brought (φέροντες) to Jesus, just as earlier in the summary sick people were brought (ἔφερον) to Jesus for healing. The similarity of 2.1-3 with the summary in 1.32-34 creates the expectation that Jesus will use his authority to heal once again.

In addition, the opening of Mk 2.1-12 is connected with the ending of Mk 1.40-45 through the repetition of a number of key words.[1] The leper, in spreading around the word (λόγον) concerning Jesus, produces a situation in which Jesus is no longer (ὥστε μηκέτι) able openly to enter (εἰσελθεῖν) into a city. At the beginning of ch. 2 Jesus enters (εἰσελθών) Capernaum and many people gather at the house where he is staying so that there is no longer (ὥστε μηκέτι) room even at the doorway. Jesus responds by beginning to speak the word (λόγον) to them. In this way, the healing of the paralytic is closely tied to the healing of the leper.

The individual who meets with Jesus in Mk 2.1-12 is described initially as a paralytic who is being carried to Jesus by four men (2.3).[2] This individual is a needy person who is suffering from a paralysis that leaves him dependent on others. Blocked by the large crowd at the door, the friends of the paralytic dig out the roof at the place where Jesus is standing and lower the paralytic on his mattress down into the house (2.4).[3] In this action, Jesus sees their faith (2.5). Jesus acknowledges the faith of the whole party, both the paralytic and his

1. Marshall, *Faith*, p. 83; Dewey, *Public Debate*, p. 67.

2. For a helpful outline of Mk 2.1-12, see Dewey, *Public Debate*, pp. 70-71.

3. A κράβαττος was the common bed for a poor man. See BAGD, p. 447; MM, p. 357; Cranfield, *Mark*, p. 97; Gnilka, *Markus*, I, p. 98; Lane, *Mark*, p. 92; Marshall, *Faith*, p. 83; Nineham, *Mark*, p. 92; Taylor, *Mark*, p. 194.

friends. The paralytic is included within the company of the believing,
since Jesus' word concerning forgiveness is addressed directly to the
paralytic.[1] By narrating the observation of Jesus, Mark communicates
more directly what he has already shown through the actions of these
individuals. The paralytic and those who brought him have a trust in
Jesus that is expressed by their determination to overcome any obstacle
in order to reach him.[2] Their faith is significant in light of Jesus'
initial proclamation which demanded faith and repentance (1.15).

After observing their faith, Jesus says to the paralytic, 'Child, your
sins are forgiven' (2.5). This term of address, τέκνον, in Mk 2.5 is a
term of endearment, and as such it is reminiscent of the compassion of
Jesus toward the leper (1.41).[3] Jesus' pronouncement of forgiveness is
unusual, since the paralytic was apparently brought to Jesus for
healing, not forgiveness. Up until this point in the narrative, sick
people are brought to Jesus for healing, and Jesus responds with compassion and heals them. According to Jesus, however, the paralytic is
sinful and stands in need not only of physical healing but also of forgiveness. This does not necessarily indicate that Jesus regards the
man's paralysis as a direct consequence of his sin.[4] Instead, Jesus wants
to help the paralytic in a way that goes beyond physical healing.[5]

Jesus' pronouncement of forgiveness opens up the debate between
Jesus and the scribes concerning his authority as the Son of Man to
forgive sins. The need of the paralytic provides the opportunity for
Mark to display the antagonism of the scribes towards the authority of
Jesus. The unbelief of the scribes is heightened in the narrative, since
it stands in contrast to the faith of the paralytic and his friends.[6] In
order to demonstrate that he has the authority to forgive sins, Jesus
commands the paralytic to arise, take up his mattress and depart to his
house (2.11). The paralytic arises, takes up his mattress and walks out
in front of the crowd (2.12). Thus, the paralytic is both healed and
forgiven, since what is seen confirms what is not seen.

1. Gnilka, *Markus*, I, p. 99; Marshall, *Faith*, 87.
2. Guelich, *Mark*, pp. 85, 94; Theissen, *Wundergeschichten*, pp. 62-63.
3. For τέκνον as a term of endearment see Cranfield, *Mark*, p. 97; Mann,
Mark, p. 224; Marshall, *Faith*, p. 88; Nineham, *Mark*, p. 93; Taylor, *Mark*, p. 195.
4. Cranfield, *Mark*, pp. 97-98; Lane, *Mark*, p. 94.
5. Anderson, *Mark*, p. 100; Guelich, *Mark*, p. 95; Lane, *Mark*, p. 94;
Schweizer, *Markus*, p. 33.
6. Dewey, *Public Debate*, p. 90.

The paralytic is needy and dependent on others who carry him to Jesus. Both the paralytic and the four who carry him express their faith by their willingness to overcome the obstacles that block their access to Jesus. Through his contact with Jesus, the paralytic is healed of his sickness and forgiven of his sin. Mark's presentation of the paralytic and his friends is positive in that they recognize the authority of Jesus and trust in him. Nevertheless, Mark does not emphasize his portrayal of the paralytic, but rather uses the need of the paralytic in order to highlight the conflict between Jesus and the scribes.

The Man with the Withered Hand (3.1-6)

The larger section on the growing conflict between Jesus and his opponents (2.1–3.6) ends with the healing of the man with the withered hand.[1] The miracle story in Mk 3.1-6 not only presents a number of similarities with the healing of the paralytic in Mk 2.1-12,[2] but also shows certain connections with the delivering of the possessed man in 1.21-28. In both 3.1-6 and 1.21-28 Jesus enters into the synagogue (εἰσελθὼν εἰς τὴν συναγωγήν, 1.21; εἰσῆλθεν πάλιν εἰς τὴν συναγωγήν, 3.1). The πάλιν in Mk 3.1 serves as a reminder of Jesus' first entrance into the synagogue in Mk 1.21.[3] In both passages, Mark

---

1. Levi should not be classified as one of the minor characters from the crowd in light of the similarities between the call of Levi in Mk 2.13-14 and the call of the disciples in Mk 1.16-20. Both scenes take place alongside the sea (παρὰ τὴν θάλασσαν, 2.13; 1.16). Jesus passes by (παράγων, 2.14; 1.16) and sees (2.14; 1.16, 19) Levi. Although Levi is busy at his occupation (2.14; 1.16, 19), Jesus calls him to follow (2.14; 1.17, 20), and Levi immediately leaves his occupation in order to follow Jesus (2.14; 1.18, 20). Jesus goes to the home of Levi (2.15) just as he went to the home of Simon and Andrew (1.29). Therefore, Levi is being characterized as a disciple of Jesus. On the characterization of Levi as a disciple, see Guelich, *Mark*, p. 100; Kingsbury, *Conflict in Mark*, p. 92. Mark makes his first explicit reference to the disciples (τοῖς μαθηταῖς) of Jesus in Mk 2.15, where he explains that there were many disciples who were following Jesus. Levi appears to be part of this large number of disciples. In Mk 3.13-19 Jesus summons and commissions the twelve. From that point on in the narrative the term 'disciples' narrows, and 'the twelve' and 'the disciples' are used interchangeably.

2. On the relationship between 2.1-12 and 3.1-6, see the previous discussion in Chapter 2.

3. Dewey, *Public Debate*, p. 176; Gnilka, *Markus*, I, p. 126; Gundry, *Mark*, p. 149; Hurtado, *Mark*, p. 35; M.-J. Lagrange, *Evangile selon Saint Marc* (EBib; Paris: Librairie Lecoffre, 8th edn, 1947), p. 57; Pesch, *Markusevangelium I. Teil*, p. 188.

simply notes the presence of a man with a particular need (καὶ εὐθὺς
ἦν ἐν τῇ συναγωγῇ αὐτῶν ἄνθρωπος ἐν πνεύματι ἀκαθάρτῳ,
1.23; καὶ ἦν ἐκεῖ ἄνθρωπος ἐξηραμμένην ἔχων τὴν χεῖρα, 3.1),
and both healings take place on the sabbath (1.21; 3.2, 4). The
similarity of these two passages raises the expectation that Jesus will
again display his authority and restore the man with the withered hand
in the same way that he restored the man with the unclean spirit.

Mark's description of the man with the withered hand is fairly
brief, and it follows the basic pattern that was established early in the
narrative. The man has a similar problem to that of the paralytic,
since he has a limb which is useless and in need of restoration. He is
not described as being brought to Jesus by others nor as taking the
initiative to contact Jesus. Instead, Mark simply portrays the man as
present in the synagogue (3.1). The need of the man provides the setting for the conflict between Jesus and his opponents, since Jesus'
opponents view the man's need as an opportunity to accuse Jesus of
breaking the sabbath (3.2). Jesus sees in this response of his opponents
an expression of their hardness of heart. Their callousness toward
human suffering and their insensitivity toward the purposes of God
cause Jesus to react with anger and grief (3.5). In contrast to his
opponents, Jesus regards the man with the withered hand as worthy of
compassion and care. He commands the man to stretch out his hand,
and when the man obeys, the hand is restored (3.5). The man with the
withered hand is needy, obedient, healed and restored. He is the
recipient of Jesus' compassion and healing power.

Mark follows his narration of the healing of the man with a withered hand with a summary concerning Jesus' ministry toward the
crowd (3.7-12). Jesus withdraws to the sea and a great multitude of
people follow him. Mark reports that Jesus responds to the crowd by
healing many and by showing his authority over the unclean spirits.
The summary serves to create the anticipation that just as Jesus has
already repeatedly healed members of the crowd, so also he will
continue to heal individuals in the following narrative. In addition,
Mark uses the juxtaposition of Jesus' healings and Jesus' exorcisms as
a preparation for the ensuing accounts on minor characters. In the following chapters, Mark will juxtapose an exorcism next to a healing
miracle.

The Response of the Reader

Early in the narrative, Mark establishes a basic pattern for the relationship between Jesus and minor characters. In this pattern, a needy individual comes into contact with Jesus. Jesus has compassion on the individual, and through his authority he heals the person. Mark uses this basic pattern as early as Mk 1.21-34 in his presentation of typical examples and a summary statement. While every episode in which Jesus deals with a minor character shows some variations and additions, this basic pattern is followed throughout the early chapters of Mark's Gospel. The establishment and repetition of the pattern encourages the reader to expect further instances in which a needy person will come to Jesus in order to be helped by him.

In the early chapters of Mark's Gospel, the appearance of minor characters often provides Mark with an opportunity to narrate Jesus' interaction with other character groups such as the demons, the disciples and the opponents. In other words, minor characters appear in mixed episodes, passages in which Jesus is dealing with more than one group of characters. Often, the demons, the disciples or the opponents play a more active role in the passage than does the minor character. In Mk 1.40-45, the leper takes a more active and prominent role in the episode. However, Mark's characterization of the leper is mixed, showing both positive and negative traits. The leper acknowledges the authority of Jesus and receives his compassion, but following his healing, he disobeys Jesus' command. In his work on the disciples, Tannehill has argued that Mark uses the early chapters of his Gospel to encourage the reader to identify with the disciples.[1] Mark's portrayal of minor characters in these early chapters of the Gospel does little to divert the reader's identification away from the disciples. Unlike the disciples, these minor characters are not called to have a special relationship with Jesus, nor are they commissioned by Jesus to help fulfill the purposes of God.

Although Mark does not encourage the reader to identify with these minor characters, he does create sympathy for them.[2] Mark shows Jesus responding to these individuals with compassion and with a

1. Tannehill, 'Disciples in Mark', pp. 392-93, 394-95, 398. See also J.M. Bassler, 'The Parable of the Loaves', *JR* 66 (1986), p. 165; Dewey, 'Point of View', pp. 99, 103-105.
2. On the concept of sympathy in characterization see Powell, *Narrative Criticism*, p. 57.

desire to help and heal. The positive response of Jesus toward these characters creates sympathy in the reader. Refusing to feel compassion for these needy people would place the reader in the position of Jesus' opponents who have hardened their hearts against the helpless and against the ways of God.

A significant theme which is introduced in the episode concerning the healing of the paralytic is that of faith. In this passage, faith is expressed by overcoming obstacles in order to come to Jesus and be helped by him. The idea of faith is clearly important in Mark's Gospel, since Jesus' initial proclamation of the gospel of God demands faith and repentance in light of the nearness of the kingdom. In the following chapters of the Gospel, faith will become a prominent feature in Mark's depiction of minor characters.

Minor Characters in Mark 4.1–8.21

Mark sets chs. 4–8 apart as a distinct section within the overall narrative through the repeated use of the boat motif.[1] Particularly prominent in this section are the three boat scenes that present Jesus with his disciples: the stilling of the storm (4.35-41), the walking on the water (6.45-52) and the conversation concerning leaven (8.14-21).[2] Jesus crosses the sea a number of times with his disciples in Mk 4.1–8.21, but these three boat scenes are the only episodes that actually take place on the sea during a crossing.[3] In each of the boat scenes, either Jesus or the narrator criticizes the disciples for their lack of faith and understanding (4.40; 6.52; 8.17-18).[4] Thus, in chs. 4–8, Mark begins to highlight the growing incomprehension and lack of trust on the part of the disciples.

Within 4.1–8.21, Mark presents passages on minor characters in

---

1.　See the discussion above in Chapter 2.

2.　Malbon, 'Echoes and Foreshadowings', p. 214; Meye, *Jesus and the Twelve*, pp. 63-73; Petersen, 'Composition', p. 195; Tannehill, 'Disciples in Mark', pp. 398-99.

3.　Petersen, 'Composition', p. 195.

4.　The first indication of a lack of understanding on the part of the disciples comes in the first episode of chs. 4–8, in the parable discourse of Jesus. See Petersen, 'Composition', pp. 206-207. Fay ('Introduction to Incomprehension') points out that the literary structure of Mk 4.1-34 introduces and highlights the incomprehension of the disciples.

pairs.[1] He juxtaposes the exorcism of the Gerasene demoniac with the intercalated healing stories of Jairus and the hemorrhaging woman in ch. 5, and then places the exorcism of the Syrophoenician woman's daughter next to the healing of the deaf man in ch. 7. Mark has prepared the reader for this pairing of exorcisms with healings through his summary statements concerning Jesus' ministry to the crowd, which connect Jesus' delivering of the possessed with his healing of the sick (1.32-34; 3.7-12).[2] In Mk 4.1–8.21 minor characters begin to serve as foils for the disciples.[3] Their response to Jesus serves as a contrast to the response of the disciples, since these minor characters exemplify faith and understanding.

At the beginning of this major section of Mark's Gospel Jesus teaches the parable of the sower and interprets it for his followers (4.1-20). The parable and its interpretation aid the reader in evaluating characters by extending the reader's knowledge of the standards that Jesus uses to judge people. The reader is able to evaluate the people in the narrative according to how they measure up to the standards or expectations of Jesus.

After teaching the parable of the sower, Jesus is questioned in private about the meaning of the parable. Jesus' initial response to this inquiry is contained in Mk 4.10-12. The purpose of the following analysis is not to solve all the interpretive problems in Mk 4.10-12, of which there are many, but to point out the standards or expectations of Jesus as they are expressed in these verses. When Jesus withdraws from the crowd, those around him together with the twelve ask him about the meaning of the parable (4.10). Mark, therefore, shows two groups of people questioning Jesus in private, those around Jesus (οἱ περὶ αὐτόν) and the twelve. 'The twelve' refers back to the twelve disciples who were chosen by Jesus in Mk 3.13-19. Within the literary context of Mark's Gospel, the title 'those around him' refers back to

---

1. Malbon, 'Fallible Followers', pp. 36-37. Malbon ('Fallible Followers', p. 37) points out that Petersen's outline of Mk 4–8 in 'Composition' obscures the pairing of passages on minor characters.

2. See also Mk 6.13, where the disciples cast out demons and heal the sick as part of the mission that Jesus has given to them.

3. On the idea of the individuals from the crowd as foils for the disciples see Kingsbury, *Conflict in Mark*, pp. 25-27; Rhoads and Michie, *Mark as Story*, pp. 132-34; Tannehill, 'Disciples in Mark', pp. 391, 404-405.

Mk 3.31-35.[1] There, a crowd is seated around Jesus (περὶ αὐτόν, 3.32). Jesus looks at those who are sitting around him (περὶ αὐτόν), and he refers to them as his relatives, because they are doing the will of God (3.34-35). Thus in Mk 4.10-12 the audience for Jesus' teaching includes both the disciples and others, those who listen to the teaching of Jesus and seek further instruction in order that they might do the will of God. Since Jesus is addressing a broader audience than simply the disciples, the expectations that Jesus expresses in his teaching are not directed toward the disciples alone, but rather toward others as well.[2]

Jesus tells this wider group that they have been given the mystery of the kingdom of God, but those who are outside receive everything in parables (4.11). In this response, Jesus points out a further group of people, that is, those who are outside (ἐκείνοις τοῖς ἔξω). In Mk 4.10 the scene changes, and Jesus meets alone with his disciples and with others who seek further teaching. 'Those who are outside' appears then to include those who have just been left behind, that is, those people in the crowd who have listened to the teaching of Jesus but have shown no further interest in what he has to say. Therefore, 'those outside' includes the unreceptive members of the crowd.[3] However, the context of Mark's Gospel helps to identify further those who are left outside. The reference to ἔξω is reminiscent of the preceding passage in Mark's Gospel. In Mk 3.31-35 the physical relatives of Jesus are twice referred to as those who are outside (ἔξω) in contrast to those who are seated around (περὶ αὐτόν) Jesus (3.31, 32). Thus, the context of Mark's Gospel shows that the members of Jesus' family are included among those who are outside, at least temporarily.[4] Inserted within the account concerning Jesus' family is the accusation of the scribes from Jerusalem against Jesus. In Mk 3.20-21 Jesus' family members begin their attempt to seize Jesus,

---

1. Guelich, *Mark*, p. 204; J. Marcus, *The Mystery of the Kingdom of God* (SBLDS, 90; Atlanta: Scholars Press, 1986), p. 89. Marcus's work is particularly helpful for this study since the emphasis of his work is on how Mark intended the parable chapter to be heard by the first readers of his Gospel. See Marcus, *Mystery*, pp. 1, 6.

2. Guelich, *Mark*, p. 204; Marcus, *Mystery*, pp. 89-92.

3. Marcus, *Mystery*, p. 93.

4. Guelich, *Mark*, p. 208; Marcus, *Mystery*, pp. 93-94; W.E. Moore, '"Outside" and "Inside": A Markan Motif', *ExpTim* 98 (1986), p. 40.

thinking that he is out of his mind. In 3.22 the scene changes and the reader's attention is focused on the scribes from Jerusalem, who accuse Jesus of casting out demons through the power of Beelzebul, the ruler of the demons. Jesus' response to the scribes is to speak to them in parables (3.23). By speaking to them in this way he is treating the scribes as outsiders.[1] Therefore, those who oppose and reject Jesus take their place among those who are outside along with those who show no enduring interest in Jesus' teaching.

Jesus presents everything in parables to those on the outside in order that they might see and yet not perceive, and hear and yet not understand, lest they repent and be forgiven (4.12).[2] The outsiders cannot ultimately see, hear or understand the true significance of Jesus' teaching and ministry. This does not mean that, in contrast to the outsiders, the insiders will always see, hear and understand. Jesus' statement in Mk 4.11-12 is not strictly antithetical. The disciples and those around Jesus have been given the mystery of the kingdom of God, but the outsiders receive everything in parables so that they might not understand. This does not exclude the possibility that the insiders, the disciples and those around Jesus, will also hear parables from Jesus. Also, Mk 4.13 clearly shows that these insiders will not always see, hear and understand. Here Jesus criticizes the insiders for their lack of understanding in light of their question concerning the meaning of the parable. Those who are on the outside find it impossible to truly see, hear and understand. Those who are on the inside should be able to see, hear and understand since they have been given the mystery of the kingdom of God, but even the insiders may have trouble comprehending all that Jesus says and does.[3] Nevertheless, Jesus expects his disciples and others who are drawn from the crowd to see, hear and understand. When they do not respond to Jesus with true insight, they are behaving like the outsiders who will not be forgiven.[4]

1. Guelich, *Mark*, p. 208; Marcus, *Mystery*, p. 94; Moore, '"Outside" and "Inside"', p. 41.

2. The τὰ πάντα of Mk 4.11 refers to Jesus' ministry in general, both his words and works. Everything that the outsiders could potentially see and hear in the ministry of Jesus is considered parabolic. See Guelich, *Mark*, p. 208; Lane, *Mark*, p. 158; Marcus, *Mystery*, pp. 108-11.

3. Guelich, *Mark*, p. 207; Marcus, *Mystery*, pp. 99, 101.

4. It is worth noting who sees, hears and understands in Mark's narrative. In

In Mk 4.14-20 Jesus interprets the parable of the sower, and this interpretation further clarifies the expectations of Jesus. Not only does Jesus expect others to see, hear and understand, but he expects them to withstand the tribulation and persecution that comes to those who accept his teaching (4.16-17). Jesus regards it as necessary for others to value his teaching more than the desires and riches of this age (4.18-19). He expects others to receive his teaching and bear fruit (4.20). These standards of judgment given by Jesus help the reader to evaluate the different people in the narrative and their responses to Jesus and his teaching.

The Gerasene Demoniac (5.1-20)

Mark follows his narration of the parable discourse with a series of miracle stories (4.35–5.43). In each miracle story, Jesus deals with people who are facing a particularly severe set of circumstances.[1] All human efforts at a solution have been exhausted and the situation seems beyond hope. The miracle immediately following the parable discourse is the stilling of the storm, the first boat scene that presents Jesus with his disciples (4.35-41). In that scene, the disciples are

---

general, when the disciples are presented as seeing or hearing, they are also portrayed as misunderstanding (6.49, 50; 9.4-6, 38, 10.41; see also 6.52; 7.17-18; 8.17-18, 21). In contrast to this, Mark leaves the reader with more hope concerning the disciples' perceptions after the resurrection of Jesus (13.7, 14, 29; 16.7). The opponents of Jesus see and hear him, but their response is to condemn Jesus and to seek his death (2.16; 3.2; 7.2-5; 11.18; 14.11, 58, 64). Even when Jesus speaks to them in parables, the opponents show a basic level of understanding, but their superficial understanding leads only to a desire for Jesus' arrest (12.1, 12). In this way, the opponents see and yet do not see, hear and yet do not understand. In the future, the opponents of Jesus will see the Son of Man seated at the right hand of God and coming with the clouds of heaven (14.62). In other words, the opponents will finally see and understand only when it is too late to be counted among God's chosen ones (13.26-27). When the crowd sees Jesus or hears about him, it quickly gathers around him (1.28, 32-33; 2.1-2; 3.7-8; 6.33-34, 54-55; 9.15). Prior to the Bartimaeus story (10.46-52), minor characters who see or hear Jesus ask him for healing (5.6, 22, 27; 7.25; 10.47). After the Bartimaeus story, minor characters who see or hear Jesus respond with insight (12.28; 15.39). For further study on the significance of hearing in Mark's Gospel see Malbon, 'Disciples/Crowds/Whoever', pp. 113-15.

1.   K.M. Fisher and U.C. von Wahlde, 'The Miracles of Mark 4:35-5:43: Their Meaning and Function in the Gospel Framework', *BTB* 11 (1981), pp. 13-14; Guelich, *Mark*, p. 293; Malbon, 'Fallible Followers', p. 36.

characterized as fearful and unbelieving. Jesus not only rebukes the wind and the waves but also rebukes the disciples for their timidity and lack of faith (πίστιν, 4.40). Moreover, the narrator points out that the disciples 'feared a great fear' (ἐφοβήθησαν φόβον μέγαν, 4.41). This fear is no longer directed at the fierce storm, but at Jesus, this one who demands the obedience of the wind and the sea.

In Mk 5.1 Jesus and the disciples arrive on the other side of the sea at the region of the Gerasenes. Immediately, Jesus is met by a man with an unclean spirit (ἄνθρωπος ἐν πνεύματι ἀκαθάρτῳ, 5.2). The initial reference to this individual is similar to the introduction of the man with an unclean spirit in Mk 1.23 (ἄνθρωπος ἐν πνεύματι ἀκαθάρτῳ). In both cases, the possessed man is described by the narrator as simply on the scene when Jesus is in a particular place. The description of the possessed man in ch. 5 is different from that in ch. 1, because Mark goes on to give a lengthy explanation concerning the suffering of this man (5.3-5). The extended description of the man's plight shows the severity of this particular case of possession and the utter helplessness of the man.[1] The man was ostracized, living among the tombs, he was untamed, breaking any restraints, and he was tormented, crying out and cutting himself with stones.

Mk 5.6 fits into the context of the story rather awkwardly. Although he has already narrated the meeting of Jesus with the man with the unclean spirit, Mark presents this meeting a second time. The possessed man sees Jesus from afar, runs to him, and prostrates himself before Jesus. The possession of the man leads Jesus to deal directly with the demons who are controlling the man (5.7-13). Jesus' conversation with the unclean spirits in this instance is reminiscent of his conversation with the unclean spirit in Mk 1.23-26. As before, the unclean spirit cries out with a loud voice (κράξας φωνῇ μεγάλῃ, 5.7; φωνῆσαν φωνῇ μεγάλῃ, 1.26). The unclean spirit rejects any basis for a relationship with Jesus (τί ἐμοὶ καὶ σοί, 5.7; τί ἡμῖν καὶ σοί, 1.24). The spirit recognizes Jesus as the Son of God ('Ιησοῦ υἱὲ τοῦ θεοῦ τοῦ ὑψίστου, 5.7; 'Ιησοῦ Ναζαρηνέ...ὁ ἅγιος τοῦ θεοῦ, 1.24). In both instances, the demons fear destruction and torment (1.24; 5.7, 10). Jesus' command to the unclean spirits to come out of the man is parallel to Jesus' earlier command of exorcism (ἔξελθε, 1.25, 5.8). As before, the unclean spirits obey the command of Jesus

---

1. Anderson, *Mark*, p. 146; Guelich, *Mark*, p. 278; Hurtado, *Mark*, p. 69; Pesch, *Markusevangelium I. Teil*, pp. 285-86.

and come out of the man (1.26; 5.13).

Nevertheless, the exorcism of the Gerasene demoniac contains a few unique features. These features serve to heighten the power and destructiveness of the unclean spirits who have possessed the Gerasene demoniac. In this exorcism, Jesus asks for the name of the unclean spirit, and the spirit responds with the reply, 'Legion is my name, because we are many' (5.9). This name, which represents a great number, emphasizes the extent of the possessed man's domination.[1] Also unique is the fact that Jesus permits the unclean spirits to enter into a nearby herd of swine (5.11-13). The legion of spirits leaves the man and enters the swine, causing them to rush down a steep bank into the sea where they drown (5.13). In this way, Mark depicts again the destructive nature and evil intent of the unclean spirits.[2]

Those who were tending the herd of swine flee and report the events throughout the region, and the people of the region come out to see what has happened (5.14). When they come to Jesus, the people see the man who had been possessed seated, clothed and having a sound mind (5.15). The calm demeanor of the man in contrast to his previous raging fury is not unlike the calm after the storm in Mk 4.35-41. The response of the onlookers is similar to the response of the disciples in the preceding episode. They become frightened (ἐφοβήθησαν, 4.41; 5.15), and, like the disciples, their fear is directed at Jesus.[3] They express their fear of Jesus by asking him to leave their region (5.17).

In contrast to the people of the region and thus in contrast to the disciples, the man who had been possessed is not afraid of Jesus. Instead of wanting to be rid of him, he begs Jesus for permission to be with him (ἵνα μετ' αὐτοῦ ᾖ, 5.18).[4] The wording of the man's request corresponds to the expression in Mk 3.14 concerning the disciples. There Jesus appoints the twelve in order that they might be

---

1. Guelich, *Mark*, p. 281; Hurtado, *Mark*, p. 69; Lane, *Mark*, p. 184; Lohmeyer, *Markus*, p. 96; Pesch, *Markusevangelium I. Teil*, p. 286.

2. Guelich, *Mark*, p. 282; Lane, *Mark*, p. 186.

3. Anderson, *Mark*, p. 149; Fisher and von Wahlde, 'Miracles', p. 14; Lane, *Mark*, p. 187.

4. παρακαλέω is used seven times in Mark's Gospel and four of those seven uses are in 5.1-20. The demons plead with Jesus that he might not send them out of the region (5.10, 12). The people of the region plead with Jesus that he might leave their area (5.17). In contrast, the healed demoniac pleads with Jesus in order that he might be with Jesus (5.18).

with him (ἵνα ὦσιν μετ' αὐτοῦ). The implication of the man's request is that he wants to become a disciple of Jesus.[1] Jesus refuses his request and sends him back to his own house and to his own family, in order that he might report to them all that the Lord in his mercy has done for him (5.19).

The command of Jesus to the healed demoniac is somewhat different from the command of Jesus to the healed leper. In Mk 1.44 Jesus sternly warns the healed leper to tell no one about his healing, but then, in disobedience to this command, the man freely spreads around the word concerning Jesus. In Mk 5.19 Jesus does not insist on complete silence by the healed demoniac, but his command does contain certain limitations. The man is to return to his house and to his family and there report what the Lord has done for him.[2] Therefore, Jesus' command to the healed demoniac is an indirect injunction to secrecy.[3] The man's response, however, is an unlimited proclamation concerning Jesus (5.20). Instead of reporting what the Lord had done for him, the man proclaims what Jesus did for him.[4] Instead of making his report at his home, the man makes his proclamation in the Decapolis, with the result that all are amazed.[5] Mark uses the same expression for the proclamation of the healed leper and the proclamation of the healed demoniac (ἤρξατο κηρύσσειν, 1.45; 5.20).[6] Mark's narration is more subtle in 5.19-20 than in 1.43-45, but the picture is much the same. Jesus commands secrecy, but the healed individuals disobey and

1. Gnilka, *Markus*, I, p. 206; Guelich, *Mark*, pp. 284-85; Pesch, *Markusevangelium I. Teil*, p. 293; Schweizer, 'Life of Faith', p. 391; Taylor, *Mark*, p. 284. See also Mk 5.40 where the phrase τοὺς μετ' αὐτοῦ refers to Peter, James and John.

2. The proximity of the possessive adjective σούς to the possessive pronoun σου in 5.19 indicates that the man's people bear some relationship with the house that belongs to him. Moulton and Milligan (MM, p. 581) point out that σός is often used substantivally in the papyri to indicate a person's household, agent or friend.

3. Gnilka, *Markus* I, pp. 206-207; Theissen, *Wundergeschichten*, p. 77.

4. Petersen, 'Composition', pp. 213-14; W. Wrede, *Das Messiasgeheimnis in den Evangelien: Zugleich ein Beitrag zum Verständnis des Markusevangeliums* (Göttingen: Vandenhoeck & Ruprecht, 1901), pp. 139-41.

5. Gnilka, *Markus*, I, pp. 206-207; Theissen, *Wundergeschichten*, p. 68; Wrede, *Messiasgeheimnis*, pp. 139-41.

6. In Mark's Gospel, ἀπαγγέλλω is used for the reporting of a particular event (5.14; 6.30), while κηρύσσω is normally used for the general proclamation of the gospel or the message concerning Jesus (1.7, 14, 38, 39, 45; 3.14; 6.12; 13.10; 14.9).

freely proclaim the miraculous work of Jesus.[1]

The traits of the Gerasene demoniac are strikingly different before and after his encounter with Jesus. Before Jesus, the man was possessed by unclean spirits, alienated, chaotic, powerful, tortured and doomed. Since he was completely controlled by demonic power, he was beyond any human subjugation. From Jesus the demoniac receives healing and freedom, with the result that he is calm, self-controlled and sane. In contrast to the people of the region and in contrast to the disciples, the man is unafraid in the presence of Jesus. Although the healed demoniac desires to become a disciple, Jesus sends the man home, moving him from a life among the tombs to a life among his own family. Nevertheless, at the end of the episode, the healed man is disobedient to the command of Jesus, because he would not be silent concerning Jesus' miraculous power.

Jairus and the Hemorrhaging Woman (5.21-43)

The series of miracle stories that began in Mk 4.35 continues with the healing of Jairus's daughter and the healing of the hemorrhaging woman in Mk 5.21-43. Once again, individuals come to Jesus when their situations seem beyond hope, when all human efforts at a solution have come to an end. Faith and fear continue to be prominent themes in 5.21-43, with Mark presenting minor characters as those who overcome fear and respond with faith.[2] Consequently, the response of these minor characters stands in contrast to that of the disciples.

Mark inserts the healing of the hemorrhaging woman within his narration concerning Jairus. The intercalation of one episode within another is a common literary technique in Mark's Gospel.[3] Mark will begin the narration of one episode, stop in the middle of it, move to another episode, and then return to the first in order to complete it. In 5.21-43 Mark begins the account concerning Jairus, but before

---

1. On the disobedience of the healed demoniac see also Tannehill, 'Narrative Christology', pp. 71, 91.

2. On the importance of the themes of fear and faith in Mk 4.35–5.43 see Fisher and von Wahlde, 'Miracles', p. 14; Tolbert, *Sowing*, pp. 164-72.

3. Donahue (*Are You the Christ?*, p. 42) lists the following passages as examples of intercalation in Mark's Gospel: 3.20-21 [22-30] 31-35; 5.21-24 [25-34] 35-43; 6.7-13 [14-29] 30-32; 11.12-14 [15-19] 20-26; 14.1-2 [3-9] 10-11; 14.12-16 [17-21] 22-25; 14.54 [55-65] 66-72.

completing it he shifts the focus of the narrative to the story of the hemorrhaging woman, and only then does he return to finish the account concerning Jairus. Mark uses intercalation, at least in part, to clarify the meaning and significance of the two episodes that have been brought together.[1] Through the use of intercalation, Mark is able to highlight both the similarities and the differences between Jairus and the hemorrhaging woman, thereby enhancing his characterization of each individual.

Jairus, a synagogue ruler, comes to Jesus and in the presence of a large crowd falls at Jesus' feet (5.21-22).[2] The ruler of a synagogue was an elected official and one who was held in esteem by the Jewish community.[3] His primary responsibilities were the supervision of the synagogue building and the arrangement of the synagogue services.[4]

---

1. Fowler, *Let the Reader Understand*, pp. 142-44; Malbon, 'Narrative Criticism', p. 39; Marshall, *Faith*, pp. 91-92; Rhoads and Michie, *Mark as Story*, p. 51. Donahue (*Are You the Christ?*, pp. 42-43, 58-63) argues that Mark has a theological motivation for using intercalations. On this theological motivation see also J.R. Edwards, 'Markan Sandwiches: The Significance of Interpolations in Markan Narratives', *NovT* 31 (1989), pp. 193-216.

2. Malbon ('Jewish Leaders', pp. 275-76) treats Jairus as a member of the religious establishment which, in general, stands opposed to Jesus. Yet instead of being a foe of Jesus, Jairus puts his faith in him. Malbon concludes that Jairus is one of the exceptions to the general rule that the religious leaders are the enemies of Jesus. Mark schematizes the group characterization of the religious leaders, but he refuses to absolutize this schema. It is true that Mark refuses to absolutize his generally negative portrayal of the religious establishment. However, it is not at all clear that Jairus should be grouped together with the opposing religious leaders in the first place. Nothing in the narrative up until this point would give any indication that there is an antagonism between Jesus and the synagogues or that a leader of a synagogue would side with the scribes and Pharisees in opposition to Jesus. Jesus seems to be welcome in the synagogues throughout Galilee, and these synagogues serve as the setting for his teaching (1.21-27, 39; 3.1-6). Mark does not introduce Jairus as someone who has ties to the religious authorities, but rather he seems to portray Jairus as one member of the large crowd that has gathered around Jesus (5.21-22).

3. W. Schrage ('συναγωγή, ἐπισυναγωγή, ἀρχισυνάγωγος, ἀποσυνάγωγος', *TDNT*, VII, p. 845) states that there are numerous references to ἀρχισυνάγωγοι in literature and inscriptions from all parts of the Roman Empire and that these synagogue rulers were highly regarded. On the election of synagogue rulers see Schrage, 'συναγωγή', p. 846.

4. Schrage, 'συναγωγή', p. 846; Cranfield, *Mark*, p. 183; Gnilka, *Markus*, I, p. 214; Guelich, *Mark*, p. 295; Gundry, *Mark*, p. 278; Hurtado, *Mark*, p. 77; Lane, *Mark*, p. 190; Marshall, *Faith*, pp. 94-95; Pesch, *Markusevangelium I. Teil*, p. 300.

Jairus, this man of high standing in the community, bows down before Jesus. Earlier in the narrative, the leper and the Gerasene demoniac bowed down before Jesus as a recognition of his authority (1.40; 5.6). In the same way, Jairus humbles himself before the authority of Jesus.[1] Jairus faces a desperate need in that his daughter is at the point of death, and so he pleads with Jesus to come and lay his hands upon her in order that she might be saved (5.23). Jairus's request reveals his confidence in the authority of Jesus to save his child.

Jesus begins to accompany Jairus to his house and the whole crowd follows along as well, pressing around Jesus (5.24).[2] Mark next turns the reader's attention to a particular woman in the crowd (5.25). His extended description of the woman and her condition reveals a number of differences between the woman and Jairus. Jairus is a prominent leader in the religious community, while the woman has a condition that would render her ritually unclean, thus isolating her from the religious community. Mark describes her ailment as a menstrual hemorrhage that has lasted for twelve years.[3] Jairus has a

---

1.　Gnilka, *Markus*, I, p. 214; Guelich, *Mark*, p. 295; Lührmann, *Markusevangelium*, p. 103; Marshall, *Faith*, p. 95; Pesch, *Markusevangelium I. Teil*, p. 300; Theissen, *Wundergeschichten*, p. 63.

2.　The language that Mark uses concerning the crowd is reminiscent of earlier instances in the narrative where the crowd gathers around Jesus. As in the episode of the paralytic's healing, many people gather around Jesus (συνήχθησαν πολλοί, 2.2; συνήχθη ὄχλος πολύς, 5.21). The gathering of the great crowd forces the paralytic and his four helpers to express their faith by overcoming the obstacle of the crowd in their approach to Jesus. The only other time that συνάγω is used with reference to the crowd is in Mk 4.1 at the beginning of the parable discourse. There, Jesus enters into a boat, presumably in order that he might maintain a safe distance from the crowd and not be pressed by it. See Mk 3.9. The press of the crowd around Jesus in Mk 5.24 (συνέθλιβον αὐτόν) recalls the potential problem of the crowd's press on Jesus in Mk 3.9 (θλίβωσιν αὐτόν). The verb συνθλίβω is only used in Mk 5.24, 31, while θλίβω is used only in Mk 3.9. In the next verse (3.10), many fall upon Jesus in order that by touching (ἄψωνται) him they might be healed of their torments (μάστιγας). Outside of Mk 3.10, μάστιξ is used only with reference to the hemorrhaging woman who touches Jesus. The gathering and pressure of the crowd, therefore, creates an expectation of faith and healing.

3.　Mark describes the woman's condition in terminology similar to that used in Lev. 15.25 (LXX) for ritually defiling bleeding (οὖσα ἐν ῥύσει αἵματος, Mk 5.25; ῥέῃ ῥύσει αἵματος, Lev. 15.25 [LXX]). Also, the phrase ἡ πηγὴ τοῦ αἵματος αὐτῆς in Mk 5.29 appears to be dependent on Lev. 12.7 (LXX). On the relationship between Mark's language and Leviticus see Cranfield, *Mark*, p. 184; Guelich, *Mark*,

daughter, while the woman's condition would preclude childbearing. Jairus is undoubtedly a man of means, while the woman has impoverished herself seeking a solution to her problem.

In spite of their many differences, Jairus and the woman have in common their extreme need. His daughter is at the point of death, and the woman's suffering has no solution. Jairus and the woman also have in common their trust in Jesus and his power. She is convinced that if she can only touch his garments, she will be saved. Unlike Jairus, who falls at Jesus' feet, the woman approaches Jesus from behind, overcoming the press of the crowd, and touches his garment (5.27). Jairus seeks help in public, but the woman seeks healing in secret.[1] As soon as the woman touches Jesus, she realizes that she has been healed of her torment (5.29).

In Mk 5.30 the narrative shifts from the woman and her healing to the dialogue between Jesus and the woman. Both the woman and Jesus are aware that a healing has taken place, but the disciples are without understanding. When Jesus turns around and asks who touched him, the disciples question the logic of Jesus' inquiry in light of the press of the crowd (5.30-31). In spite of the reaction of the disciples, Jesus continues his attempt to make a private, secret healing into a public event.

The woman knows that Jesus is looking for her, and she responds with fear and trembling (5.33). The woman's fear is similar to the fear expressed in Mk 4.41 and 5.15. Both the disciples and the inhabitants of the Gerasenes are portrayed as responding in a negative manner when they react with fear. This fear is not a feeling of awe and amazement in response to a miracle, but rather it is a feeling of terror in response to the miracle-worker, Jesus. The woman is not afraid because she has been healed, but because she has been discovered and must now present herself to Jesus.[2] In spite of her fear, she falls before Jesus and reports what she has done. In this way, she takes the same posture after her healing that Jairus took when making his initial request.

p. 296; Gundry, *Mark*, pp. 279-80; Hurtado, *Mark*, p. 77; Pesch, *Markusevangelium I. Teil*, p. 301; M.J. Selvidge, *Woman, Cult, and Miracle Recital: A Redactional Critical Investigation on Mark 5:24-34* (Lewisburg, PA: Bucknell University Press, 1990), pp. 47-51; Taylor, *Mark*, p. 290.

1.   Edwards, 'Markan Sandwiches', p. 204.
2.   Marshall, *Faith*, p. 107.

Jesus' address of the woman as daughter reveals the depth of his compassion toward her (5.34). Just as Jairus cares deeply for his sick daughter, so also Jesus cares for this needy woman. Jesus recognizes the woman's faith and refers to it as the basis for her salvation. The salvation that Jairus is seeking for his daughter (5.23) has come to this woman through faith (5.28, 34).[1] The woman expressed her faith through her complete confidence that Jesus had the authority to help her and through her willingness to overcome the press of the crowd to reach Jesus.[2] Unlike the disciples, who fear and have no faith, the woman fears but has faith. Jesus dismisses the woman in peace and health, thereby indicating that the woman has received inner wholeness as well as physical healing.[3]

The hemorrhaging woman's characterization changes through the course of the miracle story, and the turning point is her contact with Jesus. Before touching Jesus' garment, she is needy, suffering, tormented, ritually unclean, alienated from society, poor, believing and secretive. She is completely without hope apart from Jesus. After her contact with Jesus, she is healed, fearful, understanding, courageous, honest, humble and saved.

While the woman finds salvation and peace, Jairus's situation becomes more desperate. Jairus receives the news that his daughter has died (5.35). Jesus then calls on Jairus to put away his fear and instead have faith (5.36). Jairus's subsequent actions show that, like the woman who was healed, he also overcomes his fear by believing that Jesus is able to confront a desperate situation with the power of God. Jesus takes what has been a public event up until this point and turns it into a private healing. He dismisses the crowd (5.37), and puts out the many mourners who are making a commotion at Jairus's house (5.40).

When Jesus finally raises the girl, only the father, the mother and three of Jesus' disciples are present (5.40-42). The healing of Jairus's daughter is similar to the healing of the hemorrhaging woman in

---

1. Lohmeyer, *Markus*, pp. 100-101.

2. Lührmann, *Markusevangelium*, p. 104; Theissen, *Wundergeschichten*, pp. 62-63. See also Mk 2.3-5.

3. Anderson, *Mark*, p. 154; Guelich, *Mark*, p. 299; Lagrange, *Marc*, p. 142; Lane, *Mark*, p. 194; Taylor, *Mark*, p. 293. On the function of the dismissal in Synoptic miracle stories see Theissen, *Wundergeschichten*, p. 77.

several ways.[1] Both healings take place through physical contact in spite of the apparent ritual impurity of both. Both the hemorrhaging woman and Jairus's daughter are healed immediately (εὐθύς, 5.29, 42). Mark points out that Jairus's daughter was twelve years old at the time of her healing (5.42) which serves as a reminder of the hemorrhaging woman's long suffering.[2] Her affliction continued for twelve years, that is, for as long as the young girl had lived (5.25). Mark's narration concerning the healing of Jairus's daughter concludes with a secrecy command. Jesus commands the parents not to make the healing known to anyone (5.43). Mark gives no indication that this command is disobeyed, and the impression is left that Jairus and his wife are obedient to the command.

Jairus is different from the hemorrhaging woman since he is respected, influential and wealthy. Yet Jairus is also similar to the woman in that he is desperately needy, humble and obedient. Like the hemorrhaging woman he is completely without hope apart from Jesus. Mark highlights the fact that Jairus also overcomes fear and maintains his faith in Jesus even in the face of his daughter's death. On the basis of his faith in Jesus, his daughter is saved as earlier the hemorrhaging woman was saved (5.23, 28, 34). Both Jairus and the hemorrhaging woman stand in contrast to the disciples who fear and fail in their faith.

The Syrophoenician Woman (7.24-30)
As pointed out earlier, Mark 4–8 is built around three boat scenes in which the disciples respond to Jesus with a lack of courage, faith or

---

1. Marshall, *Faith*, p. 93. The healing of Jairus's daughter is also similar to earlier healings in Mark's Gospel. The raising of Jairus's daughter is narrated in a similar manner to the raising up of Simon's mother-in-law. Jesus grasps the hand of the child (κρατήσας τῆς χειρός, 5.41; 1.31) and causes her to arise (ἔγειρε, 5.41; ἤγειρεν, 1.31). Mark shows the confirmation of the miracle by portraying Simon's mother-in-law as serving a meal (1.31). In a similar way, the young girl is given something to eat as an evidence of her healing (5.43). The raising of Jairus's daughter shows some similarities to the healing of the paralytic. As in the healing of the paralytic, Jesus commands the girl to arise (ἔγειρε, 5.41; 2.9, 11) with the result that she is able to walk (περιεπάτει, 5.42; περιπάτει, 2.9). In both miracles, the response of the onlookers is amazement (ἐξέστησαν, 5.42; ἐξίστασθαι, 2.12). The verb ἐξίστημι is used to indicate the response of the onlookers to Jesus' healings only in Mk 2.12 and 5.42.

2. Marshall, *Faith*, p. 99.

understanding. The second boat scene, in which Jesus walks on the water (6.45-52), functions as an important background to Mark's presentation of the Syrophoenician woman (7.24-30). In this scene the disciples react with fear and amazement when Jesus comes to them, walking on the water. Their response of fear is shown to be negative, because Jesus immediately commands them to have courage and not to fear. Their response of amazement is also negative, because the narrator points out that their amazement grew out of their lack of understanding concerning the loaves and out of their hardness of heart. Here the disciples are portrayed in terms that are appropriate for the outsiders and the opponents of Jesus (3.5; 4.12).

Mark follows this boat scene with a summary of Jesus' healing ministry in Gennesaret (6.53-56). The healings are expressed in terms which recall Jesus' healing of the paralytic and his healing of the hemorrhaging woman. Like the miracle story concerning the paralytic, people carry (περιφέρειν, 6.55; φέροντες, 2.3) those who are sick on mattresses (τοῖς κραβάττοις, 6.55; τὸν κράβαττον, 2.4) to the place where Jesus is (ὅπου ἤκουον ὅτι ἐστίν, 6.55; ὅπου ἦν, 2.4). Like the miracle story concerning the hemorrhaging woman, those who touch even the hem of Jesus' garment (ἵνα κἂν τοῦ κρασπέδου τοῦ ἱματίου αὐτοῦ ἅψωνται, 6.56; ἐὰν ἅψωμαι κἂν τῶν ἱματίων αὐτοῦ, 5.28) are saved (ἐσῴζοντο, 6.56; σωθήσομαι, 5.28). While the preceding boat scene shows the disciples behaving as outsiders, the summary of Jesus' healing reminds the reader that there are others who respond to Jesus with faith. Up until this point in the narrative, Jesus has specifically acknowledged the faith of only the paralytic along with his friends and the hemorrhaging woman (2.5; 5.34).

Once again, in the following episode (7.1-23), Jesus criticizes the disciples for their lack of understanding. Jesus uses parabolic language to reject the teaching of the Pharisees concerning ritual defilement. In private, the disciples inquire further about the meaning of the parable, and this inquiry brings upon them the criticism of Jesus for their lack of understanding (7.17-18). Like the outsiders, the disciples are not able to comprehend the parables of Jesus. This negative portrayal of the disciples stands in contrast to the following positive presentation of a minor character.

Unlike the disciples, the Syrophoenician woman exemplifies boldness and understanding. Mark patterns his initial description of this woman after his introduction of both Jairus and the hemorrhaging woman.[1] However, the Syrophoenician woman is different from the hemorrhaging woman and Jairus in that she is a Gentile. Before presenting the woman's request concerning her daughter, Mark stresses the woman's status as a Gentile by pointing out that she is Greek, presumably in language and culture, and Syrophoenician by race (7.26).[2] This difference in race substantially affects the course of the story.

The woman asks Jesus to cast a demon out of her daughter, but Jesus responds with an enigmatic remark: 'Let the children be satisfied first, for it is not good to take the bread of the children and throw it to the dogs' (7.27). Apparently, Jesus is protecting the privileges of Israel and refusing to distribute these benefits among the Gentiles. The healing (the bread) which Jesus gives as the authoritative Son of God belongs exclusively to the Jews (the children) and should not be squandered on the Gentiles (the dogs). This harsh response of Jesus is only slightly tempered by the word πρῶτον. When Jesus says that first of all the children should be satisfied, he seems to envision the possibility that in the future the Gentiles will participate in the privileges of Israel. However, this future possibility offers little hope to the Syrophoenician woman who has an immediate concern.[3] Therefore, according to the content of his answer, Jesus appears to be refusing to help the woman because she is a Gentile. Moreover, the form of Jesus' answer also serves as a rejection of the woman. Jesus speaks to the woman with a parable, which is the language that he uses in order to speak to those on the outside (4.11). In both form and content, Jesus' answer is a rejection. Jesus refuses to help the woman because, as a Gentile, she is an outsider to the privileges of Israel.

However, it is precisely this rejection and its basis in the Gentile status of the woman that is so difficult to explain in the context of Mark's Gospel. Jesus has already been in Gentile territory before in the narrative, and there he encountered a man with a legion of unclean spirits (5.1-20). Without any hint of rejection, Jesus delivered this man from a condition far more severe than the possession of this woman's daughter. Jesus' rejection of the Syrophoenician woman is even more inexplicable in that it follows immediately after his

1. On the similarity between Mark's description of the Syrophoenician woman and his treatment of Jairus and the hemorrhaging woman see Chapter 2.

2. On Mark's stress on the Gentile character of the woman see Cranfield, *Mark*, p. 247; Guelich, *Mark*, p. 385; Hurtado, *Mark*, p. 105; Lane, *Mark*, p. 260.

3. Guelich, *Mark*, pp. 386-87.

discourse on uncleanness (7.1-23). In the discourse, Jesus insists that people are not defiled by what is outside of them, but by what is in their heart. People should not be judged by externals but by their heart. Given the context of Mark's Gospel, Jesus' rejection of the Syrophoenician woman is difficult to understand.

Nevertheless, the difficulty of Jesus' remark is significant for the influence of the text on the reader. Because of the puzzling nature of Jesus' remark, the reader lacks understanding at the same time that the woman displays understanding. Thus the difficulty of Jesus' statement highlights the insight of the woman, and interpretations that seek to clarify completely the enigmatic parable tend to diminish the woman's insight and the impact of the text on the reader.[1]

The Syrophoenician woman acknowledges the correctness of Jesus' parable, but instead of viewing it as a rejection she uses it to further her claim on behalf of her daughter. She points out that the dogs under the table are able to eat from the children's crumbs. The woman's answer shows her understanding, boldness, persistence, humility and faith.[2] The woman accepts the position of the household dog, recognizing that she can make no demand on the mercy of Jesus. She does not make any claim to the privileges that properly belong to Israel, but asks only for the crumbs that the children leave behind. She is convinced that an insignificant amount of attention from Jesus is sufficient to meet the need of her daughter. When confronted with the puzzling parable of Jesus, she shows her understanding and faith by expressing her trust in the abundance of God's mercy in Jesus.[3] On the

---

1.   On the enigmatic character of Jesus' remark and its impact on the reader see Bassler, 'Parable of the Loaves', pp. 170-71.

2.   On the woman's understanding see Guelich, *Mark*, p. 389; Kelber, *Story of Jesus*, p. 38; Lane, *Mark*, p. 259. On the woman's persistence see Hurtado, *Mark*, p. 106; Malbon, 'Narrative Criticism', p. 44; Schweizer, *Markus*, p. 86. On the woman's humility see Anderson, *Mark*, pp. 191-92; Cranfield, *Mark*, p. 249; Hurtado, *Mark*, p. 106; Lagrange, *Marc*, p. 196; Lane, *Mark*, pp. 259, 264; Schweizer, *Markus*, p. 86. On the woman's faith see Cranfield, *Mark*, p. 249; Guelich, *Mark*, p. 389; Hooker, *Mark*, p. 183; Hurtado, *Mark*, p. 106; Lane, *Mark*, pp. 259, 264; Pesch, *Markusevangelium I. Teil*, p. 390; Schweizer, *Markus*, pp. 77, 85, 86.

3.   The woman's use of κύριε in addressing Jesus may also show her understanding and faith. On κύριε as a believing confession see Gnilka, *Markus*, I, p. 293; Guelich, *Mark*, p. 388; Gundry, *Mark*, p. 374. Other commentators (Anderson, *Mark*, p. 191; Cranfield, *Mark*, p. 248; Lane, *Mark*, p. 259; Schweizer,

basis of the woman's word, Jesus grants the woman her request by delivering her daughter from the possession.

The Syrophoenician woman is needy and trusting, but she finds herself in the place of rejection because of her status as a Gentile. Yet she takes the rejection as an opportunity to emphasize again her faith in the abundance of God's mercy. In this way, she shows that she is understanding, bold, persistent, humble and believing. On the basis of her answer she is helped, and her daughter is healed. Thus, Mark's characterization of the Syrophoenician woman stands in contrast to his treatment of the disciples. The disciples lack courage and understanding (6.50, 52). Although they are insiders and have been given the mystery of the kingdom of God (4.11), the disciples comprehend neither the loaves (ἄρτοις, 6.52) nor the parables (7.17-18). In contrast to the disciples, the Syrophoenician woman has boldness and understanding.[1] Although she is initially treated as an outsider by Jesus, the Syrophoenician woman displays the insight of an insider through her understanding of Jesus' parable concerning bread (ἄρτον, 7.27).

The Deaf Man (7.31-37)

Mark uses the story of the Syrophoenician woman to exemplify understanding and then follows this episode with the healing of a deaf man, a miracle story that symbolizes the need for true perception. The miracle story itself includes a number of recurring themes that have appeared in previous passages dealing with minor characters.[2] Like the paralytic (2.3), the deaf man with the speech impediment is brought to Jesus by others (7.32).[3] Like Jairus (5.23), those who bring

---

Markus, p. 86) treat κύριε simply as a title of respect.

1. Guelich, *Mark*, p. 389; Kelber, *Story of Jesus*, p. 38; Lane, *Mark*, p. 259; Schweizer, *Markus*, pp. 77, 85.

2. On the similarity between the setting for the healing of the deaf man and the setting for the deliverance of the Gerasene demoniac see the discussion in Chapter 2.

3. The word that Mark uses to describe the deaf man's speech, μογιλάλος, is an extremely rare word. It occurs only here in the New Testament, and in the LXX it occurs only in Isa. 35.6. The Isaiah passage seems to have influenced Mark's choice of wording in 7.32 and also in the acclamation of 7.37. In 7.32 the adjective μογιλάλος means 'speaking with difficulty, having a speech impediment'. See BAGD, p. 525. Therefore, the deaf man is not described as completely mute but as having difficulty with speech. When Jesus heals the deaf man, the man is described as speaking correctly (7.35). This description implies that the man was not entirely

the deaf man plead with Jesus to lay his hand upon the man in order
that he might heal him (7.32). In a manner similar to the healing of
Jairus's daughter (5.37, 40), Jesus withdraws from the crowd and
heals in private (7.33). Jesus places his fingers in the man's ears, and,
after spitting, he touches the man's tongue.[1] Touch is one of the means
by which Jesus heals the deaf man, just as touch was a part of the
leper's healing (1.41). After touching the man's ears and tongue, Jesus
looks up into heaven and groans (7.34).[2] As in the healing of Jairus's
daughter (5.41-42), the healing of the deaf man takes place at
the moment that Jesus gives an authoritative word (7.34-35).
Immediately, the man's hearing is opened and his tongue is loosed so
that he is able to speak correctly.

Following the healing, Jesus gives a command to silence, a
command that is disobeyed.[3] In fact, Mark stresses the disobedience
by referring to it as a recurring problem. He changes to the
imperfect tense and states that the more that Jesus was commanding
(διεστέλλετο) them, the more the people were proclaiming

mute before his healing. When the acclamation of Mk 7.37 presents Jesus as giving
speech to the mute (ἀλάλους), it appears to interpret Jesus' healing more generally
in terms drawn from Isa. 35.5-6. See Cranfield, *Mark*, p. 251; Gnilka, *Markus*, I,
p. 297; Guelich, *Mark*, p. 394; Hurtado, *Mark*, p. 106; Lagrange, *Marc*, p. 197;
Mann, *Mark*, p. 323; Nineham, *Mark*, p. 202.

1.   Mark uses an unusual expression when he states that Jesus threw (ἔβαλεν,
7.33) his fingers into the man's ears. The verb βάλλω is also used in an unusual
way in the immediately preceding context. When the Syrophoenician woman went
home, she found her child having been thrown (βεβλημένον, 7.30) on the bed
delivered from the possession. Mark's choice of wording in both places may have
been influenced by Jesus' parable which involves throwing (βαλεῖν, 7.27) the
children's bread to the dogs.

2.   Both Jesus' look toward heaven and his groan appear to be gestures associated with prayer. For looking up toward heaven as a gesture of prayer see Mk 6.41.
For groaning as an expression of prayer within early Christianity see Rom. 8.23,
26. On this point see also Cranfield, *Mark*, p. 252; Guelich, *Mark*, p. 395;
Lagrange, *Marc*, p. 199; Mann, *Mark*, p. 324. For a brief treatment of Mark's
presentation of Jesus as a man of prayer see Fowler, *Let the Reader Understand*,
pp. 214-15.

3.   Mark presents Jesus' command in language similar to that of the silence
commands to the leper and to Jairus. On this point see Guelich, *Mark*, p. 396; Lane,
Mark, p. 268. Jesus commands them (διεστείλατο αὐτοῖς, 7.36; 5.43), presumably, that is, the healed man and those who brought him, that they should not speak
to anyone (μηδενὶ λέγωσιν, 7.36; μηδενὶ μηδὲν εἴπῃς, 1.44).

(ἐκήρυσσον).[1] Mark leaves the impression that Jesus repeatedly commanded silence concerning his healing miracles and that the command was repeatedly disobeyed.

The deaf man is needy, unable to hear or speak properly, yet he is befriended and brought to Jesus. Through the touch, prayer and word of Jesus, the deaf man is healed, so that he is able to hear and speak correctly. Nevertheless, in the end, the deaf man is also disobedient, since along with others he proclaims the message concerning Jesus and his healing work.

The deaf man reflects traits that are similar to those of other minor characters, but the particular disorder faced by the man is unique when compared with the problems of the suppliants in the preceding narrative. He is deaf and thus unable to speak properly. Jesus' ability to heal this particular disorder is emphasized in the conclusion to the miracle story. The people are completely amazed, and they affirm that Jesus has done all things well. He is even able to make the deaf to hear and the mute to speak (7.37).

In the context of Mark's Gospel, Jesus' healing of a deaf man takes on symbolic significance.[2] Jesus' healing of physical deafness raises the hope that Jesus will also be able to heal spiritual deafness. Earlier in Mark's narrative, defective hearing is used as a metaphor for the inability to understand Jesus' teaching and mission. In Mk 4.12 Jesus characterizes the outsiders as those who hear but do not understand. The outsiders have a defective understanding and by implication a defective hearing as well. This relationship between defective understanding and defective hearing may also be seen in that Jesus introduces his teaching with the command to hear (4.3, 9, 23, 24; 7.14). Those who do not hear are those who do not understand.

The disciples, like the outsiders, struggle to hear and understand correctly. The narrator criticizes the disciples at the end of the second boat scene for their lack of understanding (6.52). Later, in speaking to

---

1.   Mark also uses κηρύσσω to express the disobedient proclamation of minor characters in 1.45 and 5.20. The verb κηρύσσω is used with reference to minor characters only in 1.45, 5.20 and 7.36. On the use of the imperfect for repeated action see BDF, p. 169; Burton, *Moods and Tenses*, p. 12; Robertson, *Grammar*, p. 884; J.H. Moulton, W.F. Howard and N. Turner, *A Grammar of New Testament Greek* (4 vols.; Edinburgh: T. & T. Clark, 1906–76), III, p. 67.

2.   Anderson, *Mark*, p. 192; Gnilka, *Markus*, I, pp. 298-99; Hooker, *Mark*, pp. 184, 186; Schweizer, *Markus*, pp. 86-87.

the opponents, disciples and crowd in Mk 7.14, Jesus commands them all to hear and understand. In private, the disciples then ask Jesus to explain his teaching, and Jesus responds by criticizing them for their incomprehension (7.17-18). The disciples' question shows that they did not hear and understand. In contrast to the disciples, the Syrophoenician woman hears about Jesus and understands his teaching (7.25, 28). The deaf man also stands in contrast to the disciples.[1] He has a similar problem, an inability to hear, but in contrast to the disciples, he is healed of this disorder by Jesus.

The extent to which the healed deaf man stands in contrast to the disciples may be seen in the third boat scene (8.14-21). Here, Jesus commands the disciples to watch out for the leaven of the Pharisees and the leaven of Herod. The disciples react by discussing their failure to bring bread along on the journey. Jesus scolds them with a series of pointed questions that highlight their lack of understanding. In a metaphorical way, Jesus emphasizes their incomprehension by asking, 'Having eyes, do you not see, and having ears do you not hear?' (8.18). Their lack of understanding reveals their defective hearing. The disciples are spiritually deaf. The deaf man faces a physical deafness, but Jesus is able to make the deaf hear, and so he heals the man. In contrast, the disciples do not hear and understand, and Jesus has not yet healed them.

The Response of the Reader

Mark uses the early chapters of his Gospel to encourage the reader to identify with the disciples. They are called to have a special relationship with Jesus, and they are commissioned by Jesus to join with him in fulfilling the purposes of God. In chs. 1–3, Mark does not detract from the reader's identification with the disciples through his portrayal of minor characters. However, he does create sympathy for these individuals on the part of the reader by presenting Jesus as responding to them with compassion and help.

Early in his narrative, Mark establishes a basic pattern for his portrayal of minor characters. That pattern continues throughout Mk 4.1–8.21, although often with slight variations. A needy person comes into contact with Jesus, or others approach Jesus on behalf of one who needs healing. Their requests for help show that they trust Jesus to meet their needs through his authority. Jesus responds to their

---

1.   Gnilka, *Markus*, I, pp. 298-99; Tannehill, 'Disciples in Mark', pp. 399-400.

requests by bringing healing or deliverance from possession. Thus, Mark's presentation of minor characters in 4.1–8.21 shows continuity with his presentation in 1.1–3.35.

However, it also shows discontinuity. Mark's characterization of minor characters is different in 4.1–8.21 because of the extent to which he uses such characters as contrasting figures to the disciples.[1] Jesus criticizes the disciples for their lack of courage and faith, and then Mark portrays minor characters overcoming fear and responding in faith. Jesus criticizes the disciples for their inability to hear and understand, and then Mark presents minor characters as hearing and understanding. In the past, literary critics have pointed out that the minor characters serve as foils for the disciples in Mark's Gospel.[2] Rhoads and Michie go so far as to say that the minor characters 'serve throughout as "foils" for the disciples'.[3] However, it would be more accurate to say that some minor characters serve as foils for the disciples at certain points in the narrative, including Mk 4.1–8.21.

Given the contrast between minor characters and the disciples in 4.1–8.21, it would be easy to jump to the conclusion that Mark wants the reader to switch his or her loyalty from the disciples to these minor characters.[4] Such a move is too simple. Mark's characterization of the disciples in chs. 4–8 still includes material that would cause the reader to continue identifying with the disciples. In the earlier chapters of the Gospel, Mark encourages the reader to identify with the disciples by showing that Jesus has called them to follow after him. They are to be with him in order that he might send them out to preach and to have authority over demons. The reader identifies with the disciples, because more than any other group of characters in the narrative they have been given a unique relationship to Jesus and a significant commission by him. While they begin to display a lack of

---

1. Tannehill, 'Disciples in Mark', pp. 399-400. The passages on minor characters in chs. 4–8 are also different than those in chs. 1–3 because of the increase in the magnitude of the miracles and the increase in the interest that Mark shows in the minor characters themselves. See Lührmann, *Markusevangelium*, p. 93.

2. Kingsbury, *Conflict in Mark*, pp. 25-27; Rhoads and Michie, *Mark as Story*, pp. 130, 132; Tannehill, 'Disciples in Mark', pp. 399-400, 404-405.

3. Rhoads and Michie, *Mark as Story*, p. 132. Kingsbury (*Conflict in Mark*, p. 25) is more circumspect in that he regards the individuals from the crowd as contrasting figures for 'the greater part of the story'.

4. This appears to be the approach of Tolbert toward this section of Mark's Gospel. See *Sowing*, pp. 164-72.

faith and understanding in 4.1–8.21, the disciples continue to follow Jesus, taking their place with him. They fulfill the mission given to them by Jesus to preach and to cast out demons (6.7-13). When Jesus feeds the crowd, the disciples serve as Jesus' helpers in his care for the crowd (6.35-44; 8.1-10). In other words, in Mk 4.1–8.21 the disciples continue to do the very things that encouraged the reader to identify with them in the first place.

On the other hand, the minor characters in this section do not take on these disciple-like activities. Although they contrast with the disciples, the minor characters do not replace the disciples. Jesus does not allow healed individuals to become his disciples, but dismisses them after their healing (5.18-19, 34; 7.29). The suppliants are not with Jesus in the same sense that the disciples are with Jesus. Jesus does not command them to go out and proclaim a message, but rather he commands them to remain secretive and silent (5.19, 43; 7.36). The disobedience of certain individuals to these secrecy commands would also make it difficult for the reader to identify completely with these minor characters (5.20; 7.36).

In Mk 4.1–8.21 the reader begins to dissociate somewhat from the disciples, since they show a persistent lack of faith and understanding. However, the reader does not fully distance himself or herself from the disciples nor fully identify with the minor characters from the crowd.[1] Nevertheless, Mark's portrait of minor characters is still

---

1. Bassler ('Parable of the Loaves', pp. 165-67, 169-71) also argues that the reader continues to identify with the disciples up through the third boat scene where Jesus strongly criticizes the disciples (8.14-21). Bassler points out that in Mk 6–8 the narrator includes a number of enigmatic statements. The indeterminacies in these chapters of Mark's Gospel lead the reader to respond with confusion and a lack of understanding. Thus, the reader is forced to share in the disciples' lack of understanding. In the early chapters of Mark's Gospel, the reader identifies with the disciples because of the disciples' positive response to Jesus and Jesus' positive response to the disciples. This identification with the disciples, which was initially undertaken willingly, continues in Mk 6–8, although unwillingly. The gaps in Mk 6–8 force the reader to continue identifying with the disciples, because now the reader shares in the disciples' incomprehension. Tannehill ('Disciples in Mark', p. 393) points out that the surprisingly negative development in the disciples' characterization requires the reader to dissociate somewhat from them. However, Tannehill argues that something of the reader's initial identification with the disciples remains because of the similarity between the problems of the disciples and the problems that the first readers faced. The similarity between the historical situation of the initial audience and the situation of the disciples in the narrative forced the first readers to retain their

relevant to the reader's response to the narrative. These individuals exemplify for the reader the positive qualities of faith and understanding. In this way, the reader is encouraged to have a faith in Jesus that overcomes fear and to develop a clearer insight into the teaching and mission of Jesus.

Minor Characters in Mark 8.22–10.45

Mk 8.22–10.52 is built around three passion predictions by Jesus (8.31; 9.31; 10.33-34). After each passion prediction, the disciples display their misunderstanding, and in response Jesus teaches them about the nature of true discipleship.[1] Within this significant section of Mark's Gospel, the instruction of Jesus in response to the disciples' misunderstanding is particularly helpful for clarifying the expectations of Jesus. These expectations aid the reader in evaluating the people in the narrative, including minor characters. Within 8.22–10.52 Mark presents four such characters: the blind man of Bethsaida (8.22-26), the man with the possessed son (9.14-29), the rich man (10.17-31) and blind Bartimaeus (10.46-52).

The Blind Man of Bethsaida (8.22-26)
Prior to the first passion prediction, Mark includes the healing of the blind man of Bethsaida (8.22-26). Mark's narration of the healing of the blind man clearly parallels his narration concerning the deaf man (7.31-37).[2] As Fowler states, 'The two healing stories in 7:31-37 and

identification with the disciples. This tension between identification and dissociation 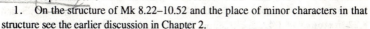 was intended to awaken the initial readers to their own failure as disciples and their need for repentance.

1.   On the structure of Mk 8.22–10.52 and the place of minor characters in that structure see the earlier discussion in Chapter 2.

2.   The extensive similarities between these two passages may be seen in a synopsis of Mk 7.31-37 and 8.22-26. Fowler (*Loaves and Fishes*, pp. 105-106) and Taylor (*Mark*, pp. 368-69) both provide a helpful synopsis of the two passages. The parallel expressions in Mk 7.31-37 and 8.22-26 are all the more impressive because for the most part they occur in the same order, with one obvious exception. In the healing of the deaf man, the people ask Jesus to lay his hand on the man (7.32), but when Jesus heals the man, he does so by touching him (7.33). The order is reversed in the healing of the blind man. The people ask Jesus to touch the man (8.22), but when Jesus heals him, he does so by laying his hands on him (8.23). Some of the differences between the two passages are necessary, because the disorders that are

8:22-26 possess as much or more verbal similarity than any two stories in Mark'.[1] The similarity between the healing of the blind man and the healing of the deaf man serves to connect Mark's portrayal of the blind man with his portrayal of other minor characters in the preceding narrative.[2]

Like the deaf man, the blind man is befriended by others who bring him to Jesus in order that he might be healed (8.22). Jesus takes the blind man outside the village, so that he is separated from the crowd (8.23). The blind man is then healed by Jesus in this private setting (8.23-25). Some of the same techniques that Jesus used to heal deafness are followed again in the healing of blindness. Jesus spits into the man's eyes and lays his hands upon him. At this point, the narrative diverges from the pattern found in the healing of the deaf man. Jesus asks the man if he sees anything, and the man answers that he sees men like trees that are walking. The man's answer implies that he has regained his sight, but that his sight is inadequate.[3] Once again, Jesus lays his hands on the man's eyes, with the result that the man's sight is completely restored and he is able to see everything clearly. After the healing, Jesus sends the man home and commands him not to enter the village (8.26).[4] Jesus' command in this instance is parallel to earlier prohibitions after miracles in which he insists on silence. By not allowing the man to return to the village, Jesus is giving an

---

treated are different. Yet the two healing stories use similar expressions to refer to the different maladies or different parts of the body. On this point see Fowler, *Loaves and Fishes*, pp. 106-107.

1. Fowler, *Loaves and Fishes*, p. 105.

2. Mark's narration of the healing of the blind man of Bethsaida also shows other lexical connections with the earlier healing stories that feature minor characters. See the use of φέρω in 1.32, 2.3 and 8.22, παρακαλέω in 1.40, 5.18, 23 and 8.22, ἅπτομαι in 1.41, 5.27, 28, 30, 31 and 8.22, ἐπιτίθημι in 5.23, 8.23, 25, and ἀποκαθίστημι in 3.5 and 8.25.

3. On the use of ἀναβλέπω to indicate the regaining of sight see Gundry, *Mark*, p. 417; E.S. Johnson, 'Mark VIII. 22-26: The Blind Man from Bethsaida', *NTS* 25 (1979), pp. 376-77; Lagrange, *Marc*, p. 213; Pesch, *Markusevangelium I. Teil*, p. 419.

4. The reading μηδὲ εἰς τὴν κώμην εἰσέλθῃς is supported by B, L, family 1 and a few other Greek manuscripts, and by Aleph and W except with μή replacing μηδέ. It is probably easier to explain the rise of the other readings in the manuscript tradition if this reading represents the earliest form of the text. See Metzger, *Textual Commentary*, pp. 98-99.

indirect command to silence.[1] Apparently, the healed man is obedient to this command and returns to his home. In 8.22-26 Mark presents an individual who is blind, needy, befriended, healed in private by Jesus, commanded to silence and obedient.

The healing of the blind man of Bethsaida serves a similar purpose in the narrative to the healing of the deaf man. The blind man functions as a contrasting figure to the disciples.[2] The similarity between Mk 7.31-37 and 8.22-26 helps to highlight the contrast between the healed individuals and the disciples as they are portrayed in Mk 8.14-21. In the latter verses Jesus scolds the disciples for their inability to see, hear and understand. Shortly before he criticizes the disciples for their lack of hearing, Jesus heals a deaf man (7.31-37). Immediately after he rebukes the disciples for their lack of sight, Jesus heals a blind man (8.22-26). Although Jesus is able to heal the deaf and the blind, the disciples remain unhealed, mired in their lack of perception.

Because of this contrast with the disciples, the healing of the blind man takes on symbolic significance. Jesus' ability to bring sight to a man who is physically blind creates the expectation that Jesus also possesses the ability to bring sight to those who are blind to his identity and mission. Jesus is able to give understanding to those who lack insight. The transition from incomprehension to understanding, like the movement from blindness to sight for the blind man, may not be simple or immediate. Jesus has already encountered greater difficulty with his disciples than with the blind man of Bethsaida. However, the healing of the blind man creates the expectation that Jesus will be able to bring true understanding to others, perhaps even to the disciples.

Consequently, the healing of the blind man of Bethsaida is a transitional episode. The healing story has significant connections with the preceding material because of its similarity to the healing of the deaf man and its contrast with the continuing blindness of the disciples. However, the healing of the blind man also encourages anticipations of the following narrative. The healing of the blind man creates the expectation that others will come to see and to understand.

Thus far, the similarity between the healing of the deaf man in

---

1. Gnilka, *Markus*, I, p. 314; Guelich, *Mark*, p. 435; Hooker, *Mark*, p. 199; Lagrange, *Marc*, p. 213; Pesch, *Markusevangelium I. Teil*, p. 419; Theissen, *Wundergeschichten*, p. 77.

2. Fowler, *Loaves and Fishes*, pp. 108, 111-12; Tannehill, 'Disciples in Mark', pp. 399-400.

Mk 7.31-37 and the healing of the blind man in 8.22-26 has been stressed. However, a comparison of analogous scenes highlights not only similarities, but also dissimilarities. There are two significant ways in which the healing of the blind man of Bethsaida differs from the healing of the deaf man. The healing of the blind man is different in that the blind man is healed in two stages. The conclusion of the blind man's healing is also different, because, unlike the deaf man, the blind man appears to be obedient to Jesus' command to silence. Both of these dissimilarities call for further comment.

The two-stage healing is unique in Mark's narrative, and thus it sets the healing of the blind man of Bethsaida apart from the healing of the deaf man and all the other healing stories in the preceding narrative. This two-part healing is commonly interpreted as symbolic. R.H. Lightfoot, one of the first to follow a symbolic reading, argued that the healing of the blind man in two stages symbolized the developing insight of the disciples as seen in the following episode, Mk 8.27-30.[1] Lightfoot supported his contention by pointing out the parallelism between Mark's narration of the healing and his narration of Peter's confession. According to Lightfoot, Jesus' initial healing touch is parallel to his initial question to the disciples concerning his identity. The unclear vision of the man corresponds to the incorrect answers of others concerning the identity of Jesus. The second healing touch of Jesus parallels his second question to the disciples concerning his identity, while the restored, clear vision of the blind man symbolizes the insight of Peter who confesses that Jesus is the messiah.

Lightfoot's view faces one formidable problem. The disciples do not see clearly in Mk 8.27-30. The clear vision of the blind man cannot symbolize the understanding of Peter and the other disciples, because they do not truly understand.[2] Peter's confession of Jesus as the messiah is intertwined with the following narrative, in which Jesus

---

1. R.H. Lightfoot, *History and Interpretation in the Gospels* (New York: Harper & Brothers, 1934), pp. 90-91. For a recent defense of the same viewpoint see Matera, 'Incomprehension of the Disciples'. See also Cranfield, *Mark*, p. 245; D.J. Hawkin, 'The Symbolism and Structure of the Marcan Redaction', *EvQ* 49 (1977), pp. 104-105; Nineham, *Mark*, p. 218; Pesch, *Markusevangelium I. Teil*, p. 420-21.

2. E. Best, 'Discipleship in Mark: Mark 8.22-10.52', *SJT* 23 (1970), pp. 325-26; *idem*, *Mark: The Gospel as Story* (Edinburgh: T. & T. Clark, 1983), p. 68; *idem*, *Following Jesus*, p. 135; Guelich, *Mark*, pp. 430-31, 436; Johnson, 'Blind Man from Bethsaida', p. 381.

reveals that he must suffer, die and rise. Peter reveals his lack of understanding by taking Jesus aside and rebuking him. Peter's confession of Jesus as messiah in Mk 8.29 cannot be isolated from his lack of understanding concerning the messiah's mission in Mk 8.32.[1] At best, the perception of Peter and the disciples is only partial. Peter confesses Jesus as messiah, which is correct, but his understanding of the nature and mission of the messiah is woefully inadequate.[2] Rather than moving from partial sight in Mk 8.14-21 to full sight in Mk 8.27–9.1, the disciples move from bad to worse. They slide from being myopic to being satanic. Jesus rebukes Peter as a satan who is devoted to a human rather than a divine perspective. The disciples are clearly not moving in the right direction.

In light of the inadequate perception of the disciples in Mk 8.27–9.1, some interpreters treat the restored vision of the blind man as symbolic of the restored understanding of the disciples after the resurrection.[3] For example, Guelich states concerning the healing of the blind man:

> The primary focus of this story, however, is on the man's total healing. The disciples show themselves to be in need of the second touch, and the story bespeaks their experiencing it. A time must come when they see all things distinctly. That time does not, however, come at Caesarea Philippi or by the time of Jesus' suffering and death in Jerusalem. In fact, it really does not come by the end of Mark's Gospel (16.8). But Mark's readers know it came for the disciples at some point after Easter.[4]

In other words, the disciples possess only a partial vision in Mk 8.27–9.1, but they finally receive a second healing touch and complete vision after the resurrection.

But does Mark use the two-stage healing of the blind man as a symbol for the developing insight of the disciples at all? The main arguments for such a contention include the juxtaposition of the healing in Mk 8.22-26 with the confession of Peter in Mk 8.27-30, and the parallels between the two passages. This line of argumentation loses its force if the disciples do not come to understand fully until

1. Johnson, 'Blind Man from Bethsaida', p. 382.
2. Kingsbury, *Christology*, pp. 92, 94.
3. Best, *Following Jesus*, p. 137; *idem, Gospel as Story*, pp. 67-68; Guelich, *Mark*, pp. 430-31, 436; Hooker, *Mark*, pp. 198; Johnson, 'Blind Man from Bethsaida', p. 383.
4. Guelich, *Mark*, p. 436.

after the resurrection. Then the full restoration of the blind man's sight simply stands in contrast to the blindness of the disciples in both the immediately preceding and following contexts. Mark does appear to leave open the possibility of the full restoration of the disciples' understanding beyond the resurrection. However, he does not narrate this healing of the disciples, choosing instead to stop their story line while they are still in the midst of failure and desertion. The healing of the blind man in two stages does not appear to symbolize primarily the developing insight of the disciples, then, since the restoration of the disciples' understanding is not stressed either in the context surrounding the blind man healing or in the narrative as a whole. The healing of the blind man is not an allegory on the story of the disciples.

The healing of the blind man in two stages symbolizes the necessity of moving from partial understanding to complete understanding and the necessity of the miraculous work of Jesus to bring about such a transformation. In this way, the two-stage healing of the blind man encourages the expectation that some in the narrative will come to a true understanding of Jesus' identity and mission. As we have seen, Mark does not appear to use the healing to symbolize the growing insight of the disciples, since he follows the healing story with a depiction of the disciples' continuing obtuseness. This raises the possibility that the healing of the blind man may anticipate further developments in Mark's portrayal of minor characters. However, in the following episodes, Mark's treatment of minor characters takes a surprisingly negative turn. Through the two-stage healing of the blind man, Mark creates an anticipation that he does not immediately satisfy. Mark's narrative avoids a quick and easy path to full sight.

A further difference between the healing of the blind man of Bethsaida and the healing of the deaf man occurs at the end of the miracle story, where the healed blind man appears to obey Jesus' indirect command to secrecy. Earlier in the narrative, the healed deaf man seemed to join with others in disobeying Jesus' command to silence. Since Jesus' secrecy command in Mk 8.26 is the last such injunction to a healed individual in Mark's Gospel, it provides a suitable opportunity to review the secrecy motif in Mark's miracle stories.

Ever since the work of William Wrede in his *Messiasgeheimnis in den Evangelien*, the secrecy motif has been an important topic of discussion within Markan studies. Wrede sought to include a number of themes under the general category of the messianic secret. Wrede included primarily the commands of silence to the demons, to those who had been healed and to the disciples, and then to these commands he also added the teaching of Jesus in parables and the misunderstanding of the disciples.[1] Wrede insisted that these separate themes must be held together and explained with a single interpretation, since together they all undergird the messianic secret in Mark.[2] On this view, the commands to silence after the miracles are specifically commands to maintain the messianic secret.[3] Wrede's own explanation for the messianic secret was that it functioned as an attempt to reconcile two conflicting traditions, one that Jesus' messiahship began at his resurrection and the other that Jesus' earthly ministry was already messianic.[4] According to Wrede, Mark used the messianic secret to show that Jesus was messiah during his earthly life, but that his true identity was hidden until the resurrection.

Recent scholarship has tended to argue that Wrede sought to squeeze too many things under the general category of the messianic secret.[5] It is seriously questioned whether Jesus' commands after his healings should be regarded as contributing to the messianic secret. Within the healing stories, it is not Jesus' messiahship which must be kept secret but the miracle itself. Thus, recent scholarship has generally sought to separate the miracle secret in Mark from the messianic secret.[6] A

---

1. On the commands to silence see Wrede, *Messiasgeheimnis*, p. 33-51. On the use of parabolic teaching to maintain the messianic secret see Wrede, *Messiasgeheimnis*, pp. 51-65. On the misunderstanding of the disciples see Wrede, *Messiasgeheimnis*, pp. 81-114.

2. Wrede, *Messiasgeheimnis*, pp. 35-47.

3. Wrede, *Messiasgeheimnis*, pp. 36-37.

4. Wrede, *Messiasgeheimnis*, p. 228.

5. C. Tuckett, 'Introduction: The Problem of the Messianic Secret', in *idem* (ed.), *The Messianic Secret* (IRT, 1; Philadelphia: Fortress Press, 1983), pp. 19-21; H. Räisänen, *The 'Messianic Secret' in Mark* (trans. C. Tuckett; Edinburgh: T. & T. Clark, 1990), pp. 71-75.

6. U. Luz, 'Das Geheimnismotiv und die Markinische Christologie', *ZNW* 56 (1965), pp. 10-11, 17, 28; J.D.G. Dunn, 'The Messianic Secret in Mark', *TynBul* 21 (1970), pp. 93-94; Räisänen, *Messianic Secret*, pp. 166-68, 173-74, 242-43. Räisänen (*Messianic Secret*, pp. 166, 243) is willing to concede that the commands to silence which are apparently obeyed (5.43; 8.26) may be linked to the messianic secret proper.

recognition of the difference between the miracle secret and the messianic secret means that it is unnecessary to develop a unitary explanation for Mark's use of both. Instead, alternate explanations may be given for the miracle secret and the messianic secret. In fact, both may serve a variety of functions within the narrative.[1]

The episodes concerning minor characters include references to miracle secrets but not to the messianic secret as such. Whenever Jesus heals someone privately, he gives a command to silence (1.44; 5.43; 7.36; 8.26), but whenever he heals in public, he does not express such a command. The one exception to this pattern takes place in the healing of the Syrophoenician woman's daughter. In that passage the secrecy motif appears at the beginning of the healing story, rather than at the end in the form of a command. Jesus enters into a house because he does not want anyone to know of his presence, but he is not able to escape notice (7.24). Beyond this one exception, all the other healings that take place in a private setting conclude with a command to silence. In fact, when Jesus heals the hemorrhaging woman in a public setting, he goes out of his way to make the healing a matter of public knowledge (5.30-33). This stands in contrast to the healing of Jairus's daughter, which has all the makings of a public healing, but Jesus turns it into a private matter (5.40). Whenever Jesus commands secrecy from a healed individual, the command makes reference to Jesus' miracle, not to Jesus' identity as the messiah. Unlike the messianic secret, which is kept by the demons and by the disciples, the miracle secret is repeatedly broken by those who are healed.

What explanation can be given for Jesus' commands to silence after healing in private, when his miraculous power is already a matter of public knowledge? In the context of Mark's narrative, the miracle secret functions in at least two ways. It points to the negative effects of unnecessary publicity concerning Jesus' miraculous power,[2] and it highlights the impossibility of concealing Jesus' authority.[3]

Jesus' secrecy command to the leper appears in a context in which Jesus is seeking to avoid publicity and its negative effects. Immediately before the healing of the leper, Jesus leaves behind the crowds in

1.   Dunn, 'Messianic Secret', p. 95.

2.   Dunn, 'Messianic Secret', p. 95; Guelich, *Mark*, p. 76; Räisänen, *Messianic Secret*, pp. 166-68.

3.   Luz, 'Geheimnismotiv', pp. 15-17, 28-30; Räisänen, *Messianic Secret*, pp. 166-68, 242-43.

Capernaum in order to pray in a deserted place (1.35). In spite of the demand for Jesus in Capernaum, he sets out for other towns in order to proclaim his message throughout Galilee (1.36-39). Immediately after the healing and disobedience of the leper, Jesus is once again out in the deserted places (1.45). Yet because of the refusal of the leper to maintain secrecy, the deserted places are no longer a place of refuge and prayer for Jesus. Even though Jesus is out in the deserted places, people come to him from everywhere. The press of the crowd also limits Jesus' travel into the cities of Galilee, which restricts the proclamation of his message. In short, the crowds created by the disobedience of the leper keep Jesus from important aspects of his mission, his time in prayer and the proclamation of his message throughout Galilee.

The constant demands of the crowd also keep Jesus from spending time with his disciples. So, for example, immediately after Jesus chooses the twelve disciples, he enters into a house to eat a meal with them, but the presence of the crowd keeps them from even eating bread together (3.20). Jesus commands secrecy concerning his private healings in order to reduce the publicity concerning his miraculous power. The crowds drawn by such publicity restrict the activity of Jesus so that he is not able to pray, proclaim his message or teach his disciples.

Mark uses the juxtaposition of scenes in order to emphasize the negative effects of unnecessary publicity.[1] Whenever Jesus commands silence concerning a miracle and the command is disobeyed, the following scene begins with the press of the crowds. However, when the command is obeyed, the following scene shows Jesus teaching his disciples or proclaiming his message in the synagogue. Thus, when the secrecy command is obeyed, Jesus is able to do what he came to do. After the disobedience of the leper (1.44-45), the following scene begins with the gathering of a great crowd, a crowd so large that there is no longer room even at the door of the house where Jesus is staying (2.1-2). After the disobedience of the deaf man and those with him (7.36-37), the next scene begins with a large, hungry crowd (8.1). The disobedience of the Gerasene demoniac also fits this pattern. After the Gerasene demoniac proclaims the message concerning Jesus (5.19-20), the following scene begins with a great crowd gathering around Jesus (5.21). The pattern changes when Jesus' com-

1.   Guelich, *Mark*, pp. 287, 397, 435.

mand to secrecy is obeyed. Apparently Jairus and his wife obey the secrecy command (5.43), and then the following passage begins with Jesus traveling with his disciples and teaching in the synagogue (6.1-2). When the blind man of Bethsaida obeys Jesus' command (8.26), the next scene shows Jesus traveling with his disciples and teaching them. The obedience of the blind man stands in contrast to the disobedience of the deaf man, and it sets up a change in scene in which Jesus interacts with his disciples.

Jesus' commands to silence concerning his miracles also highlight the impossibility of hiding his authority. This is particularly true in those passages where the secrecy command is disobeyed.[1] Jesus is able (δύνασαι, 1.40) to cleanse the leper, but because of the leper's disobedience, Jesus is no longer able (δύνασθαι, 1.45) to enter a city openly. Jesus is able to heal, but he is not able to hide his miraculous power. Jesus commands the deaf man and those with him to remain silent, but they disobey (7.36). Mark stresses the problem by stating that the more Jesus commanded people to silence, the more they proclaimed the message concerning Jesus. In the one private healing which does not include a command to secrecy, the healing of the Syrophoenician woman's daughter, Mark begins the healing story with Jesus' desire to remain hidden. However, Jesus is not able (ἠδυνήθη, 7.24) to escape notice, and the woman comes to make a request for healing. The authority of Jesus is public knowledge, and even Jesus himself is not able to restrict the proclamation of his authority. Mark's narrative creates the expectation that the miraculous power of Jesus will not be hidden and that minor characters will take part in freely proclaiming the authority of Jesus.

After narrating the healing of the blind man of Bethsaida, Mark relates the first of Jesus' passion predictions (8.27–9.1). This passage has important implications for the reader's construction of Jesus, the disciples and the minor characters who are introduced in the subsequent narrative. Jesus reveals to a greater extent the nature of his mission and his expectations for those who choose to follow him. Jesus' passion prediction is instigated by Peter's confession of Jesus as messiah (8.29). At that point, Jesus begins to teach his disciples that as the Son of Man, he must suffer, die and rise again (8.31). Peter's response to this prediction is to take Jesus aside (προσλαβόμενος) and rebuke him (8.32). Earlier Jesus took aside the deaf man

---

1.   Räisänen, *Messianic Secret*, pp. 166, 243.

(ἀπολαβόμενος, 7.33) and the blind man (ἐπιλαβόμενος, 8.23), and now, in an ironic twist, Peter takes Jesus aside as though Jesus himself must be healed of his inadequate perception. Jesus, in turn, rebukes Peter, because Peter's understanding of the messiah and the mission of the messiah is satanic (8.33). Trapped in his human mind-set, Peter fails to understand God's perspective on the mission of Jesus.

In light of Peter's misunderstanding, Jesus instructs his disciples further concerning the demands of following him. However, Jesus does not simply address his words to the disciples, but rather he calls together the crowd along with the disciples (8.34). Thus, the demands of Jesus in these verses are addressed to a broader audience than simply to the disciples. These expectations extend beyond the disciples to members of the crowd, even to those whom Jesus calls 'anyone' or 'whoever', which would include the reader.[1] Jesus demands that his listeners deny themselves, take up their cross and follow him (8.34). Jesus expects them to lose their lives for his sake and for the sake of the gospel (8.35). They should not be ashamed of him and his words in the midst of an adulterous and sinful generation (8.38). Jesus' teaching provides further standards by which the reader may evaluate the characters in the narrative, including both the disciples and members of the crowd.

Jesus' teaching in Mk 8.34-38 also opens new possibilities for the reader's identification with the characters in the narrative. Until this point in the narrative the reader has identified with the disciples because they were given a unique call to follow Jesus and be with him. Yet now in Mk 8.34-38 the call to follow Jesus is accessible to others, thus opening the possibility for the reader to identify more closely with other characters besides the disciples. If certain minor characters follow Jesus and live up to his demands while the disciples fail to follow, this would influence the nature of the reader's identification. Surprisingly, however, as I mentioned above, it is precisely at this point in the narrative that Mark's portrayal of minor characters takes a decidedly negative turn.

The Man with the Possessed Boy (9.14-29)
The healing story in Mk 9.14-29 is analogous to earlier passages on minor characters in a number of ways. Like the other suppliants, this 'one from the crowd' (εἷς ἐκ τοῦ ὄχλου, 9.17) faces a need and so

---

1.   Malbon, 'Disciples/Crowds/Whoever', pp. 109-10, 124-26.

comes to Jesus. Like Jairus and the Syrophoenician woman, the man entreats Jesus on behalf of his child (5.23; 7.25; 9.17-18). The man's son is facing a particularly severe case of demonic possession, but his problems are not unique. In fact, Jesus has already shown an ability to cope with the cause of the boy's problems, along with its symptoms, in his dealings with similar characters in the preceding narrative. Jesus is able to cast out unclean spirits (1.25-26, 34; 5.8, 12-13; 7.29). The boy is possessed with a deaf and mute spirit (9.17, 25), but Jesus makes the deaf hear and the mute speak (7.35, 37). Whenever the boy is attacked by the unclean spirit, he is left withered (ξηραίνεται, 9.18), but Jesus is able to restore what has withered (3.5; ἐξηραμμένην, 3.1; ξηράν, 3.3). After the unclean spirit leaves, the boy appears to be dead (9.26), but Jesus is able to raise those who have apparently died (5.41-42). Consequently, Jesus has already cared for similar problems with other minor characters, which makes the father's doubt concerning Jesus' ability all the more ironic (9.22).

Mark narrates the boy's deliverance in a similar manner to previous healing stories. The boy is brought to Jesus (9.20, cf. 1.32; 2.3; 7.32; 8.22), which results in the unclean spirit reacting to the presence of Jesus (9.20, cf. 1.23-24; 3.11; 5.7-8). Jesus rebukes the spirit (9.25, cf. 1.25; 3.12) and commands it to come out of the boy (9.25, cf. 1.25; 5.8; 7.29). The unclean spirit cries out (9.26, cf. 1.26; 3.11; 5.5, 7), convulses the boy (9.26, cf. 1.26), and comes out (9.26, cf. 1.26; 5.13; 7.29-30). When the boy is left for dead, Jesus grasps his hand (9.27, cf. 1.31; 5.41) and raises him (9.27, cf. 1.31; 2.9, 11, 12; 5.41).

Although Mark's narration concerning the father of the possessed boy is similar to his presentation of earlier minor characters, this similarity only serves to highlight a particularly unusual feature in the story, the father's struggle with faith.[1] The father's initial conversa-

---

1.   Mark's narration in 9.14-29 is also unusual because it is particularly repetitive. On the repetitive nature of the passage see Marshall, *Faith*, pp. 111-12, 115. For words which are repeated in 9.14-29 see Marshall, *Faith*, p. 111. The repetition in the passage is not redundant, but rather always involves variations which serve to enrich Mark's characterization of the people in the story. Mark uses the repetition especially to stress the need of the possessed boy and his father. He includes two instances of the crowd gathering around Jesus, with the second onrush of the crowd provoking the immediate deliverance of the possessed boy by Jesus (9.15, 25). Twice the father explains the nature of his son's symptoms (9.17-18, 21-22). The second description of the boy's symptoms increases the severity of the problem, since the unclean spirit has not only thrown the boy into convulsions but has also

tion with Jesus leads to a negative evaluation of his faith. The man explains to Jesus that in his absence the disciples were unable to provide any deliverance for his possessed son (9.18). Jesus responds with the words, 'O unbelieving generation, how long will I be with you? How long will I endure you?' (9.19). Jesus' exasperation is directed against his entire generation which as a whole has remained in unbelief.[1] The disciples, the scribes, the crowd, the man from the crowd, all those gathered at the scene are in some way marked by a lack of faith. Jesus includes the disciples within the unbelieving generation, since in part it is the father's description of their failure that brings about Jesus' expression of dissatisfaction.

However, Jesus' outburst is directed at a wider group than just the disciples.[2] The father of the possessed boy must also be included in the present unbelieving generation. Jesus has been in conversation with the crowd, with the father serving as a spokesman for the crowd. In Mk 9.16 Jesus' initial question is directed at them (αὐτούς), that is, at the crowd. When Jesus responds with his outcry in Mk 9.19, he directs his response at them (αὐτοῖς), presumably once again at the crowd. As a member of the crowd, the father is part of the unbelieving generation. Later in the healing story the father describes himself as unbelieving (9.24), so that he confesses his own identification with the unbelieving generation.

---

sought to destroy the boy by throwing him into fire and water. The unclean spirit is identified twice in the narrative, once by the father as a mute spirit and once by Jesus as the mute and deaf spirit. This second designation increases the extent of the boy's problems. The failure of the disciples to cast out this unclean spirit is recounted twice, by both the father and the disciples themselves (9.18, 28). Jesus reacts to the man's initial description of his problem with two rhetorical questions (9.19). In the first, Jesus questions how long he must be with this unbelieving generation, and in the second he questions how long he must endure these people. The unclean spirit attacks the boy twice in the passage, leaving the boy apparently lifeless in the second attack (9.20, 26). Twice the father cries for help (9.22, 24). He moves from the position of doubt in his first cry to that of faith mixed with unbelief in his second cry.

1. Anderson, *Mark*, p. 230; Lagrange, *Marc*, p. 239; Marshall, *Faith*, pp. 117-18; Nineham, *Mark*, p. 243; Taylor, *Mark*, p. 398.

2. For the view that Jesus' cry is directed primarily or exclusively at the disciples see Cranfield, *Mark*, p. 301; Lane, *Mark*, p. 332; Lührmann, *Markus-evangelium*, p. 161.

The deficiency of the man's faith is further reflected in his request for help in Mk 9.23.[1] After the unclean spirit throws his son into a seizure, the father entreats Jesus with the words, 'If you are able to do anything, help us and have compassion on us' (9.23). The man's request is strikingly different from the request of the leper in Mk 1.40. The father prefaces his entreaty with the words, 'if you are able to do anything' (εἴ τι δύνῃ). The leper, however, begins with the condition 'if you are willing' (ἐὰν θέλῃς), followed by the expression of confidence 'you are able to cleanse me' (δύνασαί με καθαρίσαι). Jesus responds to the leper's expression of faith with compassion (σπλαγχνισθείς, 1.41), but he responds to the father's doubting request for compassion (σπλαγχνισθείς, 9.22) with a rebuke. Jesus throws the offending words back at the father (τὸ εἰ δύνῃ, 9.23), and in this way he underlines the presence of doubt in the man's request.[2] Jesus then insists that all things are possible to the one who believes. Jesus shifts the attention away from his own ability to the man's lack of faith. By stating that all things are possible to the one who believes, Jesus calls on the father to have faith and to recognize that God's power is limitless toward those who believe.[3]

---

1. Anderson, *Mark*, p. 230; Gnilka, *Markus*, II, pp. 47-48; Hooker, *Mark*, p. 224; Lagrange, *Marc*, p. 240; Lane, *Mark*, p. 333; Lohmeyer, *Markus*, pp. 187-88; Lührmann, *Markusevangelium*, p. 162; Marshall, *Faith*, pp. 116-18; Nineham, *Mark*, p. 243; Pesch, *Markusevangelium II. Teil*, p. 92.

2. The article in the construction τὸ εἰ δύνῃ apparently functions as a marker to signal the presence of a quotation. The phrase could then be translated as 'with regard to your "if you are able"'. See BDF, p. 140; Moule, *Idiom Book*, p. 110; Moulton, Howard and Turner, *Grammar*, III, p. 182; Robertson, *Grammar*, p. 766. See also Marshall, *Faith*, pp. 116-17. The reading τὸ εἰ δύνῃ is supported by the Greek manuscripts Aleph, B, Δ, family 1, 892 and a few others. The difficulty of the expression, which introduces a quotation with an article, probably occasioned the various other readings in the manuscript tradition. See Metzger, *Textual Commentary*, p. 100.

3. τῷ πιστεύοντι could be applied to either the suppliant or to the healer. All things are possible when the petitioner believes or all things are possible when the healer believes. Jesus' statement in 9.23 appears to be primarily a call to the father to believe without doubt. At least, this is clearly how the father understands the sense of Jesus' words, since he takes them as a rebuke of his own lack of faith in 9.24. See Anderson, *Mark*, pp. 230-31; Cranfield, *Mark*, pp. 302-303; Gundry, *Mark*, pp. 490, 499; Lane, *Mark*, pp. 333-34; F.G. Lang, 'Sola Gratia im Markusevangelium: Die Soteriologie des Markus nach 9,14-29 und 10,17-31', in J. Friedrich, W. Pöhlmann and P. Stuhlmacher (eds.), *Rechtfertigung* (Tübingen:

In his second cry for help, the father moves from doubt to a faith mixed with unbelief. In response to Jesus' implicit call for faith, the father cries, 'I believe, help my unbelief' (9.24). The father's cry shows that faith and unbelief are not mutually exclusive categories in Mark's narrative, since the same individual can experience both at the same time.[1] Belief and unbelief remain in tension within the father, so that he asks for deliverance from his unbelief. To his credit, the father is at least aware of his need and sufficiently repentant to ask for aid.[2] By perceiving his own lack and requesting help, the father distinguishes himself from the disciples (4.40), the people of Nazareth (6.1-6) and others in the unbelieving generation (9.19) who show no recognition of their own lack of faith. In response to the father's weak faith and the gathering crowd, Jesus delivers the boy from his possession.

Mark characterizes the father of the possessed boy as needy, since his son is severely oppressed by an unclean spirit and since he himself lacks proper faith. In response to his needs, the man is desperate and pleading. Through his conversation with Jesus, the father progresses from unbelieving to doubting to believing and unbelieving at the same time. Although his faith is weak, he is at least aware of his problem and repentant enough to cry out for help. In the end, Jesus responds positively to the father's weak faith, and the father is helped.

Mark concludes this healing story with a private conversation between the disciples and Jesus. The disciples question Jesus about their inability to cast out the demon, and he explains that this kind comes out only by prayer (9.28-29).[3] Jesus' insistence on the necessity of prayer points beyond itself to the need for faith, so that the key to casting out this type of demon is the faith that prayer represents.[4] The

Mohr [Paul Siebeck], 1976), p. 323; Nineham, *Mark*, p. 247.

1. Gnilka, *Markus*, II, p. 50; Marshall, *Faith*, p. 121; Nineham, *Mark*, p. 244.

2. Marshall, *Faith*, p. 122.

3. The addition of the words καὶ νηστείᾳ after προσευχῇ has widespread support in the manuscript tradition. However, it would be much easier to explain the addition of these words than their omission if they were original. The reading προσευχῇ without καὶ νηστείᾳ is supported by Aleph, B, 0274, the Itala manuscript k and Clement of Alexandria.

4. Cranfield, *Mark*, p. 305; Gnilka, *Markus*, II, p. 49; Lane, *Mark*, p. 335; Lührmann, *Markusevangelium*, p. 162; Marshall, *Faith*, pp. 221-23; Schweizer, *Markus*, p. 107. See also the close relationship between faith and prayer in Mk 11.22-24. Mark's omission of any prayer by Jesus in this exorcism may be in

failure of the disciples reveals a lack of faith on their part. Thus, the disciples as well as the father of the possessed boy share in an inadequate faith.

Earlier in Mark's narrative, the faith of minor characters stood in direct contrast to the unbelief of the disciples (4.40; 5.34, 36). However, the relationship between minor characters and the disciples becomes more complex in Mk 9.14-29, because the father of the possessed boy does not stand in direct contrast to the disciples.[1] Both the father and the disciples are part of the unbelieving generation. The disciples lack faith as they seek to fulfill the mission that Jesus has given to them, while the father lacks faith as he seeks deliverance for his son. In contrast to the disciples, however, the father recognizes his unbelief and struggles to believe.

The healing of the blind man of Bethsaida raised the expectation and hope that some might respond to Jesus not just with partial insight but with complete understanding. The disciples do not fulfill this hope, since they continue in their lack of understanding and faith. The father of the possessed boy does not fulfill this hope either, since his struggle for faith indicates a lack of understanding on his part concerning the authority and identity of Jesus.

Mark follows the healing of the possessed boy with Jesus' second passion prediction (9.30-32). Once again, the disciples respond to the prediction by misunderstanding, this time by debating the extent of their own individual greatness. Jesus confronts their incomprehension with the statement, 'If anyone wants to be first, he will be last of all

keeping with his overall presentation of Jesus. Mark repeatedly portrays Jesus as a man of prayer (1.35; 6.41, 46; 8.6-7; 14.22-23, 32-39) but only rarely narrates the actual prayers of Jesus (14.36; 15.34). See Fowler, *Let the Reader Understand*, pp. 214-15.

1.   In referring to minor characters as foils for the disciples, some literary critics have treated minor characters as though they functioned as direct contrasts to the disciples in a consistent manner throughout Mark's narrative. See Kingsbury, *Conflict in Mark*, pp. 25-27; Rhoads and Michie, *Mark as Story*, pp. 130, 132-33. So, for example, Rhoads and Michie state: 'At each stage in which the little people exemplify a particular standard of Jesus' teaching, the disciples are depicted as especially failing to live up to that standard: first faith, then being least, and finally sacrificial service. Thus, the little ones serve throughout as "foils" for the disciples' (p. 132). However, minor characters do not simply serve as contrasting figures in a consistent way throughout the narrative. At times, minor characters and the disciples share traits. Minor characters serve as foils for the disciples primarily in Mk 4–8 and 14–15.

and servant of all' (9.35). Jesus directs his words to the disciples, but he opens up his demands to a broader audience than simply the disciples. The standards of judgment that Jesus expresses are applicable to 'anyone'. Jesus' expectations, then, apply not only to the disciples, but also to other characters in the narrative as well as to the reader of the narrative.[1]

The Rich Man (10.17-31)

Mk 10.17-31 begins in a similar manner to the other scenes in which Jesus has contact with a suppliant.[2] An individual (εἷς, 10.17; εἷς, 9.17, cf. 5.22) runs to Jesus (προσδραμών, 10.17; προστρέχοντες, 9.15, cf. 5.6) and falls on his knees before him (γονυπετήσας, 10.17; γονυπετῶν, 1.40, cf. 5.6, 22, 33; 7.25). The man addresses Jesus as 'Good Teacher' (διδάσκαλε ἀγαθέ, 10.17; διδάσκαλε, 9.17) and presents Jesus with his request. Although the scene begins in a familiar manner, the succeeding events follow an unusual course in light of the negative characterization of this suppliant. Having initiated a negative portrayal of the man with the possessed boy in 9.14-29, Mark continues and increases this negative trend in his presentation of the rich man in 10.17-31.

The man's initial approach to Jesus appears to be sincere and blameless enough, but it calls forth a harsh response from Jesus. The man runs up to Jesus, falls on his knees and addresses Jesus as 'Good Teacher'. With both his actions and his words, the man treats Jesus with high respect. He then poses a question to Jesus concerning the requirements for inheriting eternal life (10.17).[3] In response, Jesus immediately challenges the man's understanding of goodness, insisting that no one is good except God (10.18). Goodness is not a matter of human achievement, since God alone is the true norm and source of all goodness. Jesus challenges the man's concept of goodness, because,

---

1. Malbon, 'Disciples/Crowds/Whoever', pp. 124-26.

2. The numerous connections between 9.14-29 and 10.17-31 highlight the analogous relationship between the two passages. For a discussion of this point see Chapter 2.

3. In the context of Mark's Gospel, 'inheriting eternal life', 'entering into the kingdom of God' and 'being saved' are synonymous expressions. Note the similarity between Mk 9.43, 45 and 47 and also Mk 10.17, 23, 24, 25 and 26. See Anderson, *Mark*, pp. 248, 250; Hooker, *Mark*, p. 241; Lane, *Mark*, p. 370; Lührmann, *Markusevangelium*, p. 174.

as the following dialogue will show, the man considers himself to be good on the basis of his own adherence to the law.[1] In the second part of his answer, Jesus further directs the man's attention to God by reminding him of God's demands through a rough summary of the second table of the ten commandments (10.19).[2]

In addressing Jesus the second time, the man drops the offending adjective 'good' and refers to Jesus simply as 'Teacher'. He then claims to have kept all these commandments from his youth (10.20). At this point, Jesus responds to the man with love rather than harshness. Nevertheless, Jesus' love does not lead him to spare the man from a difficult command. In order to overcome his lack, the man must sell all that he owns, give to the poor and follow Jesus (10.21). Since Mk 8.34, the demand to follow Jesus has been placed on a broader audience than the disciples alone, so that anyone can and should follow Jesus, including this man. Following Jesus involves leaving something else behind (1.18, 20; 2.14; 8.34), and for this man, following would involve leaving all his possessions. The man's reaction to Jesus' word (τῷ λόγῳ) is one of shock, and instead of following Jesus the man departs in grief (10.22). Mark explains this reaction by telling the reader that the man owned many possessions. Thus, the rich man exemplifies the thorny ground in Jesus' parable of the sower (4.7, 18-19).[3] The thorny ground represents those who hear the word (τὸν λόγον), but the cares of this age, the deceitfulness of

---

1. For a useful list of different explanations for Jesus' refusal to accept the reference to his goodness see Taylor, *Mark*, pp. 426-27.

2. In this summary, Jesus moves the fifth commandment on honoring parents to the end of the list and apparently omits the tenth commandment on coveting, replacing it with a prohibition against defrauding others. This commandment against defrauding appears to be an expansion of the eighth commandment prohibiting theft. For a similar view on the command against defrauding see Gundry, *Mark*, p. 553; Lane, *Mark*, p. 362; Mann, *Mark*, p. 400; Taylor, *Mark*, p. 428. For other commentators who take the command against defrauding as a summary of the tenth commandment against coveting see Anderson, *Mark*, p. 249; Cranfield, *Mark*, p. 329; Lagrange, *Marc*, p. 266; Lohmeyer, *Markus*, p. 210; Lührmann, *Markusevangelium*, pp. 174-75; Nineham, *Mark*, p. 274; Pesch, *Markusevangelium II. Teil*, p. 139. In addition, Lang ('Sola Gratia', p. 331) takes the command against defrauding as simply a replacement for the tenth commandment. For Lang, Jesus uses the command against defrauding, since this command would be more relevant to a rich man than the commandment against coveting.

3. Gnilka, *Markus*, II, p. 89; Marcus, *Mystery*, pp. 67-68.

riches and the desire for other things choke out the word. The demand of Jesus reveals the man's heart, showing that he is more devoted to himself and his own possessions than he is to God. Although he claimed to have obeyed all the commandments, he neglected the first of the ten commandments, which prohibited placing anything in the way of one's devotion to God.[1] Therefore, Jesus' command becomes a call to repentance, a call that is left unheeded.[2]

The rich man initiates his conversation with Jesus as an eager, respectful and sincere inquirer. He is confident in his own ability to do all that is necessary for obtaining eternal life, and he is confident in his careful adherence to the commandments of God. However, although he is obedient, he is not good. Goodness does not come from human achievement but through God, who alone is the source and norm of goodness. In the end, he is shocked, dismayed and grieved at Jesus' command to leave everything and follow him. He is disobedient to Jesus' command and in this way reveals that he is more devoted to himself and his material possessions than he is to God.

Although the rich man displays a number of unusual traits, it is the traits that the man is lacking that clearly set him apart as unique among minor characters. The rich man is not in need physically. He is not believing. His lack of faith is all the more unusual since the last passage presenting a minor character (9.14-29) emphasized the necessity of faith so extensively. Moreover, the rich man is not understanding. He possesses little insight into the identity of Jesus or the nature of goodness. The rich man shows a lack of understanding through his desire to do something to inherit eternal life. His attitude stands in sharp contrast to the teaching of Jesus in the immediately preceding episode, for there Jesus insists that people must receive the kingdom of God as a child (10.13-16).[3] The rich man neglects the unpretentious response of a child and wants instead to be judged on the basis of his obedience from his youth on (10.20). Finally, the rich

---

1.   Cranfield, *Mark*, p. 330; Lang, 'Sola Gratia', p. 332.
2.   Cranfield, *Mark*, p. 229; Lane, *Mark*, p. 368-69.
3.   Anderson, *Mark*, p. 247; Hooker, *Mark*, p. 240; Hurtado, *Mark*, p. 150; Lane, *Mark*, p. 363. The children in 9.36-37 and 10.13-16 seem to function more as object lessons in Jesus' instruction to the disciples than as characters who respond to Jesus. Therefore, they should probably not be treated as minor characters from the crowd.

man is not healed. For the first time, a suppliant comes to Jesus but is not helped by him.

As in Mk 9.14-29, Jesus' conversation with a minor character is followed by a private discussion between Jesus and his disciples. In this way, Mark is able to emphasize the characteristics of both the rich man and the disciples, by showing the similarities and differences between them. The disciples are like the rich man in that they also display a lack of understanding. The disciples are slow to accept Jesus' teaching on the difficulty that the rich and indeed all others find in entering the kingdom (10.23-26). Entrance into the kingdom of God on the basis of human achievement is an impossibility, for God alone is able to give salvation to people, to rich and poor alike (10.27).[1] Peter, however, is quick to point out that the disciples are different from the rich man. The rich man refused to leave his many properties and follow Jesus, but the disciples had left everything in order to follow Jesus (10.28). In response to this contrast, Jesus promises abundant reward to anyone who leaves family and possessions for his sake and for the sake of the gospel (10.29-30). Yet in addition to the abundant reward, the follower of Jesus will also receive persecutions (διωγμῶν, 10.30). In the parable of the sower, the rocky soil represents those who hear the word and receive it with joy, but when tribulation and persecution (διωγμοῦ, 4.17) come because of the word, they fall away.[2] The disciples may not be like the rich man who is captivated by the deceitfulness of riches, but they are in danger of responding like the rocky soil. They need to be warned that they may stumble in the face of persecution.[3] Mark sets up both a comparison and a contrast between the rich man and the disciples, so that it would be inadequate to refer to the rich man as a foil for the disciples as though he simply served as a contrasting figure to them. The rich man and the disciples both share in a lack of understanding. When the rich man and the disciples stand in contrast to one another, the disciples are treated in a more positive manner.

At this point in the narrative, the reader is not able to identify clearly with any character or group of characters because of the

---

1. Cranfield, *Mark*, p. 332; Lang, 'Sola Gratia', pp. 229-30; Lane, *Mark*, p. 370.

2. διωγμός is used in Mark's Gospel only in 4.17 and 10.30.

3. On the relationship of the disciples to the parable of the soils see Marcus, *Mystery*, pp. 65-67.

negative picture of the rich man and the mixed presentation of the disciples. A distance is created between the reader and the rich man, because his response to Jesus with its lack of understanding and refusal to follow is at odds with the expectations of Jesus. Yet while Mark moves the reader to dissociate from the rich man, he also builds sympathy for the rich man by informing the reader of Jesus' love for the man (10.21) and by delaying the information concerning the man's wealth (10.22). Mark's inside view of Jesus' attitude toward the rich man keeps the reader from treating him in the same manner as the opponents of Jesus, the demons and religious leaders. Since the reader has already been informed of the deceitfulness of riches (4.19), Mark's delay of any information concerning the man's wealth keeps the reader from prematurely judging and rejecting the man.[1] The reader's response to the disciples would be ambivalent, since Mark's portrayal of the disciples in this episode is mixed, including both positive and negative traits. Mark reminds the reader of the disciples' commitment to follow Jesus, the commitment which encouraged the reader to identify with the disciples in the first place. However, the reader seems to be warned that the disciples may abandon their commitment in the face of persecution. The effect of Mark's treatment of the rich man and the disciples is to move the reader away from both.

Jesus' third passion prediction follows immediately after the passage concerning the rich man. For the third time, Jesus tells his twelve disciples about his coming suffering, death and resurrection (10.32-34). The misunderstanding of the disciples is then exemplified by James and John, who come to Jesus in order to seek the most prominent positions in the kingdom (10.35-40). The rest of the disciples are indignant with James and John, presumably because they also desire the most prominent positions in the kingdom (10.41). Once again, Jesus responds by instructing his disciples about the necessity of service (10.42-45). Jesus speaks to his disciples, but his teaching applies to anyone who wants to be great or first. Jesus' expectations apply to a broader audience than simply to the disciples. Whoever wants to be great will be a servant, and whoever wants to be first will be a slave of all. Jesus himself exemplifies the proper paradigm, since,

---

1. On the significance of this delay of information see Fowler, 'Rhetoric of Direction', pp. 117-18; *idem, Let the Reader Understand*, p. 98; *idem*, 'Reader-Response Criticism', pp. 70-71.

as the Son of Man, he did not come to be served but to serve and to
give his life as a ransom for many (10.45).

The Response of the Reader

By the end of the preceding section, Mk 4.1–8.21, the reader is left in
an ambivalent situation. As early as ch. 4, the disciples begin to display
negative traits that move the reader to begin dissociating from them.
The disciples show an unusual lack of faith and understanding. In
contrast, minor characters exemplify faith and insight in Mk 5.1-43
and 7.24-37. Nevertheless, the reader does not simply abandon the
disciples and identify with these minor characters, because the
disciples maintain their unique relationship with Jesus and because the
minor characters are not consistently positive in their response to
Jesus. Repeatedly, minor characters disobey Jesus' commands to
maintain silence concerning his miraculous work.

Mk 8.22–10.45 does not clear up the reader's ambivalent situation,
but rather further complicates the interplay between the disciples,
minor characters and the reader. The healing of the blind man of
Bethsaida in two stages highlights in a symbolic fashion the
inadequacy of the disciples. With the first touch of Jesus, the blind
man regains partial sight, but only with a second touch does the blind
man come to see fully. At best, the disciples possess only partial sight,
that is, partial understanding. Immediately before the healing of the
blind man at Bethsaida Jesus strongly criticizes the disciples for their
lack of perception. After the healing, the disciples show some insight
into the identity of Jesus, but their understanding proves inadequate,
since their perception of Jesus allows no room for his suffering and
death. The healing of the blind man in two stages symbolizes the need
to move from partial insight to complete understanding, and it creates
the expectation that some in the narrative will indeed come to this
complete understanding. The disciples do not fulfill this expectation,
because they continue to have only partial understanding with regard
to the person and mission of Jesus and with regard to their own
mission as his disciples. Unable to see things from God's viewpoint,
the disciples simply follow a human perspective. The disciples continue in this incomprehension throughout Mark 8–10 without any
evidence of growth or development. Thus, it becomes increasingly
difficult for the reader to identify with the disciples.

In Mk 8.34 Jesus opens up the demands and privileges of following him to a broader audience than to the disciples alone. The disciples, members of the crowd, or anyone, may deny themselves and take up their cross and follow Jesus. The unique privilege of the disciples to follow Jesus is now made available to others. Minor characters may now also follow Jesus and in this way show their complete understanding. Surprisingly, it is precisely at this point in the narrative that Mark's portrayal of minor characters becomes increasingly negative. The father of the possessed boy struggles with doubts concerning the authority and power of Jesus. The rich man refuses to deny himself and follow Jesus even when he is directly invited to do so. Thus, at the same time that it becomes increasingly difficult for the reader to identify with the disciples, it is likewise impossible for the reader to identify with minor characters. The two-stage healing of the blind man creates an anticipation in the reader that the narrative is not quick to fulfill.

Because of the negative portrayal of both the disciples and minor characters, the reader is left with no one to identify with in the narrative following the healing of the blind man of Bethsaida, except Jesus. Significantly, Mk 8.27–10.45 is the primary section of the Gospel in which Jesus serves as the paradigm for his followers. By omitting any reference to exemplary characters in the central section of the Gospel, Mark moves the reader to focus on the paradigmatic nature of Jesus and his mission. Mark's omission of any exemplary people is all the more glaring since he encouraged the anticipation of such characters through his narration of the healing of the blind man in two stages. Jesus alone becomes the paradigm for the reader within the central section of the Gospel, and 'paradigm' here means something different from 'example'. Jesus and his mission are in many ways unique, so that his identity and mission cannot simply be duplicated in the life of his follower. However, the way that Jesus chooses is determinative for the manner of life that his followers must pursue.[1] Jesus, as the Son of

---

1. Schweizer provides a useful illustration of the difference between Jesus as an example and Jesus as a paradigm in his article 'The Portrayal of the Life of Faith in the Gospel of Mark'. There Schweizer states: 'For many years I have used the imagery which the Swiss mountain town in which I was allowed to serve as a minister for nearly ten years provided me... When a heavy snowfall sets in, the boy who had gone to his friend's after school instead of going home cannot get home until his father comes, with his strong shoulders, and breaks the way through three feet of snow. The boy "follows him" in his footsteps and yet walks in a totally different

Man, must suffer many things and be killed, and so followers of Jesus must deny themselves and lose their lives for his sake (8.31, 34-37). Jesus, as the Son of Man, did not come to be served but to serve and to give his life a ransom for many (10.45). The followers of Jesus may not serve in the same sense that Jesus does, for they will not give their lives as a ransom, but Jesus' life of service is determinative for their own lives. They must take the position of servant and slave of all (10.42-44). The path that the reader must follow is difficult, but Mark leaves the reader no other choice.

Through the two-stage healing of the blind man (8.22-26) Mark creates the expectation that some in the narrative will come to genuine insight. However, Mark does not immediately fulfill this expectation, but rather refrains from any reference to an exemplary character until after Jesus has repeatedly predicted his passion and has explained the implications of his passion for his followers. In this way, the reader is moved to recognize that Jesus serves as the proper paradigm for those who choose to follow him. Immediately after Jesus' third passion prediction and his instruction to his misunderstanding disciples, Mark finally presents an exemplary character, Bartimaeus. Mark's characterization of Bartimaeus and the influence of this characterization on the reader is the subject of the next chapter.

way. Father is not merely his teacher or example—otherwise the boy would have to break his own way, only copying the action of the father' (Schweizer, 'Life of Faith', p. 393).

Chapter 4

THE CHARACTERIZATION OF BARTIMAEUS IN MARK 10.46-52

According to Tannehill, Mark moves the reader to identify with the disciples by portraying them, at least initially, in a positive manner.[1] Though true, this contention needs to be supplemented, since Mark's Gospel includes other followers besides the disciples. Some of the individuals who are drawn from the general population respond properly to the demands and expectations of Jesus. Mark's positive treatment of these individuals creates a complexity in the reader's relationship to the characters in the narrative. While Mark initially encourages the reader to identify with the disciples, he also moves the reader to associate with other characters through the course of his narrative. Mark's treatment of Bartimaeus serves as a useful example, because he is presented in a thoroughly positive manner at a point in the narrative when the disciples are portrayed in an increasingly negative manner.

This chapter will seek to show that Mark encourages the reader to identify with Bartimaeus and that this identification is not an end in itself. Instead, in the narrative following the Bartimaeus story, Mark presents a series of minor characters who serve as models for the reader. Therefore, beginning with Bartimaeus, Mark encourages the reader to identify with a number of minor characters. In order to analyze the rhetorical effect of Mk 10.46-52 this chapter will examine Mark's characterization of Bartimaeus, showing that Mark portrays him as both an exemplary figure and a transitional figure in the narrative. Thus, an attempt will be made to show the relationship between Mark's characterization of Bartimaeus and his strategy for influencing the reader.

---

1. Tannehill, 'Disciples in Mark', pp. 392-93, 394-95, 398.

Bartimaeus as an Exemplary Figure

Mark frames the central section of his Gospel (8.22–10.52) with analogous episodes in which Jesus heals a blind man. Between these two
healing stories Mark highlights Jesus' teaching concerning his own
destiny and the implications of this destiny for those who follow him.
At the beginning of the central section Jesus heals the blind man of
Bethsaida (8.22-26), and at the end he heals blind Bartimaeus (10.46-
52). These passages begin in a similar fashion. Mark introduces the
story of the blind man of Bethsaida with the words καὶ ἔρχονται εἰς
Βηθσαϊδάν, and then begins the Bartimaeus story in an almost
identical way with καὶ ἔρχονται εἰς Ἰεριχώ. In both passages, a
blind man (τυφλός, 8.22, 23; 10.46, 49, 51) comes to see
(ἀναβλέπω, 8.24, 10.51, 52) through the miraculous power of Jesus.
The similarities between these two healing stories serve to connect the
Bartimaeus narrative with earlier episodes in which Jesus meets with a
suppliant.[1] The Bartimaeus story is best interpreted against the
background of these earlier passages.

Prior to Mk 10.46-52, minor characters have been exemplary
primarily because of the nature of their supplication. They approach
Jesus with confidence in his authority to heal them. Bartimaeus serves
as a model in a similar way, since he calls out with a persistent faith in
the mercy of Jesus, but Bartimaeus is exemplary in ways that move
beyond the manner of his supplication. Thus, as an example, he sur-
passes the pattern of earlier minor characters. Mark enhances the
exemplary character of Bartimaeus by including within the story
motifs that until this point in the narrative have been associated with
discipleship passages.[2]

---

1.   In addition, Mark ties the Bartimaeus story to earlier passages on minor characters through a number of lexical connections. See the use of ὁδός (10.17, 46, 52),
ἀκούω (5.27; 7.25, 37; 10.47), Ναζαρηνός (1.24; 10.47), κράζω (9.24; 10.47),
ἐλεέω (5.19; 10.47, 48), ἐγείρω (1.31; 2.9, 11, 12; 3.3; 5.41; 9.27; 10.49),
ἱμάτιον (5.27, 28, 30; 10.50), θέλω (1.40, 41; 10.51), ὑπάγω (1.44; 2.11; 5.19,
34; 7.29; 10.21, 52), πίστις (2.5; 5.34; 10.52), σώζω (3.4; 5.23, 28, 34; 10.26,
52), and ἀκολουθέω (10.21, 52).
2.   On the idea that Bartimaeus functions as an example to the reader see
J. Dupont, 'L'aveugle de Jéricho recouvre la vue et suit Jésus (Marc 10,46-52)',
Revue Africaine de Théologie 8 (1984), pp. 165, 172, 178; Kingsbury, *Christology*,
p. 105; Malbon, 'Fallible Followers', p. 31.

The Characterization of Bartimaeus as Exemplary

Mark structures the Bartimaeus story in 10.46-52 around the blind man's meeting with Jesus, resulting in a narrative that takes place in three scenes. In vv. 46-49 Mark records the blind man's attempt to reach Jesus, in vv. 50-52b he presents the blind man's encounter with Jesus, and then in v. 52c he gives the result of this meeting. Each of the three scenes is initiated by a report of the physical posture of Bartimaeus. At first, Bartimaeus is sitting alongside the way (10.46), next he throws aside his garment, jumps up and comes to Jesus (10.50), and finally, he follows Jesus in the way (10.52c).[1]

Bartimaeus Calls Out to Jesus (10.46-49). The setting for the story is on the outskirts of Jericho. Bartimaeus, a blind beggar, is sitting beside the way while Jesus passes by accompanied by his disciples and a great crowd (10.46). Like earlier minor characters, the blind man is needy and helpless, since he faces a physical difficulty that has reduced him to poverty and begging. Unlike earlier minor characters, the blind man is introduced by name, 'the son of Timaeus, Bartimaeus'.[2] In the preceding narrative, Jairus is the only member of the crowd to be specifically named (5.22). More commonly, disciples are named when they are called by Jesus (1.16, 19; 2.14; 3.16-19).[3] In the narrative following the Bartimaeus story there is an increase of instances in which minor characters are introduced by name (15.21, 40, 43). Bartimaeus is sitting alongside the way, presumably in order that he might beg for alms from those who are passing by. Like the two pairs of brothers who are involved with fishing (1.16, 19) and

1.   For a similar outline see Marshall, *Faith*, p. 126.

2.   A number of commentators explain the naming of Bartimaeus by positing that he was a Christian and known to the early Christian community. See J.A. Brooks, *Mark* (New American Commentary; Nashville: Broadman, 1991), p. 173; Cranfield, *Mark*, p. 334; E.P. Gould, *A Critical and Exegetical Commentary on the Gospel according to Saint Mark* (ICC; New York: Charles Scribner's Sons, 1896), p. 204; Lagrange, *Marc*, p. 284; Lane, *Mark*, p. 387; Mann, *Mark*, pp. 421, 423; A.E.J. Rawlinson, *St Mark* (Westminster Commentaries; London: Methuen, 3rd edn, 1931), p. 149; Roloff, *Kerygma*, p. 122; Taylor, *Mark*, p. 448. Although this historical explanation may be accurate, it overlooks the possibility that the naming of Bartimaeus may have some function within the narrative itself.

3.   On the naming of an individual as a typical feature of a discipleship call story see Marshall, *Faith*, p. 141; M.G. Steinhauser, 'The Form of the Bartimaeus Narrative (Mark 10:46-52)', *NTS* 32 (1986), pp. 588-89.

like Levi who is sitting at the tax office (2.14), Bartimaeus is engaged in his occupation when he is called by Jesus.[1]

When he hears that Jesus the Nazarene is present,[2] Bartimaeus begins to cry out, 'Son of David, Jesus, have mercy on me' (10.47). Bartimaeus's cry expresses his faith, since he is confident that Jesus is both able and willing to have mercy on him, that is, to heal him.[3] Moreover, Bartimaeus displays his understanding, for he addresses Jesus with a messianic title, Son of David.[4] Until this point in the narrative, the only other human character to ascribe to Jesus a messianic title has been Peter (8.29). Bartimaeus is similar to the disciples in that he shows insight into the messianic identity of Jesus.[5]

The people traveling with Jesus respond to Bartimaeus's cry by rebuking him and calling on him to be silent (10.48a). At times in the preceding narrative, minor characters were commanded to be silent or at least to limit their communication in some way (1.44; 5.19, 43; 7.36; 8.26). However, the rebuke in Mk 10.48 stands in contrast to these earlier commands to silence.[6] Before, the commands to silence always came from Jesus, but now the crowd expresses the rebuke. Earlier, the commands came after the healing miracle, but here Bartimaeus is commanded to silence before his healing.[7] The rebuke

1.   M.G. Steinhauser, 'Part of a "Call Story"?', *ExpTim* 94 (1983), p. 205.

2.   In the preceding narrative, the hemorrhaging woman hears of Jesus and comes to him for healing (5.27). In addition, the Syrophoenician woman hears about Jesus and approaches him in order to request help for her possessed daughter (7.25). In a similar way, Bartimaeus hears about Jesus and cries out to him for mercy (10.47).

3.   Kingsbury, *Christology*, p. 103.

4.   For a helpful discussion on the use of 'Son of David' as a messianic title within first-century Judaism see E. Lohse, 'υἱὸς Δαυίδ', *TDNT*, VIII, pp. 480-82. According to Mk 12.35-37, the scribes taught that the messiah is the Son of David. For the use of 'Son of David' as a messianic title see also *Pss. Sol.* 17.21.

5.   Robbins, 'Healing of Blind Bartimaeus', p. 227; Tolbert, *Sowing*, p. 190.

6.   Best, *Following Jesus*, p. 140; Räisänen, *Messianic Secret*, pp. 230-31.

7.   Noticing the difference between this rebuke of the crowd and other commands to silence in Mark's Gospel, Wrede (*Messiasgeheimnis*, pp. 278-79) argued that the command in 10.48 had nothing to do with the messianic secret. Wrede has been followed in this judgment by a vast array of interpreters. See Achtemeier, 'Miracles and Discipleship', p. 118; Busemann, *Jüngergemeinde*, p. 168; Gnilka, *Markus*, II, p. 110; W. Grundmann, *Das Evangelium nach Markus* (THKNT; Berlin: Evangelische Verlagsanstalt, 9th edn, 1984), p. 298; Gundry, *Mark*, p. 602; Johnson, 'Blind Bartimaeus', pp. 196-97; W. Kirchschläger, 'Bartimäus—

from the crowd in Mk 10.48 is similar, however, to the rebuke from the disciples in 10.13.[1] There, people bring their children to Jesus in order that he might touch them, but the disciples rebuke (ἐπετίμησαν) them, presumably because they feel that the children would be a nuisance to Jesus. The crowd traveling with Jesus rebukes (ἐπετίμων) Bartimaeus in a similar manner, since they apparently feel that Jesus should continue on his way to Jerusalem and not be bothered with the cries of a blind beggar.[2]

Although Bartimaeus is pressured to be silent, he cries out all the more, 'Son of David, have mercy on me' (10.48b). Like previous minor characters, Bartimaeus refuses to be silent (1.45; 7.36-37), but in contrast to these free-speaking members of the crowd, Bartimaeus is not disobedient to Jesus in the process. Bartimaeus's refusal to be silent reveals the extent of his faith, in that it is persistent[3] and able to overcome obstacles.[4] Bartimaeus is similar to previous suppliants who have found it necessary to move past the crowd in order to gain access

---

Paradigma einer Wundererzählung (Mk 10,46-52 par)', in F. Van Segbroeck *et al.* (eds.), *The Four Gospels 1992* (Leuven: Leuven University Press, 1992), II, p. 1114; Koch, *Wundererzählungen*, pp. 130-31; Lohmeyer, *Markus*, p. 224; Lührmann, *Markusevangelium*, p. 183; Marshall, *Faith*, p. 129; Räisänen, *Messianic Secret*, pp. 230-31; Rawlinson, *Mark*, p. 149; Schenke, *Wundererzählungen*, p. 357; J. Schmid, *Das Evangelium nach Markus* (RNT; Regensburg: Pustet, 4th edn, 1958), p. 204. Burger (*Davidssohn*, pp. 60-62) argues against this consensus, insisting that the command in 10.48 is bound up with the messianic secret.

1. See especially Robbins, 'Healing of Blind Bartimaeus', pp. 231-32, 235. See also Busemann, *Jüngergemeinde*, p. 169; Gundry, *Mark*, p. 594; Lührmann, *Markusevangelium*, p. 183; Räisänen, *Messianic Secret*, p. 231; Wrede, *Messiasgeheimnis*, pp. 278-79.

2. Cranfield, *Mark*, p. 345; Gnilka, *Markus*, II, p. 110; Grundmann, *Markus*, p. 298; Lagrange, *Marc*, p. 285; Lane, *Mark*, p. 388; Räisänen, *Messianic Secret*, p. 231; Rawlinson, *Mark*, p. 149; Schmid, *Markus*, p. 204.

3. Achtemeier, 'Miracles and Discipleship', pp. 118-19; Johnson, 'Blind Bartimaeus', p. 197; Kingsbury, *Christology*, p. 103; Nineham, *Mark*, p. 283; Rhoads and Michie, *Mark as Story*, p. 131; Schweizer, *Markus*, p. 128; S.G. Sinclair, 'The Healing of Bartimaeus and the Gaps in Mark's Messianic Secret', *Saint Luke's Journal of Theology* 33 (1990), p. 253.

4. Guelich, *Mark*, pp. 85, 94; Rhoads and Michie, *Mark as Story*, p. 131; W. Schmithals, *Das Evangelium nach Markus* (Ökumenischer Taschenbuch-kommentar zum Neuen Testament; Gütersloh: Gütersloher Verlagshaus/Gerd Mohn, 1979), II, p. 475; Theissen, *Wundergeschichten*, pp. 62-63.

to Jesus (2.2-4; 5.24-27). Jesus sees this persistence as an evidence of faith (2.5; 5.34).

Jesus stops and commands the crowd to call the blind man (10.49a). Jesus is the kind of messianic king who hears the cry of a blind beggar and stops in order to show him mercy. In contrast to their previous reaction to the beggar, the people now encourage Bartimaeus with the words, 'Have courage, arise, he is calling you' (10.49b). The actions of Bartimaeus throughout the episode mark him as one who already possesses courage, so that the crowd's encouragement is unnecessary for the blind man. Nevertheless, the message of the crowd draws the reader's attention to the beggar's fearless behavior. In the preceding narrative, the hemorrhaging woman and Jairus both responded with a faith that overcomes fear (5.33-34, 36). Their faith and courage stood in contrast to the unbelief and fear of the disciples (4.40-41). The courageous examples of these suppliants do not seem to influence the disciples, for their fear continues to be a problem. When Jesus comes to the disciples walking on the water, the disciples become unsettled, and Jesus must tell them to have courage and not be afraid.[1] The disciples continue to respond with fear in the central section of the Gospel as they travel with Jesus on the way to Jerusalem, the place of suffering and death (9.32; 10.32). In contrast to the disciples, Bartimaeus reacts with faith rather than fear. Although Bartimaeus is different from the disciples because of his courage, he is similar to them in that he receives a call. Jesus' call of Bartimaeus is clearly important in the narrative, since the verb φωνέω is repeated three times in v. 49: by Jesus, by the narrator and by the crowd.[2] As he did previously with disciples (1.17, 20; 2.14; 3.13-19), Jesus takes the initiative to call Bartimaeus, and this summoning does more than create an opportunity for the blind man to be healed; it also makes it possible for Bartimaeus to follow Jesus.[3]

Bartimaeus Encounters Jesus (10.50-52b). In response to the call of Jesus, Bartimaeus throws aside his garment, jumps up and comes to

1.   θαρσέω is used twice in Mark's Gospel, both times in a command: once to the disciples when they are afraid (6.50), and once to Bartimaeus who is not afraid (10.49).

2.   Marshall, *Faith*, pp. 125, 141.

3.   Marshall, *Faith*, pp. 125, 141; Steinhauser, 'Call Story', p. 205; Tolbert, *Sowing*, p. 190.

Jesus (10.50). Perhaps the most striking feature in Bartimaeus's response is the casting aside of his mantle. This action of the blind man has been variously explained as a sign of his eagerness,[1] an attempt to throw away any hindrance that might impede his hasty run to Jesus,[2] an expression of his dramatic decisiveness[3] and a demonstration of his belief that he would be healed.[4] While any of these explanations may contain an element of truth, they appear to be unrelated to the broader narrative. In the broader narrative, those who have been called by Jesus leave something behind in order to follow him. Simon and Andrew abandon their nets to follow Jesus (1.18), while James and John leave their father in the boat with the hired servants (1.20). Levi walks away from his occupation to go with Jesus (2.14). Jesus commands the rich man to sell all of his possessions and give away what he has to the poor in order to follow (10.21). In view of the rich man's failure, Peter points out that the disciples have left everything in order to be with Jesus (10.28). In a similar way, Bartimaeus has been called by Jesus and he leaves behind his mantle.[5] Lohmeyer suggested that it was the custom at that time for a beggar to place a garment along the road, so that passersby could lay their alms on it.[6] Like the fishermen and the tax collector, Bartimaeus would then be leaving behind his occupation and means of income by throwing aside his mantle. On the other hand, 'beggars' customs are not often the stuff of recorded history'.[7] Mark may simply be indicating that Bartimaeus left behind what he possessed in order to be with Jesus, so that the beggar does what the rich man refused to do.

When the blind man approaches, Jesus asks him, 'What do you want that I might do for you?' (τί σοι θέλεις ποιήσω, 10.51a). Jesus put

---

1. Gnilka, *Markus*, II, p. 110; Gould, *Mark*, p. 204; Kingsbury, *Christology*, pp. 103-104.

2. Gnilka, *Markus*, II, p. 110; Grundmann, *Markus*, p. 298; Gundry, *Mark*, p. 596; Lagrange, *Marc*, p. 285; Rawlinson, *Mark*, p. 149; Schmithals, *Markus*, II, p. 476; H.B. Swete, *The Gospel according to Mark* (London: Macmillan, 3rd edn, 1909), p. 244.

3. Lane, *Mark*, p. 388; Taylor, *Mark*, p. 449.

4. Hurtado, *Mark*, p. 165; Pesch, *Markusevangelium II. Teil*, p. 173.

5. Busemann, *Jüngergemeinde*, p. 170; R.A. Culpepper, 'Mark 10:50: Why Mention the Garment?', *JBL* 101 (1982), pp. 131-32; Hooker, *Mark*, p. 253; Marshall, *Faith*, pp. 129, 141-42; Steinhauser, 'Call Story', p. 205.

6. Lohmeyer, *Markus*, p. 226.

7. Steinhauser, 'Call Story', p. 205.

the same question to James and John, the sons of Zebedee, in the immediately preceding context (τί θέλετέ με ποιήσω ὑμῖν, 10.36). The response of James and John to this question stands in direct contrast to the answer of Bartimaeus.[1] The request of James and John reveals their blindness, for they want to receive places of honor and privilege in the coming kingdom. They want to sit (καθίσωμεν) with Jesus, one at his right and one at his left, when he comes into his glory (10.37). Jesus is unable to grant their request, because the places at his right and left have been prepared for others (10.40). When Jesus receives his glory at the baptism of his death, two thieves are crucified along with him, one at his right and one at his left (15.27).[2] In other words, James and John do not know what they are requesting (10.38). In contrast to these disciples, Bartimaeus, the son of Timaeus, who has been sitting (ἐκάθητο) alongside the way, asks for the restoration of his sight.

The blind beggar responds to Jesus' question with the words, 'Rabbouni, that I might see' (10.51b). Here, Bartimaeus changes his address of Jesus, moving from 'Son of David' to 'Rabbouni'.[3] The blind man's use of titles reveals not only his recognition of Jesus' messianic identity but also his acknowledgment of Jesus' authority as his teacher.[4] Bartimaeus's plea for sight is a request that Jesus is able

1. Brooks, *Mark*, p. 172; Dupont, 'L'aveugle', p. 170; Marshall, *Faith*, pp. 130, 140; Robbins, 'Healing of Blind Bartimaeus', p. 239; Schmithals, *Markus*, II, p. 477.

2. Note the similarity between the words of James and John in 10.37 (εἷς σου ἐκ δεξιῶν καὶ εἷς ἐξ ἀριστερῶν) and the words of the narrator in 15.27 (ἕνα ἐκ δεξιῶν καὶ ἕνα ἐξ εὐωνύμων αὐτοῦ).

3. The title ῥαββουνί, which appears twice in the New Testament (Mk 10.51; Jn 20.16), does not differ significantly from the more common form ῥαββί. See E. Lohse, 'ῥαββί, ῥαββουνί', *TDNT*, VI, p. 964. The address ῥαββί is used by disciples for their teacher elsewhere in Mark's Gospel (9.5; 11.21; 14.45), which agrees with the usage of the word outside of Mark's Gospel. See Lohse, 'ῥαββί, ῥαββουνί', pp. 961-62. Thus, Bartimaeus responds to Jesus like a disciple addressing his teacher.

4. Kelber (*Kingdom in Mark*, pp. 94-95) argues that Bartimaeus's use of both 'Son of David' and 'Rabbouni' reveals a lack of understanding on his part and that Mark shows this by having Bartimaeus use these terms while he is still blind. Thus, Bartimaeus's christological awareness is no better than that of the blind disciples. A similar argument may be found in Best, *Following Jesus*, p. 140; Johnson, 'Blind Bartimaeus', p. 197; Lührmann, *Markusevangelium*, p. 183. Kelber appears to move away from this argument, placing Bartimaeus in a more positive light in *Story*

to grant. In Mark's Gospel, people receive when their desires align with God's will, but those who seek after comfort or privilege suffer loss. This principle is clearly presented in Jesus' teaching concerning the demands of discipleship, which are often set forth in terms of what a person wants (θέλει, 8.34; 9.35; θέλῃ, 8.35; 10.43, 44).[1] Whoever wants to save his life will lose it, but whoever is willing to set aside selfish concerns for the sake of Jesus and the gospel will in the end receive life (8.35). Bartimaeus wants to receive his sight, and his sight allows him to follow Jesus on the way. Thus, the blind man's desires are in accord with God's point of view.

In response to Bartimaeus's request, Jesus says, 'Depart, your faith has saved you' (10.52a). The command to depart functions as a typical feature of healing miracles in Mark (1.44; 2.11; 5.19, 34; 7.29; 10.52).[2] After being healed, the suppliants are frequently dismissed without receiving any specific call to follow Jesus or continue on with him. However, in Mk 8.34 Jesus summons the crowd along with the disciples and opens up his commission to anyone who wants to follow after him. From that point on in the narrative the opportunity to follow Jesus is open to anyone, including members of the crowd. Thus, while Bartimaeus is granted permission to depart, he is also given the opportunity to follow.[3] When dismissing Bartimaeus, Jesus commends the blind beggar for his faith. Jesus himself attests to the fervent trust of Bartimaeus that has been evident from the beginning of the story through the blind man's persistent attempts to be healed by Jesus. In addition, Jesus declares that Bartimaeus's faith has led to his salvation. Jesus' words indicate that the blind man has received his sight, but they go beyond an indication of physical restoration to a

---

of Jesus, pp. 55-56. Kingsbury (*Christology*, pp. 105-106) argues that both titles show a proper understanding of Jesus on the part of Bartimaeus. According to Kingsbury, it is beside the point that Bartimaeus uttered these titles when he was physically blind. Unless the story is completely rewritten, when else could Bartimaeus have addressed Jesus except while blind? Kingsbury also shows that when Jesus restores the sight of Bartimaeus, he is responding positively to one who has addressed him as Son of David and Rabbouni. This response of Jesus would leave the reader with a positive view of Bartimaeus and the titles that he uses.

1. On the relationship between Jesus' discipleship teaching and the question put to Bartimaeus see Robbins, 'Healing of Blind Bartimaeus', p. 239.

2. Theissen, *Wundergeschichten*, p. 77.

3. Marshall, *Faith*, p. 143.

declaration of salvation in the spiritual realm as well.[1] By acknowledging the faith of Bartimaeus and healing him, Jesus accepts the designation 'Son of David'.[2] Moreover, this title is not insignificant for Mark, since he has the blind man repeat the address twice when calling on Jesus for mercy (10.47, 48). Thus, Bartimaeus shows true insight into the nature of Jesus' identity through his address.[3]

Mark reports the healing only briefly by stating that the blind man regained his sight immediately (10.52b). The narration of the healing (ἀνέβλεψεν) corresponds directly to the wording of the blind man's request in 10.51 (ἀναβλέψω). Thus, by faith, Bartimaeus receives his request and is healed of his blindness. Unlike the healing of the blind man of Bethsaida, this healing takes place immediately.

Bartimaeus Follows Jesus (10.52c). After his healing, Bartimaeus follows Jesus in the way. Some have interpreted this action in strictly literal terms as implying no more than that Bartimaeus joins the pilgrimage and walks behind Jesus on the road to Jerusalem.[4] Apparently, the only function for the action within this interpretation

---

1. Anderson, *Mark*, p. 259; Best, 'Discipleship in Mark', p. 336; *idem, Following Jesus*, p. 141; *idem, Gospel as Story*, pp. 60-61; Brooks, *Mark*, p. 174; Busemann, *Jüngergemeinde*, p. 171; Gnilka, *Markus*, II, p. 111; Johnson, 'Blind Bartimaeus', p. 200; Kirchschläger, 'Bartimäus', p. 1117; Lagrange, *Marc*, p. 286; Nineham, *Mark*, p. 283; Rawlinson, *Mark*, p. 149; Swete, *Mark*, p. 245.

2. Hurtado, *Mark*, p. 162; Kingsbury, *Christology*, p. 105; Kingsbury, *Conflict in Mark*, p. 45; Marshall, *Faith*, p. 127; Nineham, *Mark*, p. 282; Robbins, 'Healing of Blind Bartimaeus', p. 227.

3. Kingsbury (*Christology*, pp. 108-14, 149-50; *idem, Conflict in Mark*, p. 46) points out that the title 'Son of David' is a correct designation for Jesus, but in some sense one that is also insufficient to convey completely the identity of Jesus. Later in the narrative, Jesus challenges the teaching of the scribes that the messiah is the Son of David, because David himself calls the messiah Lord (12.35-37). Jesus is able to accept the 'Son of David' title as correct (10.46-52), but he is also able to regard himself as something more than the Son of David. He is David's Lord (12.35-37). On the idea that the 'Son of David' title is correct but insufficient see also J. Marcus, *The Way of the Lord: Christological Exegesis of the Old Testament in the Gospel of Mark* (Louisville, KY: Westminster Press/John Knox, 1992), pp. 137-45, 149-51.

4. See especially Kingsbury, *Christology*, pp. 104-105. See also Gundry, *Mark*, p. 595; E. Haenchen, *Der Weg Jesu: Eine Erklärung des Markus-Evangeliums und der kanonischen Parallelen* (Berlin: de Gruyter, 2nd edn, 1968), p. 372; Lane, *Mark*, p. 389; Mann, *Mark*, p. 423; Pesch, *Markusevangelium II. Teil*, p. 174; Swete, *Mark*, p. 245.

is to demonstrate the reality of the healing.[1] Following Jesus, however, seems to be an unlikely demonstration for the healing of a blind man, especially since this blind man was able to jump up and come to Jesus before he was healed. Following Jesus would perhaps be a more appropriate sign for the healing of a lame person.[2] A strictly literal interpretation of Bartimaeus's action appears less likely when it is viewed within the context of the broader narrative. Although the verb ἀκολουθέω is used in a strictly literal sense in Mark's Gospel (3.7; 5.24; 11.9; 14.13), it always contains some metaphorical significance, indicating a personal allegiance to Jesus, when it is used of individuals following Jesus (1.18; 2.14; 8.34; 10.21, 28; 14.54; 15.41).[3] In other words, these individuals are not simply walking behind Jesus in a physical sense, but they have also become his followers, taking on his demands. In addition, ἀκολουθέω is used in Mark's Gospel with metaphorical overtones in the vast majority of instances in which people, whether in groups or as individuals, are said to follow Jesus (1.18; 2.14, 15; 6.1; 8.34; 10.21, 28, 32; 14.54; 15.41).[4] The only exceptions to this in Mark's Gospel take place when a large crowd follows Jesus (3.7; 5.24; 11.9). In light of the use of ἀκολουθέω in the broader narrative, most interpreters understand Bartimaeus's following of Jesus as carrying a metaphorical meaning.[5] Bartimaeus not only walks behind Jesus on the way, but he also becomes a follower of

---

1. Gundry, *Mark*, pp. 595-96; Kingsbury, *Christology*, p. 104; Pesch, *Markusevangelium II. Teil*, p. 174.

2. Marshall, *Faith*, p. 142.

3. Marshall, *Faith*, p. 142.

4. See also the metaphorical use of ἀκολουθέω in 9.38, where someone is said to be casting out demons in Jesus' name, but not following Jesus and his disciples.

5. Achtemeier, 'Miracles and Discipleship', p. 124; Anderson, *Mark*, p. 258; Best, *Following Jesus*, pp. 142-43; Brooks, *Mark*, p. 174; Busemann, *Jüngergemeinde*, pp. 165-66; Cranfield, *Mark*, p. 346; Gnilka, *Markus*, II, pp. 111-12; Johnson, 'Blind Bartimaeus', pp. 202-203; Kertelge, *Wunder*, p. 181; Kirchschläger, 'Bartimäus', pp. 1117-18; Koch, *Wundererzählungen*, pp. 131-32; Lohmeyer, *Markus*, pp. 226-27; Lührmann, *Markusevangelium*, p. 183; Marshall, *Faith*, pp. 142-43; Nineham, *Mark*, p. 283; Rawlinson, *Mark*, p. 149; Reploh, *Lehrer der Gemeinde*, pp. 224, 225-26; Roloff, *Kerygma*, pp. 125-26; Schenke, *Wundererzählungen*, pp. 351, 355, 367-69; Schmithals, *Markus*, II, p. 477; R. Schnackenburg, *Das Evangelium nach Markus* (Düsseldorf: Patmos, 1971), II, pp. 120-21; Schweizer, *Markus*, p. 127; Sinclair, 'Bartimaeus', p. 253; Tannehill, 'Disciples in Mark', p. 400; *idem*, 'Narrative Christology', p. 72; Taylor, *Mark*, p. 449; Tolbert, *Sowing*, p. 190.

Jesus. The healed man takes on a commitment to Jesus and seeks to fulfill his demands.

When he states that Bartimaeus follows Jesus in the way, Mark uses another word, ὁδός, that has taken on symbolic significance in the narrative.[1] A number of references to the way are clustered in the central section of Mark's Gospel. While Jesus is in the area of Caesarea Philippi and while he is on the way (8.27), he asks his disciples about their understanding of his identity. After Peter makes his confession, Jesus begins to teach his disciples that he must suffer and die at the hands of the religious hierarchy and then be raised again. From this point on, Jesus' way leads to Jerusalem where he will suffer and die. Throughout the central section of the Gospel, Jesus is described by the narrator as on the way (9.33, 34; 10.17, 32, 46), and Mk 10.32 makes it clear that this travel along the way is leading up to Jerusalem. References to Jesus' travel on the way in Mark's Gospel end when Jesus reaches the city of Jerusalem (11.8). The final reference to 'the way' in Mark's Gospel takes place in Jerusalem, when Jesus' opponents flatter him by professing that he teaches the way of God in truth (12.14). Ironically, the way of God for Jesus leads to death at the hands of his opponents. Having been healed, Bartimaeus follows in the way of Jesus, but in Mark's Gospel the way of Jesus is a path that leads necessarily to suffering. The blind man who was sitting along the way is now the healed man who is following Jesus in the way.[2]

Bartimaeus possesses a number of traits that make him similar to other minor characters in the preceding narrative. He is needy and helpless apart from the help of Jesus, since he is blind and poor, reduced to begging for his existence. Yet Bartimaeus is also perceptive, for when he hears that Jesus the Nazarene is present he understands that Jesus has the authority to heal him. So he cries out to Jesus for mercy, and his repeated cries show that he is trusting, persistent and courageous. When the blind man is called, he responds with eagerness by jumping up and coming to Jesus. In his conversation with Jesus, Bartimaeus is believing and sincere, and so Jesus heals him of

1.   On the way motif in Mark's Gospel see E.S. Malbon, *Narrative Space and Mythic Meaning in Mark* (San Francisco: Harper & Row, 1986), pp. 68-71, 104-105; Rhoads and Michie, *Mark as Story*, pp. 64-65.

2.   Dupont, 'L'aveugle', p. 173; Lane, *Mark*, p. 389; A. Paul, 'Guérison de Bartimée: Mc 10,46-52', *AsSeign* 61 (1972), pp. 47-48, 51.

his blindness. At the end of the story, Bartimaeus is healed, seeing and saved. Because of his persistent and fervent faith, the blind man serves as an exemplary figure for the reader.

Although Bartimaeus belongs to the crowd, he also possesses a number of traits that are normally associated with the disciples of Jesus. Like the disciples, he is named and he is busy at his occupation when he is called by Jesus. He possesses insight into the messianic identity of Jesus, since he addresses Jesus as the Son of David. Moreover, he addresses Jesus as his teacher, so that he expresses the commitment of a disciple. Like the twelve disciples, he is also sacrificial, leaving behind what he has in order to follow Jesus on the way. Thus, Bartimaeus is exemplary not only because of his faith, but also because he is a follower of Jesus.

Nevertheless, Bartimaeus is not a disciple.[1] He is an exemplary follower, but it is important for the course of the narrative that this ideal follower does not belong to the company of the disciples, but to the crowd. Following Jesus, although central to discipleship, is not limited to the disciples. Within Mark's narrative, the category of 'followers' is broader than that of 'disciples'.[2] In Mk 8.34 Jesus opens up the possibility of following him to anyone who has the will to do so, with the result that the disciples, members of the crowd, the reader or anyone may follow Jesus. Bartimaeus is similar to the disciples in a number of ways, but he is not a disciple, and he succeeds where the disciples fail. Unlike the disciples, the blind man does not struggle with unbelief and fear. After his messianic confession, Peter rejects the idea of a suffering messiah, but after declaring Jesus to be the Davidic king Bartimaeus proceeds to follow Jesus in the way to Jerusalem. The blind man does not desire position and privilege, but simply wants to see. Although Mark presents Bartimaeus as an exemplary follower, he does not depict him as becoming a disciple.[3]

1. Kingsbury, *Christology*, pp. 104-105; Malbon, 'Fallible Followers', p. 31; Tolbert, *Sowing*, p. 189.

2. Malbon, 'Disciples/Crowds/Whoever', pp. 109-10.

3. Numerous studies identify Bartimaeus as a disciple, but such an identification fails to make a distinction between disciples and followers in Mark's narrative and thus confuses the story of the disciples with the story of minor characters who follow. Studies that refer to Bartimaeus as a disciple include the following: Achtemeier, 'Miracles and Discipleship', pp. 124-25, 132; Best, *Following Jesus*, pp. 142-43; H.D. Betz, 'The Early Christian Miracle Story: Some Observations on the Form Critical Problem', *Semeia* 11 (1978), p. 75; Brooks, *Mark*, p. 174;

The Response of the Reader

In Bartimaeus, the reader is presented with a figure who is shown in an entirely positive light, who lives up to the expectations of Jesus. Bartimaeus responds to Jesus with faith and yet moves beyond faith to following Jesus as well. Up until this point in the narrative he is the only character to both trust and follow Jesus. Bartimaeus thus becomes the exemplary figure whom the reader has been anticipating since the healing at Bethsaida. In the presence of Jesus this blind beggar sees immediately and his actions show that his perceptiveness goes beyond physical sight. Bartimaeus displays an unusual insight into both the identity of Jesus and the appropriate response to Jesus.

Because of his exemplary response to Jesus, Bartimaeus stands in contrast to the disciples.[1] The juxtaposition of the request of James and John (10.36-37) and the blind beggar's request (10.51) brings this contrast out clearly. When Jesus asks the sons of Zebedee what they want him to do for them, their answer reveals their values. They want to be guaranteed places of power and privilege in the time of Jesus' glory. This answer shows just how little they understand about the destiny of Jesus and the cost involved in following him. When the same question is put to Bartimaeus, he gives an answer that displays a different set of values. The blind man wants to see, and with this gift of sight he desires to follow Jesus in the way.

Not only is Bartimaeus different from the disciples, but he also stands in contrast to the other minor characters within the central section of the Gospel, the father of the possessed boy (9.14-29) and the rich man (10.17-31). The healing stories in Mk 9.14-29 and 10.46-52 are similar in that both deal with the theme of faith.[2] However, Bartimaeus is different from the father of the possessed boy, because he displays an exuberant faith, while the father struggles with doubt. Therefore, the cry of the blind man stands in contrast to

Busemann, *Jüngergemeinde*, p. 166; Gnilka, *Markus*, II, pp. 111-12; Grundmann, *Markus*, p. 299; Hooker, *Mark*, pp. 252-53; Johnson, 'Blind Bartimaeus', p. 201; Lohmeyer, *Markus*, p. 226; Marshall, *Faith*, pp. 142-43; Reploh, *Lehrer der Gemeinde*, pp. 225-26; Robbins, 'Healing of Blind Bartimaeus', pp. 230, 239; Schenke, *Wundererzählungen*, p. 368; Schnackenburg, *Markus*, II, p. 120; Schweizer, *Markus*, p. 128; Steinhauser, 'Bartimaeus Narrative', p. 589.

   1.   Kingsbury, *Conflict in Mark*, pp. 25-26; Hooker, *Mark*, p. 252; Marshall, *Faith*, pp. 124, 139; Tannehill, 'Disciples in Mark', pp. 404-405.

   2.   Johnson, 'Blind Bartimaeus', p. 200; Koch, *Wundererzählungen*, p. 121; Lührmann, *Markusevangelium*, p. 182.

the cry of the father. Bartimaeus repeatedly cries out (ἤρξατο κράζειν, 10.47; ἔκραζεν, 10.48) for Jesus to have mercy on him even though he is pressured to be silent. When the father cries out (κράξας, 9.24) to Jesus, he expresses his request in faith mixed with doubt. Jesus criticizes the father's doubt but commends the blind man's faith.

The most striking contrast, however, is between Bartimaeus and the rich man.[1] Mk 10.17-31 and 10.46-52 both begin with similar genitive absolute constructions (καὶ ἐκπορευομένου αὐτοῦ, 10.17, 46), and both episodes use the way as their setting (εἰς ὁδόν, 10.17; παρὰ τὴν ὁδόν, 10.46), but from that point on the stories diverge.[2] Bartimaeus is a blind beggar (10.46), while the rich man has many possessions (10.22). The rich man addresses Jesus as Good Teacher (10.17), while Bartimaeus recognizes Jesus as the Son of David (10.47, 48). The rich man asks Jesus what he should do (ποιήσω) to inherit eternal life (10.17), but in the healing of the blind man, the roles are reversed and Jesus asks Bartimaeus what he might do (ποιήσω) for him. Jesus responds to the rich man's request with a rebuke (10.18-19), but responds to the blind man's cry for mercy with a call (10.49). The rich man wants to be judged on the basis of his obedience to the commandments (10.20), while Bartimaeus comes to Jesus in faith (10.52). Jesus commands the rich man to go (ὕπαγε), sell his possessions, give to the poor and then follow (ἀκολούθει) him (10.21). Likewise, Jesus tells Bartimaeus to go (ὕπαγε), but instead Bartimaeus chooses to follow (ἠκολούθει) Jesus in the way (10.52). The rich man will not sell all that he has in order to follow Jesus (10.22), while the blind beggar leaves behind his mantle and follows

---

1. Culpepper, 'Mark 10:50', p. 132; Dupont, 'L'aveugle', pp. 169-70.

2. A number of studies have pointed out that 10.46-52 begins awkwardly with two statements about the movement of Jesus, the first with Jesus entering into Jericho and the second with Jesus departing from Jericho. Normally either the first or the second introductory statement is assigned to Mark's redactional activity. However, it should be noted that both introductory statements find significant parallels in earlier passages. The first sentence (καὶ ἔρχονται εἰς Ἰεριχώ, 10.46) is almost identical to the introduction to the healing of the blind man of Bethsaida (καὶ ἔρχονται εἰς Βηθσαϊδάν, 8.22). The genitive absolute construction (καὶ ἐκπορευομένου αὐτοῦ) in the second introductory statement of 10.46 is found also in 10.17, the introduction to the passage on the rich man. Mark may be using this awkward double introduction to connect 10.46-52 with earlier passages on minor characters.

(10.50, 52). For the rich man, the path to the kingdom of God is too hard, the cost of eternal life too high. Jesus uses the rich man as an illustration for his disciples of how difficult it is for those who have wealth to enter into the kingdom of God (10.23-25). At this, the perplexed disciples ask, 'Who is able to be saved?' (σωθῆναι, 10.26). Bartimaeus serves as an answer to this question, for he is saved (σέσωκεν, 10.52) on account of his faith. The exemplary character of Bartimaeus is enhanced, because he stands in such striking contrast to the rich man who will not follow.

Since Bartimaeus is presented in entirely positive terms and is set in contrast to those who have responded negatively to Jesus, the reader comes to identify with Bartimaeus. In the article 'The Parable of the Loaves' Bassler points out that the continuing incomprehension of the disciples throughout the central section of the Gospel causes the reader to begin dissociating from the disciples.[1] Then, according to Bassler, at the end of the section, when blind Bartimaeus receives his sight, 'the reader has a new figure with whom to identify'.[2] Bassler continues,

> It has always been puzzling that this unit would close with a miracle clearly symbolizing the achievement of insight, since the disciples appear as blind as ever. Yet if the text has 'worked', the disciples and the reader are no longer one. The disciples continue their blind way through the narrative, but the newly enlightened reader can now identify with the newly sighted Bartimaeus and has, like him, the potential of following Jesus.[3]

Bassler is correct when she claims that the reader comes to identify with Bartimaeus. Moreover, the reader's identification with Bartimaeus has important implications for the overall rhetorical effect of Mark's narrative. The identification with Bartimaeus affects the reader's relationship with the disciples especially in light of the disciples' unchanging incomprehension. While the reader will continue to have sympathy for the disciples and remain interested in the outcome of their story, the reader will no longer identify with the disciples as in the earlier part of the narrative. Bartimaeus, who believes, sees and follows, now exemplifies what it means to fulfill the demands of Jesus.

---

1. Bassler, 'Parable of the Loaves', p. 167.
2. Bassler, 'Parable of the Loaves', p. 167.
3. Bassler, 'Parable of the Loaves', p. 167.

Bartimaeus as a Transitional Figure

Mk 10.46-52 has been treated as a transitional passage in past studies on the Gospel of Mark.[1] It is transitional in terms of geography, moving the narrative from Jesus' journey on the way to Jesus' ministry in Jerusalem. In addition, this passage marks a boundary in the narrative in terms of content, since it completes a section that emphasizes Jesus' instruction to the disciples and leads to a section that presents Jesus' confrontation with the religious establishment in Jerusalem. I shall try to show that Mk 10.46-52 is transitional in two further ways. First, Mark's treatment of Bartimaeus establishes a development in his overall characterization of minor characters. Secondly, this passage is transitional in terms of the reader's relationship with the characters in the narrative.

The Characterization of Bartimaeus as Transitional

When listing the characters in Mark's story who are on the side of Jesus, Malbon includes together the 'suppliants and exemplars— although these two overlap'.[2] Malbon's terminology is helpful for understanding the nature of minor characters in Mark's narrative. The minor characters from the crowd encompass both the suppliants and the exemplars, and these two groups do overlap, but primarily in Mk 10.46-52. Prior to the Bartimaeus story, minor characters serve primarily as suppliants, while after the Bartimaeus story minor characters function as exemplars. Bartimaeus himself is a transitional figure, since he serves as both a suppliant and an exemplar.

Early in the narrative, through typical examples and summary statements, Mark sets forth a basic pattern for the interaction between suppliants and Jesus. A needy individual comes into contact with Jesus. Often the individual will request healing or others will make this request on the needy person's behalf. Jesus responds with compassion for the suppliant, and through his authority he heals the person. This basic pattern is found repeatedly in the first ten chapters of Mark's Gospel. Certain minor characters who appear in the narrative before

---

1. The idea that this healing miracle is transitional is usually associated with the work of Eduard Schweizer and Norman Perrin. See Schweizer, *Markus*, p. 214; *idem*, 'Life of Faith', p. 389; *idem*, 'Leistung des Markus', p. 184; Perrin, 'Towards an Interpretation', pp. 3-9; *idem*, *New Testament*, pp. 155-58.

2. Malbon, 'Jewish Leaders', p. 277.

Bartimaeus function as exemplars as well as suppliants. Thus, the paralytic, Jairus and the hemorrhaging woman exemplify genuine faith, and the Syrophoenician woman typifies true understanding. However, these minor characters serve as examples because of the nature of their supplication. Their exemplary traits are those that cause them to bring their requests to Jesus effectively. While in a sense these minor characters are exemplars, they function primarily as suppliants within the narrative.

Bartimaeus is an ideal suppliant who reflects the positive characteristics and actions found in the previous suppliants.[1] Bartimaeus, the blind beggar, hears that Jesus is passing by and cries out for mercy. With persistence and courage, the blind man continues to cry out even when he is pressured to be silent. Jesus recognizes a fervent faith within this persistent plea for help, and so he heals his sight and sends him on his way. Thus, the story of Bartimaeus picks up the common features of earlier episodes on minor characters. Bartimaeus is a suppliant, and he is also exemplary in his supplication, because he responds to Jesus with a persistent faith.

However, unlike minor characters in the preceding narrative, Bartimaeus is exemplary in ways that move beyond the nature of his supplication.[2] The blind beggar shows insight into the messianic identity of Jesus. Jesus calls Bartimaeus, and Bartimaeus regards Jesus as his teacher. In the end, Bartimaeus follows Jesus in the way. Thus, Bartimaeus is an exemplar who typifies what it means to be a follower of Jesus.

Bartimaeus is the last of the suppliants in Mark's Gospel. In the narrative after the Bartimaeus story minor characters are no longer suppliants, since they do not come to Jesus with requests for healing or deliverance. Instead, like Bartimaeus, they are exemplars who display for the reader a commitment to the expectations of Jesus. Bartimaeus thus stands at the beginning of a series of minor characters who function in the narrative as exemplary figures, and as both suppliant and exemplar he is a transitional figure in the narrative.

The transitional nature of the Bartimaeus story may also have important implications for other interpretive issues related to the

---

1. Tolbert, *Sowing*, pp. 189-90.

2. For a helpful discussion on the way in which Bartimaeus typifies the ideal suppliant, but beyond this also typifies the ideal follower see Tolbert, *Sowing*, pp. 189-92.

study of Mk 10.46-52. For example, the form of the passage has often perplexed interpreters. Bultmann listed the Bartimaeus story as a healing miracle story, but he noted that this passage does not follow the pattern of a conventionally narrated miracle story. For Bultmann, the unconventional nature of the pericope marked it as having a secondary character.[1] In a similar way, many commentators refer to Mk 10.46-52 as a miracle story, although they often find it necessary to explain the unusual features of the story that set it apart from a conventional miracle story.[2] More recently, some have argued that the Bartimaeus narrative is not a miracle story, but rather a call story that shows how Bartimaeus became a follower of Jesus.[3] However, since Mk 10.46-52 is a transitional passage in the Gospel, it functions in the narrative as both a miracle story and a call story.[4] Any attempt to consider the passage simply as a miracle story or as a call story would inevitably result in certain parts being ignored. Bartimaeus is both healed and called to be a follower of Jesus.[5]

1.   R. Bultmann, *Die Geschichte der synoptischen Tradition* (FRLANT, 29; Göttingen: Vandenhoeck & Ruprecht, 3rd edn, 1957), p. 228. M. Dibelius (*Die Formgeschichte des Evangeliums* [Tübingen: Mohr (Paul Siebeck), 6th edn, 1971], p. 49) also found difficulty with the form of the Bartimaeus story, classifying it as a paradigm of a less pure type, a paradigm being a brief and simple illustrative story.

2.   Gnilka, *Markus*, II, pp. 108-109; Hurtado, *Mark*, p. 160; Kertelge, *Wunder*, p. 180; Kingsbury, *Christology*, pp. 103-105; Lohmeyer, *Markus*, p. 224; Lührmann, *Markusevangelium*, pp. 182, 184; Pesch, *Markusevangelium II. Teil*, pp. 168-69; Roloff, *Kerygma*, pp. 123-24; Schenke, *Wundererzählungen*, pp. 362-65; Schmithals, *Markus*, II, pp. 472-73; Taylor, *Mark*, p. 447.

3.   Achtemeier, 'Miracles and Discipleship', pp. 124-25; A.J. Droge, 'Call Stories in Greek Biography and the Gospels', in K.H. Richards (ed.), *Society of Biblical Literature Seminar Papers 1983* (Chico, CA: Scholars Press, 1983), p. 252; Steinhauser, 'Bartimaeus Narrative'; *idem*, 'Call Story'. For a similar classification see Kirchschläger, 'Bartimäus', pp. 1118-19. Betz ('Miracle Story', p. 74) argues that in vv. 49-50 the miracle story 'flips over' into a call story.

4.   For a similar point see Marshall, *Faith*, pp. 124-25, 140-41.

5.   The transitional nature of 10.46-52 may also serve to explain the unusual juxtaposition of the Son of David title with a request for healing. Since Bartimaeus is a suppliant, he is portrayed as asking for healing. Then, since he is an exemplary follower, he is presented as understanding the Davidic sonship of Jesus. This passage may include the juxtaposition of the Son of David title with the plea for mercy, not because the Son of David historically was expected to be a healer, but because the passage is transitional within Mark's narrative. On the difficulty of presenting the Son of David as a healer in Mk 10.46-52 see Achtemeier, 'Miracles

The Response of the Reader

Mark encourages the reader to identify with Bartimaeus through his presentation of the blind man as an exemplary figure. However, this identification with Bartimaeus is not an end in itself, because Bartimaeus is also a transitional figure. Mark does not encourage the reader to identify with a minor character only to drop this identification from the narrative altogether. Instead, beginning with Bartimaeus, Mark presents a series of minor characters who serve as exemplary figures and who display through their actions the values of Jesus. The reader is therefore able to identify with a number of minor characters beginning with Bartimaeus.

The portrayal of blind Bartimaeus signals a development in Mark's presentation of minor characters, but it also creates a change in the reader's relationship to the characters in the narrative. In light of the continuing negative picture of the disciples in the central section of the Gospel, the reader is moved to dissociate from them. In place of the disciples, the reader is given a series of minor characters who live up to the expectations of Jesus in contrast to the disciples. The reader continues to maintain sympathy for the disciples, because Jesus himself does not appear to give up on them. However, the reader comes to identify more closely with minor characters than with the disciples after the Bartimaeus story.

Through the identification with Bartimaeus and subsequent minor characters, the reader is encouraged to move beyond faith in Jesus and his power toward a more faithful acceptance of the demands and values of Jesus. Prior to the Bartimaeus story, minor characters are exemplary primarily because of the nature of their faith. They believe that Jesus has the authority from God to heal and deliver them, and so they will move beyond any obstacle in order to come to Jesus. Bartimaeus possesses this same kind of faith, but while his faith leads to healing, his healing leads to devotion to Jesus. After the Bartimaeus story, minor characters exemplify a proper devotion to the values of Jesus. In this way, the reader is encouraged to move beyond faith in Jesus to a more faithful following of Jesus.

and Discipleship', pp. 125-26; Burger, *Davidssohn*, pp. 44, 61-62; F. Hahn, *Christologische Hoheitstitel: Ihre Geschichte im frühen Christentum* (FRLANT, 83; Göttingen: Vandenhoeck & Ruprecht, 1963), pp. 262-64; Robbins, 'Healing of Blind Bartimaeus', pp. 233-34.

In addition, this identification with minor characters in the later part of the narrative functions to move the story out toward the reader, so that the demands of Jesus may be pressed upon him or her. As long as the reader identifies solely with the disciples, he or she is able to maintain some distance from the expectations of Jesus. There are some ways in which the situation of the disciples in the narrative is unique. The reader does not receive a specific call to discipleship from Jesus as the disciples do (1.16-20; 3.13-19). The reader is also different from the disciples in that Jesus gives to the disciples a unique commission to preach and to have authority (3.13-19; 6.7-13). Later in the narrative Mark will show that Jesus foresees significant responsibilities for the disciples in the post-Easter community (13.9-13). The situation of the reader is closer to that of the minor characters from the crowd than to that of the disciples. The reader, like the minor characters, must respond to the general call to follow Jesus through self-denial and a willingness to suffer (8.34). Thus, Mark encourages the identification with minor characters in order to move the reader to acknowledge that anyone can be a follower of Jesus.

Chapter 5

MINOR CHARACTERS FOLLOWING THE BARTIMAEUS NARRATIVE

Following the Bartimaeus story, Mark includes a series of episodes in which he presents minor characters as exemplary figures. He continues this positive portrayal until the final scene in the Gospel, in which another significant development takes place in Mark's depiction of minor characters. Mark 11–16 includes a section on Jesus' relationship to the temple and the religious establishment (11.1–13.2), Jesus' eschatological discourse (13.3-37) and the passion narrative (14.1–16.8). Besides appearing in the passion narrative, minor characters appear in the section in which Jesus visits the temple and challenges the religious authorities.

Minor Characters in Mark 11.1–13.37

Mark organizes his material in chs. 11–13 around Jesus' activity in the temple on three consecutive days. Two minor characters appear in the midst of the controversy stories that take place on Jesus' third day in the temple: the scribe (12.28-34) and the poor widow (12.41-44).[1] Both individuals are commended by Jesus, because in some way they reflect his values. Also, both individuals are similar to Bartimaeus in that they stand in contrast to the rich man. The scribe and the poor widow serve as contrasts to the rich man by responding positively in areas where the rich man failed.

The Scribe (12.28-34)

After Bartimaeus, Jesus' next interaction with an individual is unusual, because it involves a conversation with a scribe. Until this point in the narrative Mark's characterization of the scribes has been uniformly

---

1. On the outline of Mk 11–13 and the place of episodes concerning minor characters in that outline see Chapter 2.

negative.[1] His first reference to the scribes portrays them as those who teach without authority (1.22). Along with the other members of the religious establishment, the scribes spend most of their time in the narrative disputing with Jesus (2.6-7, 16; 3.22; 7.1-5; 9.14; 11.27-28) and seeking to destroy him (8.31; 10.33-34; 11.18). Until this point, the scribes have always appeared as a group and often in tandem with other members of the religious hierarchy. This pattern of presentation changes in Mk 12.28-34, in which Jesus has a conversation with an individual scribe who responds positively to his teaching.

The scribe in Mk 12.28-34 is the first of several individuals who are portrayed as exceptional figures. These individuals come into contact with Jesus, and although they have some relationship to a larger group that is antagonistic to Jesus, they themselves are not in opposition to Jesus. The scribe in Mk 12.28-34 is clearly an exceptional scribe, since although the scribes as a whole oppose Jesus and seek to destroy him, this scribe accepts Jesus' teaching.[2] Later in the narrative, Mark will present the centurion as an exceptional soldier and Joseph of Arimathea as an exceptional council member. The religious and political leaders as a whole are opponents of Jesus, but Mark's categories are not so hard and fast that this enmity cannot be set aside in individual cases.[3] Although the scribe is a member of the religious establishment, he is not an opponent of Jesus. Therefore, he is an individual belonging to the general mass of people who function in the narrative as neither Jesus' disciples nor his opponents.

Mark introduces the scribe as 'one of the scribes' (εἷς τῶν γραμματέων, 12.28). He uses similar descriptions to introduce earlier minor characters: Jairus is 'one of the synagogue rulers' (εἷς τῶν

---

1. For an overall description of Mark's characterization of the scribes see Malbon, 'Jewish Leaders', pp. 264-65.

2. Malbon ('Fallible Followers', p. 31; *idem*, 'Jewish Leaders', pp. 275-76) also treats the scribe of Mk 12.28-34 as an exceptional figure who stands apart from the group characterization of the Jewish religious establishment. J.D. Kingsbury ('The Religious Authorities in the Gospel of Mark', *NTS* 36 [1990], pp. 47-48; *idem, Conflict in Mark*, pp. 14, 81-82) does not want to treat the scribe of Mk 12.28-34 as an exception who breaks the otherwise united front of the religious authorities who militantly oppose Jesus. Instead, Kingsbury understands the scribe as an ironic character who vindicates Jesus by acknowledging that Jesus rather than the authorities declares the will of God. However, it is unclear why, as an ironic character, the scribe is not also an exceptional character.

3. Malbon, 'Jewish Leaders', pp. 275-76, 280.

ἀρχισυναγώγων, 5.22), the man with the possessed boy is 'one from the crowd' (εἷς ἐκ τοῦ ὄχλου, 9.17) and the rich man is simply 'one' (εἷς, 10.17). The scribe both hears and sees, hearing Jesus disputing with the other religious leaders and seeing that he answered well. In this way, Mark portrays the scribe as unusually perceptive. In light of Jesus' profound answers, the scribe is moved to ask a question concerning the foremost of all the commandments. In contrast to the preceding questions of the religious leaders, which were intended to trap, the question of the scribe is sincere. Jesus answers the question in a straightforward manner, stating that the first commandment is to love the Lord God and the second is to love one's neighbor (10.29-31). The scribe responds by acknowledging the truth of Jesus' answer and in this way shows himself to be open to the will of God and the teaching of Jesus (10.32-33).[1]

Just as the scribe perceived the wisdom of Jesus' answers, so also Jesus recognizes the value of the scribe's answer. Mark uses similar wording to narrate the perception of the scribe (ἰδὼν ὅτι καλῶς ἀπεκρίθη, 12.28) and the recognition of Jesus (ἰδὼν αὐτὸν ὅτι νουνεχῶς ἀπεκρίθη, 12.34). In response to his wise answer, Jesus commends the scribe by saying, 'You are not far from the kingdom of God' (12.34). Although expressed in a negative form, the emphasis of Jesus' words lies on the nearness of the scribe to God's kingdom rather than on some lack on the part of the scribe.[2] Jesus' words serve as a commendation of the scribe and as an acknowledgment of his wise response. Because of his openness to God's demands, this scribe, in contrast to the other scribes, is now also open to the kingdom of God. Mark ends his narration concerning the scribe by emphasizing his receptivity to the kingdom of God.[3]

1. Cranfield, *Mark*, p. 380.
2. Nineham, *Mark*, p. 328.
3. To some extent the interpretation of Mk 12.34, where Jesus states that the scribe is not far from the kingdom of God, depends on the interpretation of Mk 1.15, where Jesus states that the kingdom of God has come near (ἤγγικεν ἡ βασιλεία τοῦ θεοῦ). The significance of this latter passage, however, is debated. C.H. Dodd (*The Parables of the Kingdom* [London: Nisbet, 3rd edn, 1936], p. 44) has argued that ἤγγικεν in Mk 1.15 should be translated as 'has come', implying the idea that the kingdom has already arrived. W.G. Kümmel (*Verheissung und Erfüllung: Untersuchungen zur eschatologischen Verkündigung Jesu* [Zürich: Zwingli-Verlag, 3rd edn, 1956], pp. 13-18) has championed the view that ἤγγικεν in Mk 1.15 should be translated as 'has come near', implying the imminent arrival of the kingdom. For a

As one who is near to the kingdom of God, the scribe stands in contrast to the rich man who refuses to enter the kingdom. The passage on the scribe is analogous to the passage on the rich man in a number of ways, but in the end the scribe stands in contrast to the rich man. In both passages, one (εἷς, 10.17; 12.28) approaches Jesus and asks (ἐπηρώτα, 10.17; ἐπηρώτησεν, 12.28) a question. In both passages, Jesus' answer refers to the oneness of God (εἷς ὁ θεός, 10.18; κύριος ὁ θεὸς ἡμῶν κύριος εἷς ἐστιν, 12.29) and to the commandments (ἐντολάς, 10.19; ἐντολή, 12.31). In responding to Jesus' answer, both the rich man and the scribe address Jesus as 'Teacher' (διδάσκαλε, 10.20; 12.32). Yet in spite of the similarities, Mark uses the scribe as a contrast to the rich man. Both characters recognize the importance of the commandments, but the scribe shows a greater understanding by inquiring about the most important of the commandments. Jesus answers the scribe's inquiry by insisting on the need to love God and one's neighbor. Although the rich man claims to have kept the commandments from his youth on, his refusal to sell his possessions in order to care for the poor and follow Jesus reveals that he does not genuinely love God or his neighbor. In contrast to the rich man, Jesus himself expresses true obedience to the foremost commandments because he protects the honor of God's goodness (10.18) and he loves the rich man (10.21). The scribe also contrasts with the rich man, because, unlike the rich man who responds to Jesus' teaching with self-justification and disobedience, he affirms the truth and wisdom of Jesus' teaching concerning the commandments. In the end, the scribe is not far from the kingdom of God (12.34), while the rich man would rather retain his wealth than enter into the kingdom of God (10.23-25).

The scribe is exceptional among the religious authorities because he is not antagonistic to Jesus. He is perceptive enough to recognize the

summary concerning the debate on this passage see G.R. Beasley-Murray, *Jesus and the Kingdom of God* (Grand Rapids: Eerdmans, 1986), pp. 72-73; Kelber, *Kingdom in Mark*, pp. 7-9. If the kingdom is present, then the scribe is near to the kingdom in that he recognizes God's demands and is open to God's kingdom and ready to become a part of it. If the kingdom is future, then the scribe is near to the kingdom in that he is open to it and ready to become a part of it at its arrival. In either case, the scribe shows a remarkable openness to the kingdom of God, and Jesus commends him for this.

1.   The verb ἀγαπάω is used in Mark's Gospel only in 10.21 and 12.30-33. The noun ἀγάπη is not used in Mark's Gospel at all.

wisdom of Jesus' teaching and sincere enough to ask a genuine question. He does not seek to trap Jesus but rather to learn from Jesus. The scribe's response to Jesus reveals that he is also wise for he acknowledges the truth of Jesus' answer. Thus, Mark characterizes the scribe as open and receptive to the demands of God and to the kingdom of God.

The Poor Widow (12.41-44)
As Jesus is in the temple debating and teaching, he commends not only the wisdom of a scribe but also the gift of a widow.[1] Jesus takes up a position opposite the treasury and observes the crowd putting their gifts into the treasury (12.41). The gift that stands out to Jesus is that of one poor widow who gives two small copper coins. Like earlier minor characters, she is introduced as 'one' (μία, 12.42; cf. 5.22; 9.17; 10.17), and like earlier minor characters she is needy, since she is poor. References to her poverty are repeated throughout the passage. Both the narrator and Jesus refer to her as 'poor' (12.42, 43), and Jesus also refers to her lack or need (ὑστερήσεως, 12.44). Unlike the earlier minor characters, she remains in her need and lives sacrificially regardless of her station in life. Jesus gathers together his disciples in order that he might commend to them her exemplary giving (12.43). While others gave out of their abundance, she gave out of her lack, putting in the treasury all that she had (12.44). Her act of giving all represents a complete surrender of herself to God and his mercy.[2] In addition, her action stands in contrast to actions of the scribes who are described by Jesus in Mk 12.38-40.[3] The poor widow gives all, while the scribes take all, even devouring widows' homes. The poor widow makes no show about her sacrificial action, while the scribes seek recognition and pretentiously display their acts of piety in order to call attention to themselves.

Jesus continues his commendation of the widow by telling his disciples that the poor widow gave 'her whole life' (ὅλον τὸν βίον αὐτῆς, 12.44). In Mk 12.30 Jesus pressed upon the individual scribe

1. On the connection between the scribe in 12.28-34 and the widow in 12.41-44 see the discussion in Chapter 2.
2. Anderson, *Mark*, p. 287; Cranfield, *Mark*, p. 387; Lane, *Mark*, p. 443; Pesch, *Markusevangelium II. Teil*, p. 263; Schweizer, *Markus*, p. 148.
3. Lane, *Mark*, p. 442; Malbon, 'Fallible Followers', p. 38; *idem*, 'Poor Widow', pp. 595-96; Pesch, *Markusevangelium II. Teil*, p. 263.

the necessity of loving God with one's whole (ὅλης) heart, whole (ὅλης) soul, whole (ὅλης) mind and whole (ὅλης) strength. In Mk 12.33 the scribe agrees with Jesus on the importance of loving God with one's whole (ὅλης) heart, whole (ὅλης) understanding and whole (ὅλης) strength. In Mk 12.44 the poor widow becomes an example of such a whole-hearted response to God by giving her whole (ὅλον) life.[1] The poor widow also exemplifies for the disciples the type of complete giving that Jesus desires of his followers.[2] As the Son of Man, Jesus has come 'to give his life' (δοῦναι τὴν ψυχὴν αὐτοῦ, 10.45) for many, and Jesus expects his follower to lose 'his life' (τὴν ψυχὴν αὐτοῦ, 8.35) in order to truly save it. Thus, Jesus commends the sacrificial action of the poor widow as an example to follow.[3]

1. Pesch, *Markusevangelium II. Teil*, p. 263.
2. Malbon, 'Fallible Followers', p. 38; *idem*, 'Poor Widow', p. 596.
3. A.G. Wright ('The Widow's Mites: Praise or Lament?—A Matter of Context', *CBQ* 44 [1982], pp. 256-65) rejects any interpretation of 12.41-44 that treats the poor widow as an example to be followed. Wright insists that the literary context of this passage shows that Jesus' words concerning the widow are a lament rather than a commendation. For his view, Wright depends largely on the immediate context surrounding 12.41-44. Just prior to the story of the widow's gift, Jesus condemns the scribes because they devour widows' houses (12.40). According to Wright, Mark includes the story of the widow as a tragic example of a widow who has just been 'devoured'. Immediately following the story in 12.41-44, Jesus announces the destruction of the temple (13.2). For Wright, the future destruction of the temple means that the widow's gift was totally misguided and a tragic waste. On this point, Wright's argument is open to objection, because it assumes that permanence is a necessary characteristic for a worthy recipient of charity. However, a different set of values is operating in 14.7: 'For you always have the poor with you, and you are able to do good to them whenever you wish, but you do not always have me'. In his commentary on Mark (*Mark*, pp. 493-95), Mann follows the position of Wright and understands Jesus' words in 12.43-44 as an expression of disapproval. The same view may be found in R.S. Sugirtharajah, 'The Widow's Mites Revalued', *ExpTim* 103 (1991), pp. 42-43. Malbon ('Poor Widow', pp. 589-604; *idem*, 'Fallible Followers', p. 38) agrees with Wright that the context is important in interpreting 12.41-44 and that the widow should not be used as an exemplum for a stewardship campaign, but she counters his argument by showing that he defines the context too narrowly. She shows that within the broader context of Mark's Gospel, the woman's action must be treated as commendable. The widow's gift of her whole life (12.44) is comparable to Jesus' gift of his life (10.45). The value of the woman's gift is not diminished because she is a victim any more than the value of Jesus' gift is negated because he is victimized by the chief priests, scribes and elders. 'Wright's narrow contextual focus results in an unfortunate, if not unusual, case of "blaming

Like Bartimaeus and the scribe, the poor widow stands in contrast to the rich man.[1] There are several connections between the passage on the rich man and that on the poor widow, but in the end the widow serves as a contrasting figure to the rich man. Both passages deal with the rich (πλούσιον, 10.25; πλούσιοι, 12.41) and the poor (πτωχοῖς, 10.21; πτωχή, 12.42, 43).[2] In both passages, Jesus uses the action of a minor character as an opportunity to teach his disciples, and in both passages Jesus introduces a portion of this teaching with the words 'truly, I say to you' (ἀμὴν λέγω ὑμῖν, 10.29; 12.43). Nevertheless, the poor widow gives all that she has (ὅσα εἶχεν, 12.44) in contrast to the rich man who is commanded to give all that he has (ὅσα ἔχεις, 10.21), but refuses to do so. The poor widow gives all out of her lack (ὑστερήσεως, 12.44), while the rich man lacks (ὑστερεῖ, 10.21) one thing, a willingness to give all and follow Jesus.

The widow of Mk 12.41-44 is poor and needy, but in the midst of her poverty she acts in a way that is sacrificial and self-denying. The gift of her life is made in an unobtrusive manner without any show, so that only Jesus notices her gift. Her action reveals that she is devoted to God and dependent on his mercy, and thus she is offered as an exemplary individual to the disciples. During his activity in the temple, Jesus commends two individuals, the scribe who acknowledges God's demands for love and the widow who displays sacrificial piety. Together these individuals represent what might have been, if the religious leaders had not turned the temple into a den of thieves.

Minor Characters in Mark 14.1–16.8

Following his narration of Jesus' activity in the temple, Mark narrates Jesus' eschatological discourse (13.3-37) and the passion narrative (14.1–16.8). In ch. 14, at the beginning of the passion narrative, Mark substantially changes his characterization of the disciples. He splits off

the victim"' (Malbon, 'Poor Widow', p. 596). As a final note, why would it be exemplary for the rich man to give away all that he has (10.21) but lamentable for the poor widow to do the same (12.44)?

1. M.A. Beavis, 'Women as Models of Faith in Mark', *BTB* 18 (1988), p. 6.

2. πλούσιος is used only in 10.25 and 12.41 in Mark's Gospel. πτωχός is used only in the passage on the rich man (10.21), the passage on the poor widow (12.42, 43) and the passage on the woman who anoints Jesus, who is the next minor character in Mark's Gospel (14.5, 7).

the story line of the disciple Judas from that of the rest of the disciples. While Judas turns into a traitor, betraying Jesus to the chief priests for silver, the rest of the disciples move from misunderstanding to failure.[1] The disciples have displayed an incorrigible lack of understanding concerning the necessity of suffering and sacrificial service for Jesus' followers, and so when they are called upon to suffer, they cease following Jesus. When Jesus is arrested, all the disciples flee except Peter (14.50). Although Peter continues to follow Jesus from afar for a time, he also displays his inability to follow by denying Jesus three times (14.54, 66-72). Mark's portrayal of the disciples ends with Peter weeping after his denials. Although the disciples are referred to later, they never appear again in the remaining narrative.

The failure and absence of the disciples affects Mark's treatment of minor characters and the reader's relationship with them. Once again, in the passion narrative, the minor characters begin to serve more directly as contrasting figures to the disciples.[2] Minor characters serve Jesus as the disciples should serve him but are unable to because of their failure and desertion. Sometimes these individuals fulfill the duties of Jesus' followers unwittingly and beyond their intention. However, since the reader is able to see their actions within the broader context of the narrative, he or she is able to perceive the significance of their activity. Thus, Mark presents minor characters in a positive manner at the same time that he portrays the disastrous failure of the disciples. In light of this contrast, the reader will identify more closely with these minor characters than with the disciples in the passion narrative.

In spite of the identification with the minor characters, the reader is never able completely to distance himself or herself from the disciples in the same way that he or she is completely distant from the enemies of Jesus. Mark continues to create sympathy for the disciples on the part of the reader by indicating a future hope for them. In Mk 14.28 and 16.7, first Jesus and then the young man at the tomb point to a future meeting in Galilee between Jesus and the disciples after the resurrection. Mark ends his Gospel without narrating this meeting, but the reader is left with the impression that the purpose for the

---

1. Tannehill, 'Disciples in Mark', pp. 393, 402-403.
2. Kingsbury, *Conflict in Mark*, p. 27; Rhoads and Michie, *Mark as Story*, pp. 132-33; Tannehill, 'Disciples in Mark', pp. 404-405.

future meeting is the restoration of the faithless disciples. The death of
the shepherd scatters the sheep (14.27), and the meeting in Galilee
appears to be for the purpose of regathering the scattered sheep
(14.28). The restoration of the disciples is necessary, because in the
eschatological discourse Jesus predicts a time between the resurrection
and the parousia when the disciples will share in the proclamation of
the gospel and in suffering for the sake of Jesus (13.9-13). The
misunderstanding of the disciples results in disaster for them during
the passion of Jesus, but Mark holds open the hope that the disciples
will eventually be 'fishers of men'.[1]

The Woman who Anoints Jesus (14.3-9)

The passion narrative begins with an episode depicting a minor character inserted between the plot of the religious leaders to kill Jesus and
the plot of Judas to betray him. Thus the eschatological discourse is
framed by analogous scenes that present minor characters, the poor
widow immediately before the discourse and the woman who anoints
Jesus immediately after it.[2] In Bethany at the home of Simon the leper
a woman anoints Jesus' head with a costly perfume (14.3). Some who
are at the scene respond with indignation at the wastefulness of this
gesture, since the perfume could have been sold for as much as 300
denarii and the proceeds given to the poor (14.4-5).[3] Jesus defends the
woman's action and insists that she has done a good (καλόν) work
(14.6). Jesus' description of the woman's deed as good is unique in
Mark's narrative, and it recalls the language that Jesus used to
describe the good (καλήν) earth (4.8, 20). The good earth represents
those who hear the word, receive it and produce abundant fruit. Jesus
further defends the woman against the complaint of the onlookers by
pointing out that the poor will always be with them, and they are able
to give to them at any time (14.7). Jesus' statement does not imply that
care for the poor is unimportant, but simply that it should not be used

---

1.   For a discussion on the end of the disciples' story in Mark see Tannehill,
'Disciples in Mark', pp. 403-405.
2.   For a discussion of the analogy between 12.41-44 and 14.3-9 see Chapter 2.
See Chapter 2 also for a discussion of the placement of episodes on minor characters
in the overall outline of the passion narrative.
3.   A denarius was a typical day's wage (Mt. 20.2), so that the perfume was
worth nearly a year's salary. See Anderson, *Mark*, p. 306; Cranfield, *Mark*, p. 416;
Hooker, *Mark*, pp. 328-29.

as a reason for criticizing the woman's devotion to him.[1] For Jesus, the woman's gift symbolized her recognition of his priority over all others. In addition, her gift revealed that she recognized the present moment as a unique occasion for expressing her love and devotion to him. Mark underlines this love and devotion by placing it in contrast to the hatred of the religious leaders (14.1-2) and the treachery of Judas (14.10-11).[2]

While the woman shows understanding through her gift, Jesus expresses a greater understanding, because he is able to see an even greater significance to the woman's action. Through her gift, the woman has anticipated Jesus' death and has provided the anointing for his burial beforehand (14.8). Anointing Jesus for his burial was beyond the woman's conscious intention, but Jesus interprets her action in this way.[3] The gift of the woman becomes a prophetic sign of the approaching death of Jesus. At the same time that some are determined to bring about Jesus' death, the body of Jesus is prepared for burial through the woman's act of devotion. Her undivided loyalty toward Jesus will be remembered wherever the gospel is proclaimed (14.9), so that instead of receiving criticism for wastefulness, she will receive honor throughout the world for her attention to Jesus. Because of what she forfeits for the sake of Jesus, she is able to gain a place of prominence in the whole world (ὅλον τὸν κόσμον, 14.9, cf. τὸν κόσμον ὅλον, 8.36).

The woman who anoints Jesus is sacrificial and self-denying in giving her costly perfume. While her gift may have been directed toward others, she pours out the entire flask of perfume in her anointing of Jesus as a reflection of the fact that she is completely devoted to him. For this complete devotion, she is criticized by some, defended by Jesus and ultimately remembered and honored throughout the world. The woman is understanding because she recognizes the

---

1. Cranfield, *Mark*, pp. 416-17; Lane, *Mark*, p. 494.
2. S.C. Barton, 'Mark as Narrative: The Story of the Anointing Woman (Mk 14.3-9)', *ExpTim* 102 (1991), p. 231; Hurtado, *Mark*, p. 216; Lane, *Mark*, p. 492; Malbon, 'Fallible Followers', p. 40; Pesch, *Markusevangelium II. Teil*, pp. 335-36.
3. Cranfield, *Mark*, p. 417; Hurtado, *Mark*, p. 217; Lane, *Mark*, p. 493; Lohmeyer, *Markus*, p. 295; Mann, *Mark*, p. 558; Taylor, *Mark*, p. 533.

unique importance of Jesus and the unique opportunity of the present moment to honor him.[1]

Simon of Cyrene (15.21)

Although Jesus has been the chief actor and speaker up until this point in the narrative, after his arrest he becomes almost entirely passive and silent.[2] During his trials before the Sanhedrin (14.55-65) and before Pilate (15.1-5), Jesus is unusually silent, speaking apparently only to assure his condemnation. In the scenes surrounding his crucifixion, Jesus is not so much an actor as the one who is acted upon. During his crucifixion, Jesus' only actions are to cry out loudly to God concerning his forsakenness (15.34) and then to cry out a second time before breathing his last (15.37). This development in the characterization of Jesus has an effect on Mark's treatment of minor characters. After the arrest, Mark does not narrate scenes that depict minor characters interacting and speaking with Jesus, because for the most part Jesus no longer acts or converses. Instead, Mark focuses the reader's attention on an individual, showing the person's contact with Jesus and response to him.

Immediately preceding his narration of Jesus' crucifixion, Mark focuses on a certain passerby, a man named Simon of Cyrene, who was coming from the countryside (15.21). Shortly before in the narrative, the crowd in Jerusalem, under the influence of the religious leaders, demanded the crucifixion of Jesus. Mark's description of Simon of Cyrene separates him from the hostile crowd that joined forces with the religious leaders to demand Jesus' death. Mark tells the reader little about Simon of Cyrene except that he was the father of Alexander and Rufus and that he was compelled to take up the cross of Jesus (ἄρῃ τὸν σταυρὸν αὐτοῦ). Mark expresses the action of Simon

---

1. In passing, it should be observed that the anointing of Jesus takes place at the home of Simon the leper, who should perhaps also be classified as a minor character (14.3). Simon the leper is presented in a different manner than the leper of Mk 1.40-45. Here, Mark makes no mention of a supplication or a healing. The giving of sight to Bartimaeus serves as the last healing in the narrative. After this last healing, minor characters are no longer presented as suppliants but as exemplars who respond like followers of Jesus. Thus, Simon the leper welcomes Jesus into his home, responding like Simon and Andrew after their call to follow Jesus (1.29-31) and like Levi after his call (2.15). Note the use of κατάκειμαι in 1.30, 2.15 and 14.3.

2. Kingsbury, *Conflict in Mark*, pp. 49-50; Tannehill, 'Narrative Christology', p. 81.

with words that recall Jesus' demands upon his followers.[1] In Mk 8.34 Jesus insists that those who choose to follow him must deny themselves, take up their cross (ἀράτω τὸν σταυρὸν αὐτοῦ) and follow him. The wording of Mk 15.21 concerning the action of Simon is almost exactly the same as the expression of Jesus' demand in Mk 8.34, but the referent of αὐτοῦ has changed. At this crucial point in the narrative there is a cross to be carried, and it is not just any cross, but the cross of Jesus himself. Simon's act of service, even though it is done under compulsion, highlights the failure of the disciples. The disciples have not taken up their own cross, nor are they available to carry the cross of Jesus. Instead, Simon of Cyrene serves Jesus by taking up his cross. Just as the woman at Bethany served Jesus in a way that went beyond her conscious intention, so now Simon of Cyrene helps Jesus although not by his own intention. Simon of Cyrene is characterized by Mark as one who is both compelled and able to serve.

The Centurion (15.39)

At the climax of the crucifixion narrative Mark presents another individual who responds to Jesus in a positive way, the centurion. Just as the wise scribe in Mk 12.28-34 was an exceptional scribe, so also the centurion is an exceptional soldier.[2] Until this point in the narrative Mark has presented the soldiers in a uniformly negative manner. The soldiers mock Jesus, pretending to honor him as a king while they beat him and spit at him (15.16-20). They crucify Jesus and divide up his garments as the spoils for their work (15.24-27). By their actions, the soldiers show that they are cruel and ignorant rejecters of Jesus. Although the centurion is in a sense a member of the soldiers as a group, he is an exception to the overall group characterization. The centurion shows an openness to Jesus and a perceptiveness concerning him that is unique among the soldiers.

Mark records the death of Jesus on the cross by stating that Jesus uttered a great cry and breathed out his last (15.37). At the death of Jesus, Mark immediately changes the scene, moving from Golgotha to the temple where the veil is torn from top to bottom (15.38). In his

---

1. Gnilka, *Markus*, II, p. 315; Hooker, *Mark*, p. 372; Kingsbury, *Conflict in Mark*, p. 27; Lührmann, *Markusevangelium*, p. 259; Schweizer, *Markus*, pp. 198-99; Tannehill, 'Disciples in Mark', p. 404.
2. Malbon, 'Fallible Followers', p. 31.

description of the rending of the temple's veil, Mark uses language that is reminiscent of the baptism scene in the prologue of the Gospel.[1] He uses the verb σχίζω only twice in his narrative, for the tearing of the temple veil (ἐσχίσθη, 15.38) and for the tearing of heaven at the baptism of Jesus (σχιζομένους, 1.10). In the baptism scene, after heaven is opened, God declares that Jesus is his beloved son (1.11). The connection between the baptism and the death of Jesus serves to remind the reader that Jesus fulfills his destiny as the Son of God through his death. The connection between Jesus' baptism and death also verifies the truth of the centurion's confession. The centurion views Jesus from God's perspective, since he affirms what God has previously declared, that Jesus is the Son of God.[2]

The centurion is standing (παρεστηκώς) opposite Jesus and sees (ἰδών) him breathe his last (15.39). Through this description, Mark places the response of the centurion in contrast to that of earlier bystanders at the cross.[3] Jesus' first cry on the cross is a question directed at God concerning his abandonment: 'Eloi, Eloi, lama sabachthani?' (15.34). Some of those who are standing near (παρεστηκότων, 15.35) hear Jesus' cry and misunderstand, assuming that Jesus is calling out for Elijah. They mock Jesus, stating their desire to see (ἴδωμεν, 15.36) Elijah come and rescue him by taking him down from the cross. This response of the bystanders is in keeping with the mocking of the chief priests and scribes, who say, 'He saved others; he cannot save himself. Let the Messiah, the King of Israel come down from the cross now, in order that we may see (ἴδωμεν) and believe' (15.31b-32a). Both the bystanders and the religious leaders claim to possess sight, but what they want to see is Jesus coming down from the cross in order to establish his identity and vindicate himself. Thus, while they have eyes to see, they do not see. After Jesus' second cry from the cross (15.37), the centurion responds by truly seeing and believing in contrast to the earlier

---

1. F.J. Matera, *The Kingship of Jesus: Composition and Theology in Mark 15* (SBLDS, 66; Chico, CA: Scholars Press, 1982), pp. 47, 139; 'Prologue', pp. 14-15.

2. The connection between Jesus' baptism and death is further strengthened by the fact that Jesus refers to his death as a baptism in 10.38-39. See Matera, *Kingship of Jesus*, p. 139.

3. Hurtado, *Mark*, p. 258; Kingsbury, *Christology*, p. 129; Matera, *Kingship of Jesus*, pp. 135-36.

bystanders. He recognizes that Jesus has established his identity and vindicated himself not by coming down from the cross but by dying on the cross.

The centurion sees Jesus breathe his last, and he then responds with his confession. Thus, his believing response arises out of his observation of Jesus' death.[1] Appropriately, the centurion states in his confession that Jesus *was* the Son of God. In this way, the imperfect verb ἦν points back to Jesus' death as the moment in which his identity was clearly seen.[2] The proclamation of the divine sonship of Jesus must be viewed in connection with his death, since Jesus' identity cannot be separated from his destiny. In the context of Mark's Gospel, any attempt to understand the identity of Jesus apart from the necessity of his death is simply an exercise in misunderstanding.

In response to Jesus' death, the centurion confesses that 'in truth, this man was the Son of God' (15.39),[3] and for the first time in

---

1. Anderson, *Mark*, pp. 347, 348; Cranfield, *Mark*, p. 460; Gnilka, *Markus*, II, p. 325; Lane, *Mark*, p. 576; Lührmann, *Markusevangelium*, p. 264; Pesch, *Markusevangelium II. Teil*, p. 499.

2. Gnilka, *Markus*, II, p. 325; Kingsbury, *Christology*, p. 131; Kingsbury, *Conflict in Mark*, p. 54.

3. The predicate nominative υἱὸς θεοῦ is best understood as definite and should be translated 'the Son of God'. According to E.C. Colwell ('A Definite Rule for the Use of the Article in the Greek New Testament', *JBL* 52 [1933], pp. 13, 20), if the context suggests that an anarthrous predicate nominative which precedes the verb is definite, then it should be translated as definite in spite of the absence of the article. This is because a definite predicate nominative does not normally have the article when it precedes the verb. The context of Mark's Gospel certainly suggests that υἱὸς θεοῦ should be regarded as definite. References to Jesus' divine sonship in Mark's Gospel repeatedly use υἱός with the article (1.11; 3.11; 9.7; 13.32; 14.61). Outside of 15.39, Mark's Gospel includes only two other clear references to Jesus' divine sonship where the article is not used with υἱός. In 1.1 the narrator uses υἱοῦ θεοῦ without an article. Nevertheless, the narrator's point of view is always consistent with God's point of view in Mark's Gospel. God's perspective is that Jesus is 'the Son' (1.11; 9.7), and this viewpoint is determinative for the narrator. In 5.7 Jesus is referred to as 'Son of the Most High God' and here again υἱός is used without the article. However, υἱός is in the vocative case, so that it is grammatically impossible for it to take the article. Therefore, Mark's Gospel consistently presents Jesus as 'the Son of God', and it is unlikely that Mark would use the centurion's confession toward the end of the Gospel to introduce a completely different concept using the words υἱὸς θεοῦ. For a similar argument see P.G. Davis, 'Mark's Christological Paradox', *JSNT* 35 (1989), pp. 11-12.

Mark's narrative a human character, other than Jesus himself, acknowledges the divine sonship of Jesus.[1] Mark does not have the centurion address his confession to anyone within the narrative. He records the centurion's confession for the reader's benefit, and it is the reader who is able to grasp the significance of the confession within the broader context of the narrative.[2] In the context of the overall narrative, the centurion's confession stands in agreement with God's perspective on Jesus, since at the baptism and at the transfiguration God himself declares that Jesus is his beloved Son (1.11; 9.7).[3] Within the broader context, the centurion's confession stands in contrast to the high priest's condemnation.[4] For the high priest, Jesus' confession of his divine sonship is blasphemy, and Jesus is worthy of death for his claim (14.61-64). By way of contrast, the centurion acknowledges the truth of Jesus' divine sonship when he sees Jesus die. Within the larger narrative, the centurion's confession also stands in contrast to Peter's confession.[5] In Mk 8.29 Peter confesses Jesus as the messiah. Peter is correct in acknowledging that Jesus is the messiah, but his confession is inadequate because his understanding of the mission of the messiah is faulty (8.31-32). In contrast to Peter's confession, that of the centurion adequately expresses Jesus' identity, because it is made in the face of Jesus' suffering and death. The centurion makes the confession that the disciples failed to make because of their unwillingness to accept the suffering of the messiah.[6] Thus, the broader context of Mark's narrative gives to the centurion's confession a more profound meaning than he himself may have intended, so that the centurion exemplifies for the reader the true understanding of

---

1. Kingsbury, *Christology*, pp. 132-33; *idem, Conflict in Mark*, p. 54; Matera, *Kingship of Jesus*, p. 140; *idem*, 'Prologue', p. 14.

2. Hurtado, *Mark*, p. 258; Kingsbury, *Christology*, p. 131; *idem, Conflict in Mark*, pp. 53-54.

3. Kingsbury, *Christology*, p. 133; *idem, Conflict in Mark*, p. 54; Matera, *Kingship of Jesus*, p. 140; *idem*, 'Prologue', p. 14; Tannehill, 'Narrative Christology', p. 88.

4. Gundry, *Mark*, p. 951; Kingsbury, *Christology*, p. 131; *idem, Conflict in Mark*, p. 54.

5. Schweizer, 'Life of Faith', pp. 389-90; Tannehill, 'Disciples in Mark', p. 404.

6. Kingsbury, *Conflict in Mark*, p. 27; Rhoads and Michie, *Mark as Story*, pp. 132-33; Tannehill, 'Disciples in Mark', pp. 404-405.

Jesus. Jesus is the Son of God who reveals himself as such not in spite of his death but in his death.

The centurion is an exceptional individual, particularly when compared with the other soldiers who mock and reject Jesus. Because he is perceptive and insightful, he is able to understand that Jesus reveals himself as the Son of God in his death. The centurion is believing, in contrast to the chief priests and scribes who will believe only if Jesus comes down from the cross. The centurion believes when he sees Jesus die, and in his confession he expresses his faith.

The Women at the Cross (15.40-41)

At the end of the crucifixion account Mark attaches a short reference concerning three women, Mary Magdalene, Mary the mother of James the Less and Joses, and Salome.[1] The women do not respond to Jesus or to the events of the crucifixion, but rather they are simply present as witnesses of Christ's death. Mark states that they were watching from a distance (15.40). Apparently, Mark refers to the presence of the women simply as a way of introducing them into the story in order that they might play a more significant role in the following narrative.[2]

According to Mark's description, the women respond properly to the demands of Jesus. When the women were in Galilee, they were following Jesus (ἠκολούθουν, 15.41), and then they also came up to Jerusalem with him along with many others.[3] In Mk 8.34 Jesus calls on both the disciples and members of the crowd to deny themselves

---

1.   Although Mark's description of Mary is ambiguous, she appears to be the mother of both James the Less and Joses. See Gundry, *Mark*, pp. 976-77; Lagrange, *Marc*, pp. 438-39; Matera, *Kingship of Jesus*, pp. 49-50; Taylor, *Mark*, p. 598. Mark includes further references to these women in 15.47 and 16.1 although with variations in his descriptions. In 15.47 Mark refers again to Mary Magdalene, but Mary is described only as the mother of Joses while a reference to Salome is omitted. In 16.1 Mark again introduces Mary Magdalene and Salome while Mary is described as the mother of James.

2.   Hooker, *Mark*, p. 379; Nineham, *Mark*, p. 431; Schweizer, *Markus*, p. 209; Taylor, *Mark*, p. 598.

3.   W. Munro ('Women Disciples in Mark?', *CBQ* 44 [1982], pp. 39-43) argues that 15.40-41 points to the existence of women disciples and that Mark arranged his narrative in order to obscure this historical reality. For a reply to Munro's argument see M.J. Selvidge, 'And Those Who Followed Feared (10:32)', *CBQ* 45 (1983), pp. 396-400.

and follow (ἀκολουθείτω) him. The women fulfill Jesus' expectations and follow him all the way up to the cross. Thus, they are watching at the crucifixion scene long after the disciples have all fled. The women also live up to Jesus' demands in that they serve (διηκόνουν, 15.41) him. In response to the disciples' desire to attain positions of prominence and honor, Jesus tells them that they should take a lowly position in which they are the servant (διάκονος) of all (9.35; 10.43). Even Jesus as the Son of Man did not come to be served (διακονηθῆναι), but to serve (διακονῆσαι) and to give his life (10.45). Like Jesus, the women take on the responsibility of service in contrast to the disciples who reject lowly service in order to seek honor.

Mark offers a positive description of the women at the cross, but he also includes one detail that foreshadows a negative response from the women.[1] Mark states that the women watch the crucifixion scene at a distance (μακρόθεν, 15.40). Shortly before, Peter followed Jesus but remained at a distance (μακρόθεν, 14.54). Then, after following at a distance, Peter denied Jesus three times in the courtyard of the high priest (14.66-72). Following at a distance is dangerous and may lead to failure. On the whole, however, Mark presents the women at the cross in a positive manner, and they exemplify for the reader individuals who are following and serving. The women are committed to Jesus and to his ideals, and they stand in contrast to the disciples who have ceased to follow and have failed to serve.

Joseph of Arimathea (15.42-47)

The crucifixion scene is framed by references to individuals who serve Jesus, Simon of Cyrene coming immediately before the crucifixion scene (15.21) and Joseph of Arimathea coming immediately after it (15.42-47). The two are similar in that they are both introduced by name along with a geographical designation. Simon helps Jesus by carrying his cross, while Joseph helps Jesus by taking him down from the cross. Both Simon of Cyrene and Joseph of Arimathea function as replacements for the disciples of Jesus who have long since fled from their master.[2]

1. Malbon, 'Fallible Followers', p. 43.
2. Kingsbury, *Conflict in Mark*, pp. 27, 123-24; *idem*, 'Religious Authorities', pp. 49-50; Rhoads and Michie, *Mark as Story*, pp. 132-33; Tannehill, 'Disciples in Mark', pp. 404-405.

Mark introduces Joseph of Arimathea as a prominent council member (εὐσχήμων βουλευτής, 15.43). Mark's use of βουλευτής with reference to Joseph is ambiguous, indicating either that Joseph is a member of the Sanhedrin or a member of some local or provincial council.[1] Since no other council is mentioned or even assumed in Mark's narrative beyond the Sanhedrin, it seems likely that Mark is presenting Joseph of Arimathea as a member of the Sanhedrin.[2] Thus, he is treated by Mark as an exception to the overall characterization of the Sanhedrin and its members.[3]

Joseph of Arimathea is an exceptional member of the Sanhedrin in the same way that the wise scribe is an exceptional scribe and the centurion is an exceptional soldier. Mark's overall characterization of the Sanhedrin is uniformly negative. The whole (ὅλον) Sanhedrin seeks to find testimony against Jesus in order that they might condemn him to death (14.55). The members of the council are even willing to resort to using false testimony against Jesus (14.56-59). In response to Jesus' claim to be the Son of God, all the members of the council condemn Jesus as worthy of death (14.64). They end the trial by spitting at Jesus, beating him and mocking him (14.65). The whole (ὅλον) Sanhedrin joins together in handing Jesus over to Pilate (15.1). Thus, the Sanhedrin as a whole is hostile, ruthless and determined to bring about Jesus' death. Yet in spite of this uniformly negative picture, Mark seems to isolate Joseph of Arimathea as an exceptional member

---

1. For a useful presentation of the options for interpreting βουλευτής see Matera, *Kingship of Jesus*, p. 55.

2. For others who take the position that Joseph of Arimathea is a member of the Sanhedrin see R.E. Brown, 'The Burial of Jesus (Mark 15:42-47)', *CBQ* 50 (1988), pp. 238-39; Cranfield, *Mark*, p. 462; Gundry, *Mark*, pp. 980-81, 984-85; Lagrange, *Marc*, p. 440; Lane, *Mark*, p. 577; Lohmeyer, *Markus*, p. 350; Mann, *Mark*, p. 657; Pesch, *Markusevangelium II. Teil*, p. 513. See also Josephus, *War* 2.17.1, where he uses βουλευτής for members of the Sanhedrin.

3. Malbon, 'Jewish Leaders', p. 276. Kingsbury ('Religious Authorities', pp. 44-50) insists that Mark treats the religious authorities as a united front in their opposition to Jesus and that Mark does not allow any exceptions to break this united front. In line with this reasoning, Kingsbury argues that Joseph of Arimathea cannot belong to the larger group of religious authorities. For Kingsbury, Joseph is not a member of the Sanhedrin, but a prominent member of a local, or provincial, council. However, it is unclear why Mark's allowance for individual exceptions would negate his overall characterization of the religious authorities.

of the Sanhedrin.[1] Mark creates a tension by presenting the Sanhedrin as uniformly and comprehensively antagonistic to Jesus at the same time that he allows an individual exception in Joseph, who remains open to Jesus and the kingdom. Yet Mark is apparently willing to allow this tension in the same way that he is willing to permit such a tension in his treatment of the scribes and the soldiers.[2]

Mark further characterizes Joseph of Arimathea as one who was waiting for the kingdom of God (15.43). Joseph of Arimathea is similar to the wise scribe who was not far from the kingdom (12.34), since they are both described in ways that show them to be open to the kingdom of God.[3] Joseph is not only receptive of God's kingdom, but he is sufficiently courageous to approach Pilate and request the body of Jesus (15.43). In the preceding narrative, the religious authorities respond with fear when faced with any threat to their positions of power and respect (11.18, 32; 12.12, 34; 14.1-2). By way of contrast, Joseph of Arimathea exemplifies courage and a lack of concern for his own safety or prominence. In response to Joseph's request, Pilate finds it difficult to believe that Jesus has already died, but with the confirmation of Jesus' death Pilate grants the body to Joseph (15.44-45).

Joseph of Arimathea takes the corpse of Jesus down from the cross, wraps it in a linen cloth and lays it in a tomb (15.46). By taking responsibility for Jesus' burial, Joseph acts in a manner that has been associated with discipleship earlier in Mark's narrative.[4] After John the Baptist is beheaded, his disciples come and take his corpse (τὸ πτῶμα αὐτοῦ) and lay it in a tomb (ἔθηκαν αὐτὸ ἐν μνημείῳ, 6.29). After the crucifixion, Jesus' disciples are absent, and instead

---

1. In a similar way, Mark goes out of his way to report that the whole (ὅλην) cohort of soldiers was called together in order to participate in the hostilities directed at Jesus (15.16). This general characterization of the soldiers, however, does not negate any possible exception, since in contrast to the other soldiers, the centurion accepts Jesus as the Son of God.

2. Pesch (*Markusevangelium II. Teil*, p. 513) seeks to resolve the tension by positing that Joseph of Arimathea was not present during the trial of Jesus. Pesch also argues that Joseph's access to Pilate presupposes his high rank and thus probably also his membership in the Sanhedrin.

3. Brown, 'Burial', p. 239; Malbon, 'Jewish Leaders', p. 276.

4. See especially Matera, *Kingship of Jesus*, pp. 54, 98. See also Fowler, *Let the Reader Understand*, p. 245; Kingsbury, *Conflict in Mark*, p. 27; *idem*, 'Religious Authorities', pp. 49-50; Rhoads and Michie, *Mark as Story*, p. 133; Tannehill, 'Disciples in Mark', pp. 404-405.

Joseph of Arimathea assumes responsibility for the burial. Joseph receives access to the corpse (τὸ πτῶμα, 15.45) from Pilate, takes Jesus down from the cross and lays him in a tomb (ἔθηκεν αὐτὸν ἐν μνημείῳ, 15.46).[1]

Mark characterizes Joseph of Arimathea as a prominent individual who holds a position of great authority and respect. Yet Joseph is exceptional, because unlike others within the religious establishment he is neither threatened by Jesus nor antagonistic to him. Joseph is not only open to the kingdom of God and waiting for its arrival, but his actions show that he is also open and receptive to Jesus. By coming to Pilate and asking for the body of Jesus, Joseph shows that he is a courageous man who places his respect for Jesus above his own safety and position. In the end, Joseph responds to Jesus like a devoted and committed follower, in that he takes the responsibility for his burial.

In this passage on Joseph of Arimathea Mark refers again to certain minor characters that he has introduced previously in the narrative. This is an unusual feature, since until this point minor characters have never appeared again once they have left the scene. The centurion returns to the narrative in order to report to Pilate that Jesus has indeed died (15.44-45). Mary Magdalene and Mary the mother of Joses appear again at the tomb in order to observe the place where Joseph of Arimathea lays Jesus (15.47). Therefore, the centurion serves as a witness of Jesus' death, and the two women function as witnesses of Jesus' burial.

The Women at the Tomb (16.1-8)
Early on the first day of the week Mary Magdalene, Mary the mother of James and Salome bring spices to the tomb in order to anoint the body of Jesus (16.1-2). In this way, Mark begins and ends the passion narrative with analogous scenes in which women, minor characters, seek to anoint Jesus.[2] This passage on the women at the tomb presents the interpreter with a number of problems, not the least of which is a

---

1. Mark uses virtually identical expressions for the placement of both John the Baptist and Jesus in the tomb, and he uses the word for corpse (πτῶμα) only in 6.29 and 15.45.

2. For other connections between 16.1-8 and earlier passages on minor characters see the use of ἀναβλέπω (8.24, 10.51, 52; 16.4), ἐκθαμβέομαι (9.15; 16.5, 6), Ναζαρηνός (1.24; 10.47; 16.6), ὑπάγω (1.44; 2.11; 5.19, 34; 7.29; 10.21, 52; 16.7), ἔκστασις (5.42; 16.8), and φοβέομαι (5.15, 33, 36; 16.8).

major text-critical problem. Mark's Gospel ends in different ways in the manuscript tradition. Some manuscripts end the Gospel at 16.8, other manuscripts continue after 16.8 with the so-called longer ending of 16.9-20, one manuscript omits the longer ending while concluding instead with the so-called shorter ending and finally some manuscripts include both the shorter and the longer endings.[1] Based on external and internal evidence, the general consensus among New Testament scholars is that both the longer ending and the shorter ending are secondary, later additions to Mark's Gospel.[2]

If the longer and the shorter endings are secondary, then three basic options are open to the interpreter: first, that Mark intended to conclude his Gospel at 16.8; secondly, that Mark was unable to complete his Gospel, and that although he stopped at 16.8, that was not his intended ending; and thirdly, that the real ending of Mark's Gospel has been lost.[3] When treating the end of Mark's Gospel, literary

1. For a detailed presentation of both the external and internal evidence with regard to this textual problem see J.K. Elliott, 'The Text and Language of the Endings to Mark's Gospel', *TZ* 27 (1971), pp. 255-62. See also K. Aland, 'Der Schluss des Markusevangeliums', in M. Sabbe (ed.), *L'Evangile selon Marc: Tradition et rédaction* (Leuven: Leuven University Press, 2nd edn, 1988), pp. 436-55; Metzger, *Textual Commentary*, pp. 122-24. The ending of the Gospel at 16.8 is attested by Aleph, B, 304 and a number of version manuscripts. Clement of Alexandria and Origen appear to have no knowledge of 16.9-20, while both Eusebius and Jerome state that the longer ending was absent from almost all the manuscripts known to them. The longer ending of 16.9-20 is included in the vast majority of witnesses, although some of the witnesses also contain scribal notes indicating that these verses are not found in older manuscripts. The Itala manuscript k includes the shorter ending but not the longer one, with the result that this manuscript stands as further evidence for the circulation of Mark's Gospel without 16.9-20. Several witnesses including L, Ψ, 099, 0112 and others contain the shorter ending followed by the longer ending.

2. As Metzger states, 'Almost all textual studies and critical commentaries on the Gospel according to Mark agree that the last twelve verses cannot be regarded as Marcan' (B.M. Metzger, *The Text of the New Testament: Its Transmission, Corruption, and Restoration* [New York: Oxford University Press, 2nd edn, 1968], p. 228). See also Metzger, *Textual Commentary*, p. 126. For an isolated objection to this general consensus see W.R. Farmer, *The Last Twelve Verses of Mark* (SNTSMS, 25; London: Cambridge University Press, 1974). A refutation of Farmer's position may be found in J.N. Birdsall, review of *The Last Twelve Verses of Mark*, by W.R. Farmer, *JTS* 26 (1975), pp. 151-60.

3. For an explanation of these three possibilities see Cranfield, *Mark*, pp. 470-71; Metzger, *Text of the New Testament*, 228; *idem*, *Textual Commentary*, p. 126.

critics have typically accepted Mk 16.8 as the intended conclusion of the Gospel.[1] Instead of looking for a different conclusion, literary critics have sought to understand the ending as it stands in 16.8 and to show that this ending provides a meaningful closure to the narrative as a whole. Literary critics are not alone in this position, since, as

Those who argue for the second or third options should recognize that they are providing a historical explanation for what is essentially a literary problem. The problem, first of all, is whether or not the ending of Mark's Gospel at 16.8 makes adequate sense, and as such this is a literary problem dealing with the meaning and function of the text. At times, historical explanations are necessary in order to deal with literary problems, but a literary solution should be sought first. Pesch comes to a similar conclusion when he states: 'Der Kommentator des Mk-Ev hat allen Grund, davon auszugehen, dass mit Mk 16, 1-8 der ursprüngliche Abschluss des Evangeliums gegeben ist. Die Eigenart dieses Schlusses ist Anstoss zur Interpretation, nicht zu konjekturaler Rekonstruktion oder Vermutung' (Pesch, *Markusevangelium I. Teil*, p. 47).

1. Two common objections have been raised against the notion that Mark intended to end his Gospel at 16.8. First, some have argued that it would be virtually impossible for a book to end with γάρ. See, for example, Gundry, *Mark*, p. 1011; Metzger, *Text of the New Testament*, p. 228; Taylor, *Mark*, p. 609. This objection is answered by P.W. van der Horst ('Can a Book End with ΓΑΡ? A Note on Mark XVI.8', *JTS* 23 [1972], pp. 121-24) who points to a treatise by Plotinus that ends with a γάρ. In addition, he presents the commonsense argument that if a sentence or paragraph can end with γάρ, then so can a book. Secondly, some have argued that while a suspended, open ending may be appropriate in modern literature, it would be entirely out of place in ancient literature. A classic statement of this objection may be found in W.L. Knox, 'The Ending of St. Mark's Gospel', *HTR* 35 (1942), pp. 13-23. Knox argued that Mark could not have intended to end his Gospel at 16.8, since this abrupt ending would be completely at odds with the canons of popular storytelling in the ancient world which required the author to develop fully the ending of the narrative. T.E. Boomershine and G.L. Bartholomew ('The Narrative Technique of Mark 16:8', *JBL* 100 [1981], pp. 213-33) argue against Knox's position by comparing Mark's ending at 16.8 with the endings of earlier pericopes in the Gospel. Boomershine and Bartholomew demonstrate that Mark uses suspended, open endings in narrating earlier stories within the Gospel in ways that parallel the ending in 16.8. J.L. Magness (*Sense and Absence: Structure and Suspension in the Ending of Mark's Gospel* [SBLSS; Atlanta: Scholars Press, 1986], pp. 6-9, 25-85) surveys Hebrew, Greek and Roman literature in order to demonstrate that ancient literature abounds in open or suspended endings. In this way, Magness questions the widespread opinion that ancient writers and readers were not sophisticated enough to produce or understand open endings.

Kümmel states, 'There is an increasingly strong inclination to the view that 16.8 is the intended ending of Mk'.[1]

Literary critics have examined Mk 16.1-8 perhaps more than any other passage in Mark's Gospel, but this concentrated attention has produced a variety of results. Among the many explanations offered by literary critics for Mark's enigmatic ending, the most satisfying solution, I believe, is that of Andrew T. Lincoln.[2] The following discussion will deal primarily with the various literary approaches to Mark's ending in analyzing the characterization of the women at the tomb. This analysis will generally follow Lincoln's explanation for the ending of Mark's Gospel, while seeking also to point out certain inadequacies in other literary approaches.

Mark begins his presentation of the woman at the tomb in a sympathetic manner. Mary Magdalene, Mary the mother of James and Salome bring spices to the tomb in order to anoint the body of Jesus (16.1). As they are coming to the tomb very early on the first day of the week, they discuss among themselves the difficulty presented by the large stone in front of the door of the tomb (16.2-3). Upon arriving at the tomb, however, they see that the stone has already been

---

1. W.G. Kümmel, *Introduction to the New Testament* (trans. H.C. Kee; Nashville: Abingdon, 1975), p. 100. In a similar manner, Telford (*Interpretation*, p. 26) states: 'While a number of scholars would still adhere to the view that the Gospel originally extended beyond 16.8, more and more are coming to the opinion that it was intended to end at 16.8, and that it does so indeed, in literary terms, with dramatic appositeness'. On 16.8 as the original ending of Mark's Gospel see also Aland, 'Schluss', pp. 464-65, 469.

2. See Lincoln, 'Promise and the Failure', pp. 283-300. In explaining the ending of Mark's Gospel, Lincoln wants to stress equally the promise implied in the young man's message in 16.7 and the failure of the women in 16.8. Lincoln insists that the juxtaposition of promise and failure must be allowed its full force. For other literary-critical explanations for the ending of Mark see T. Boomershine, 'Mark 16:8 and the Apostolic Commission', *JBL* 100 (1981), pp. 225-39; Kelber, *Story of Jesus*, pp. 83-90; Kingsbury, *Christology*, pp. 135-37; *idem*, *Conflict in Mark*, pp. 112-15; Magness, *Sense and Absence*, pp. 87-105; Malbon, 'Fallible Followers', pp. 43-45; N.R. Petersen, 'When is the End not the End? Reflections on the Ending of Mark's Narrative', *Int* 34 (1980), pp. 151-66; *idem*, *Literary Criticism*, pp. 77-78; *idem*, 'Reader in the Gospel', p. 49; M.A. Powell, 'Toward a Narrative-Critical Understanding of Mark', *Int* 47 (1993), pp. 344-45; Rhoads and Michie, *Mark as Story*, pp. 61-62, 96-100, 129, 134, 140; Tannehill, 'Disciples in Mark', pp. 403-404; *idem*, 'Narrative Christology', pp. 82-84; Tolbert, *Sowing*, pp. 288-99.

rolled away (16.4). When the women enter the tomb, they see a young man clothed in a white robe and they respond with amazement (16.5).[1] The young man rebukes their amazement and reports to them the resurrection of Jesus (16.6). The one sought by the women, Jesus the Nazarene, is not in the tomb, because he has been raised. Until this point in the narrative, the women are presented in a positive manner. The women are followers of Jesus who are sufficiently humble and self-denying to serve others. They express their devotion and loyalty to Jesus by following him to the cross and by attempting to anoint his body even after his burial. They respond to the miraculous events at the tomb with amazement, but this amazement is understandable since Jesus predicted his coming resurrection only to his disciples (8.31; 9.9, 31; 10.34; 14.28).[2]

In Mk 16.7 the young man gives a command to the women, a command that should be obeyed. The nature of this command and the preceding report of Jesus' resurrection identify the young man as a reliable character. Since his words confirm the teaching and promises of Jesus, the young man must be treated as a reliable and authoritative spokesman for God. The young man's announcement of the resurrection confirms the predictions of Jesus concerning the event. He also restates Jesus' promise to the disciples that he will go before them into Galilee after the resurrection. The young man's words clearly point back to the promise of Jesus in Mk 14.28,[3] and the young man himself

---

1. Mark apparently uses νεανίσκον in 16.5 to refer to an angel. The description 'young man' may be used in order to narrate the scene from the perspective of the women. See Pesch, *Markusevangelium II. Teil*, p. 532. For the view that the young man is an angel see also Anderson, *Mark*, p. 355; Cranfield, *Mark*, p. 465; Gnilka, *Markus*, II, pp. 341-42; Gundry, *Mark*, pp. 990-91; Hooker, *Mark*, p. 384; Lagrange, *Marc*, p. 446; Lane, *Mark*, p. 587; Lohmeyer, *Markus*, p. 354; Nineham, *Mark*, pp. 444-45; Schweizer, *Markus*, pp. 215-16; Taylor, *Mark*, pp. 606-607. Taylor gives a number of parallels in Jewish and Christian literature in which angels are described in similar terms.

2. On the positive portrait of the women at the tomb prior to the command of the young man see Boomershine, 'Apostolic Commission', pp. 231-32; Lincoln, 'Promise and the Failure', p. 288. Malbon ('Fallible Followers', pp. 43-44) also points out that the women should not be faulted either for their attempt to anoint Jesus or for their amazement at his resurrection.

3. Several words link the promise of Jesus in 14.28 and the message of the young man in 16.6-7. The verb ἐγείρω is only used twice with regard to Jesus' resurrection, by Jesus in 14.28 (ἐγερθῆναι) and by the young man in 16.6 (ἠγέρθη). Note also the similarity between Jesus' statement προάξω ὑμᾶς εἰς τὴν

indicates that he is referring back to Jesus' words when he says καθὼς εἶπεν ὑμῖν. With authority, then, the young man commands the women to depart and report to the disciples and to Peter that Jesus is going before them into Galilee where they will see him.

The predicted meeting between Jesus and his disciples is apparently intended to bring about the restoration of the disciples, so that they might fulfill their responsibilities as Jesus' apostles between the resurrection and the parousia.[1] Jesus called the disciples to be his followers and 'fishers of men' (1.16-20), and he also appointed them as his apostles in order that they might preach and have authority (3.13-19; 6.7-13). Jesus predicted that between the resurrection and the parousia, the disciples would testify on his behalf and suffer for his sake (13.9-13), and at least some of them would suffer martyrdom (10.39). Yet in spite of their lofty calling, the disciples have failed miserably. At the moment that called for faithfulness and courage, they all fled except for Peter, who continued to follow only long enough to deny Jesus three times (14.50, 54, 66-72). The disciples have failed, but now the predicted meeting in Galilee holds open the possibility of restoration.[2] The message concerning the meeting in Galilee is addressed directly to the disciples and to Peter, to those who fled and above all to the one who denied his master. Thus, the message from the young man holds open the hope that there is an enduring relationship with Jesus even after failure. This promise of restoration is also implied in Jesus' words in Mk 14.27-28.[3] There, Jesus' prediction of a meeting in Galilee after the resurrection (14.28) stands in contrast to his prediction of the stumbling and scattering of the disciples (14.27). Therefore, the meeting appears to be a time for the shepherd to gather together his scattered sheep, a time for Jesus to

Γαλιλαίαν in 14.28 and the young man's statement προάγει ὑμᾶς εἰς τὴν Γαλιλαίαν in 16.7.

1. Thus, Mk 16.7 refers to a resurrection appearance in Galilee and not to the parousia of Jesus in Galilee. See Lincoln, 'Promise and the Failure', p. 285. See also R.H. Stein, 'A Short Note on Mark XIV.28 and XVI.7', *NTS* 20 (1974), pp. 445-52.

2. Kingsbury, *Christology*, pp. 136-37; *idem, Conflict in Mark*, pp. 113-15; Lincoln, 'Promise and the Failure', p. 289; Rhoads and Michie, *Mark as Story*, p. 97; Tannehill, 'Disciples in Mark', pp. 403-404; *idem, 'Narrative Christology'*, pp. 83-84.

3. Tannehill, 'Disciples in Mark', pp. 403-404; *idem, 'Narrative Christology'*, p. 83.

restore his failed disciples. The place for the meeting is in Galilee, which has been the primary location for the ministry of Jesus and the mission of the disciples. At the meeting, Jesus will regroup and restore the disciples, so that they might once again be sent out on their mission.[1]

Mark follows the command of the young man in 16.7 with the surprisingly negative reaction of the women in 16.8. The women flee from the tomb with trembling and terror, and instead of reporting this message to the disciples they speak to no one because of their fear. Every aspect of the women's response in Mk 16.8 is negative. The flight (ἔφυγον) of the women from the tomb is similar to the cowardly flight of the disciples after the arrest of Jesus in the garden (ἔφυγον, 14.50).[2] The trembling and terror that causes the women to flee is also an inappropriate response. Earlier, the young man commanded the women not to be amazed after their initial response of astonishment at the miraculous events at the tomb. Instead of setting aside their amazement in obedience to the young man's command, the women increase their level of emotion to trembling and terror. In addition, the silence of the women is an act of disobedience to the young man's command, and this silence is clearly negative because it arises out of fear.[3] In Mark's Gospel, fear is related to a lack of trust and an unwillingness to face suffering and self-sacrifice. This unbelief and lack of self-denial is especially evident in the fear of the disciples (4.41; 6.50; 9.32; 10.32). Out of fear, the women say nothing to anyone, with the result that they disobey the command of the young man and fail to pass on the message to the disciples. This disobedient and fearful silence, along with the women's flight and amazement, is part of a wholly negative response on their part.[4]

1. Lincoln, 'Promise and the Failure', p. 289.
2. Boomershine, 'Apostolic Commission', p. 229; Lincoln, 'Promise and the Failure', p. 287.
3. For arguments concerning the negative nature of the women's fear see Boomershine, 'Apostolic Commission', pp. 227-30; Lincoln, 'Promise and the Failure', pp. 285-87.
4. Therefore, the view taken in this study stands in contrast to interpretations that regard the actions of the women in 16.8 as positive and typical responses to a miracle. In such interpretations, the silence of the women is generally treated as a momentary, awe-inspired silence before the miraculous. The best defense of this position is perhaps found in D. Catchpole, 'The Fearful Silence of the Women at the Tomb', *Journal of Theology for Southern Africa* 18 (1977), pp. 3-10. Magness

Mark's characterization of the women at the tomb, then, takes an unusual and surprising turn. Mark initially characterizes the women as committed to Jesus and to his values. However, after the young man's announcement of the resurrection and his command to report a message to the disciples, the women make a dramatic turn for the worse. Mark characterizes them as fleeing, trembling, disturbed, astonished, silent, fearful and disobedient. Like the disciples before them, the women followers also fail. In this way Mark's characterization of the women followers is similar to his treatment of the disciples, since he begins with a positive presentation but then shifts to a negative one.

In a number of ways, Mark leaves the reader unprepared for the failure of the women and their disobedient silence. His sympathetic treatment of the women prior to 16.8 encourages the reader to expect obedience from the women. In addition, the women stand in line with a series of similar individuals who have been portrayed as those who live up to the expectations of Jesus. From Bartimaeus to the women at the tomb, Mark presents a series of minor characters who respond to Jesus in a positive manner, and so he encourages the reader to identify with these individuals. Yet although the women at the tomb are unlikely failures, they still fail and in an unlikely manner. They disobey by remaining in silence, when they have been commanded to speak. In the preceding narrative, minor characters have not been given to silence, even when they are commanded to remain silent. When the leper is sternly warned by Jesus to say nothing to anyone, he disobeys by freely spreading around the word concerning Jesus (1.43-45).[1] After healing the deaf man, Jesus is unable to enforce silence,

(Sense and Absence, pp. 87-105) offers a literary interpretation of Mark's ending in which the response of the women in 16.8 is treated as appropriate and positive. For Magness, the fearful silence of the women at the tomb is not negative, because such a reaction is simply a typical feature of miracle stories. Also, for Magness, the silence of the women is only temporary. 'Their immediate awe-struck silence may not have been permanent; they may have said "nothing to anyone" only until, passing soldiers changing the guard and merchants opening their stalls and shoppers heading for the market, they reached the disciples' (Magness, *Sense and Absence*, p. 100). According to Magness, the women may have kept silence in the midst of inappropriate audiences only to give a full report to the appropriate audience, that is, the disciples. Magness also argues that the fear of the women was the appropriate response to the miraculous. For a similar literary approach see Malbon, 'Fallible Followers', pp. 43-45.

1. The similarity between Jesus' command to the leper (ὅρα μηδενὶ μηδὲν

because, as the narrator adds, the more Jesus commanded people to silence the more they proclaimed (7.36). Bartimaeus is another individual from the crowd who refuses to be silent. When others seek to silence him, he cries out all the more for Jesus to have mercy on him (10.48). The action of the women at the tomb is almost the complete reverse of what has taken place up until this point in the narrative. Mark has created the expectation that the women at the tomb, like earlier individuals from the crowd, will freely speak, but then he shatters this expectation with the women's silence.[1] Not only do the women disobey in an unlikely manner, but they do so at an unlikely time. In Mk 9.9 Jesus states that the time of silence will be over after his resurrection. Thus, the women remain silent at a time when all restrictions on speaking have been lifted.[2] Mark has led the reader to assume that the women at the tomb will respond with joyful obedience, but instead they flee in fearful silence.

The unexpected failure of the women forces the reader to reflect again on the message of hope given in Mk 16.7.[3] Does the disobedience of the women negate the promise implied in the young man's message to the disciples? No; the promise still holds true because it is based on the word of Jesus. The message of the young man is related to the prediction of Jesus in Mk 14.28, where Jesus indicates that after his resurrection he will go before his disciples to Galilee. The context implies that Jesus is going to Galilee in order to restore and regroup his disciples. In Mark's narrative, the predictions of Jesus are consistently fulfilled, so that the reader is able to recognize that Jesus' promises will come true even if they must be fulfilled beyond the end of the narrative.[4] Jesus' predictions always come true even when Jesus

εἴπῃς, 1.44) and Mark's description of the women's silence (οὐδενὶ οὐδὲν εἶπαν, 16.8) heightens the irony of the women's disobedience.

1. Lincoln, 'Promise and the Failure', pp. 290-91.

2. Lincoln, 'Promise and the Failure', pp. 290-91.

3. Lincoln, 'Promise and the Failure', p. 291; Petersen, 'When is the End not the End?', pp. 153-54, 162-63.

4. Kingsbury, *Christology*, pp. 135-36; *idem, Conflict in Mark*, p. 113; Petersen, 'When is the End not the End?', pp. 154-56. Repeatedly in Mark's narrative, the predictions of Jesus are fulfilled. Jesus predicts the presence of a colt for his entry into Jerusalem (11.2), the rejection of the religious leaders in Jerusalem (8.31), the availability of a guest room for his celebration of the Passover (14.13-15), the betrayal of Judas (9.31; 10.33; 14.18-21), the desertion of the disciples (14.27), the denials of Peter (14.30), his trial before the religious leaders and before

is faced with the failure or antagonism of others.[1] Heaven and earth may pass away, but Jesus' word will never pass away (13.31). Therefore, the anticipated meeting predicted by Jesus and confirmed by the young man will take place in spite of the disobedience of the women.[2] Mark never tells the reader how the promise in 14.28 and

the Gentiles (10.33), the mocking of his enemies (10.34), his own suffering (8.31), his death (8.31; 9.31; 10.34; 12.8) and his resurrection (8.31; 9.9, 31; 10.34). All of these predictions come true within the course of the narrative. This consistent fulfillment of Jesus' predictions within the course of the narrative encourages the reader to expect that Jesus' other predictions will continue to be fulfilled beyond the end of the narrative.

1. Lincoln, 'Promise and the Failure', pp. 291-92; Petersen, *Literary Criticism*, p. 78; *idem*, 'When is the End not the End?', pp. 154-56.

2. Kingsbury, *Christology*, pp. 135-36; *idem*, *Conflict in Mark*, p. 113; Lincoln, 'Promise and the Failure', pp. 291-93. Within Mark's narrative, the predictions of Jesus are certain, so that the reader assumes the fulfillment of Jesus' predictions concerning a future meeting with the disciples and concerning a future ministry for the disciples. The certainty of these predictions creates difficulties for literary approaches to Mark's ending in which the disobedience of the women actually or potentially destroys any hope for the disciples. Kelber (*Story of Jesus*, pp. 83-87) argues that the silence of the women is disastrous for the disciples. For Kelber, a meeting with Jesus in Galilee after the resurrection is the last hope remaining for the disciples. Yet because of the fearful silence of the women, the message concerning the meeting in Galilee is never delivered to the disciples, and the fate of the disciples is sealed forever. They never return to Galilee to become part of the kingdom community. Thus, the ending of the Gospel finalizes Mark's polemic against the disciples. In contrast to Kelber's position, I would argue that the promise of Jesus holds true, so that the silence of the women does not destroy all hope for the disciples. To some extent, the certainty of Jesus' promise also creates difficulty for the view of Tannehill ('Disciples in Mark', pp. 403-404; *idem*, 'Narrative Christology', pp. 81-84). According to Tannehill, the future restoration of the disciples is left ambiguous because of the silence of the women. The predicted meeting in 16.7 holds open the possibility that the disciples may be reinstated as followers of Jesus, but Mark never directly tells the reader that the disciples have changed their ways and become true followers. For Tannehill, the failure of the women in 16.8 gives an ambiguous quality to the ending of the Gospel, since the women may never have informed the disciples of the possibility of a new beginning. Both positive and negative possibilities are suggested at the end of the Gospel, and this open ending leaves the readers with decisions to make concerning their own failure and restoration. For a similar description of the ending of Mark's Gospel see Powell, 'Narrative-Critical Understanding', pp. 344-45; Rhoads and Michie, *Mark as Story*, pp. 96-100, 129. Fowler (*Let the Reader Understand*, pp. 219, 258-59) also emphasizes the opacity and open-ended nature of the final episode in Mark's Gospel. I would argue that

16.7 is fulfilled, but the reader is given every reason to believe that it will be fulfilled.[1]

The failure of the women does not negate the promise to the disciples, but neither does the promise to the disciples negate the failure of the women.[2] The significance of the women's role in Mark's ending should not be neglected, because Mark has encouraged the reader to identify with the women through his initially positive characterization of them.[3] In addition, he has prepared for this sympathetic response to the women by encouraging the reader's identification with a series of similar minor characters who have lived up to the expectations of Jesus. By the end of Mark's Gospel, the reader is not simply interested in the fate of the disciples, but is also attentive to the response of the women. The women at the tomb respond with failure, since they disobey the young man's command to deliver a message to the disciples and to Peter concerning a meeting with the risen Jesus in Galilee. Since the disobedience of the women is tied to the specific details of the narrative, their disobedience does not serve as a

since Jesus' predictions hold true, the situation of the disciples is not completely open-ended. Instead, the reader is left with hope for the disciples. In addition, it would be difficult to imagine a first-century audience for whom the restoration of the disciples following the resurrection would be merely a possibility to be considered.

1. Lincoln, 'Promise and the Failure', p. 292.

2. Lincoln, 'Promise and the Failure', pp. 292-96. Petersen (*Literary Criticism*, pp. 77-78; *idem*, 'Reader in the Gospel', p. 49; *idem*, 'When is the End not the End?') argues for the certainty of the meeting in Galilee as promised in 16.7, but in the process he diminishes the failure of the women in 16.8. Petersen notes the difficulty of Mark's juxtaposition of 16.7 and 16.8. Mark creates the expectation of a meeting between the disciples and Jesus in 16.7 and then cancels this expectation with the silence of the women in 16.8. Since Jesus has also predicted a meeting in Galilee with the disciples, the reader is led to expect that the prediction in 16.7 will be fulfilled. For Petersen, the fulfillment of the promise in 16.7 means that Mark does not mean what he says in 16.8. The reader should not take the silence of the women literally but should recognize that it is intended to be ironic. After reflecting on this irony, the reader should supply the proper closure to the narrative by imagining the meeting between Jesus and his disciples in Galilee. In following Petersen's approach, Kingsbury (*Christology*, pp. 135-37; *idem*, *Conflict in Mark*, pp. 112-15) also tends to diminish the significance of the women's failure in 16.8, choosing instead to concentrate on the fulfillment of the young man's prediction in 16.7 and on the purpose for the meeting in Galilee.

3. On the identification of the reader with the women at the tomb see Boomershine, 'Apostolic Commission', pp. 231-33.

challenge for the reader to fulfill the task left undone by the women. The reader is not in a position to pick up where the women failed and so report the message to the disciples and to Peter.[1] Nevertheless, the failure of the women carries a significant warning for the reader, because this failure takes place after the resurrection.[2] Thus, the women's failure informs the reader that disobedience and fear are not simply part of the disciples' condition before the resurrection. The time between the resurrection and the parousia, that is, the time of the reader, is also a period of potential failure and fear.

In 16.7-8 Mark juxtaposes promise and failure. The prediction of 16.7 implies a promise that a restoration to discipleship is possible in spite of failure, the failure of the disciples and even the failure of the women. Consequently, Mark's ending serves as an encouragement to the reader. Yet Mark's ending is not only an offer of hope, but is also a warning. Mark moves the reader to identify with the women at the tomb, and then he creates a distance between the reader and the women because of their disobedience. In moving away from an identification with the women, the reader must acknowledge that

1. Because the disobedience of the women is tied to the specific details of the narrative, their failure cannot simply be treated as an attempt at reverse psychology by the narrator. In some literary approaches, the failure of the women to go and tell becomes a general appeal to the reader to go and tell others about the resurrection. According to Boomershine ('Apostolic Commission', pp. 213-23), Mark concludes his Gospel with a commission to announce the resurrection followed by the silence and fear of the women. The effect of the ending is first to shock the reader into the realization that silence is wrong and secondly to appeal to the reader to participate in the proclamation of the resurrection regardless of fear. Thus, Mark ends his Gospel with the same theme as the other Gospel writers, the apostolic commission to proclaim the gospel, but he does so through his description of the failure of the women. Tolbert (*Sowing*, pp. 288-99) points out that the reader is encouraged to anticipate the obedience of the women at the tomb. Nevertheless, the women like the disciples prove to be faithless, because they refuse to obey the command to go out and sow the word. Since the women will not go and tell, then the task is left up to the reader. Only the reader has faithfully followed Jesus to the very end, and now it becomes the reader's task to go and tell. Mark has used the narrative to form the reader into the perfect disciple. Rhoads and Michie follow a similar approach to that of Tolbert in *Mark as Story*, pp. 61-62, 140, 159. This literary approach to Mark's ending does not work, however, because technically the women are not told to announce openly the gospel or the resurrection, but to report to the disciples a coming post-resurrection meeting.

2. Lincoln, 'Promise and the Failure', pp. 297-98.

failure, fear and disobedience are all still possible in the period between the resurrection and the parousia.

The Response of the Reader

In the central section of the Gospel (8.22–10.52) Mark presents minor characters in negative terms only to end the section with a positive portrait of a minor character. The reader is moved to dissociate from the father of the possessed boy and the rich man, but then to identify with Bartimaeus. In the final sections of the Gospel (11.1–16.8) the situation is reversed, since Mark presents minor characters in positive terms only to conclude his Gospel with a negative portrait of these characters. Mark encourages the reader to identify with a series of individuals, but then creates a distance between the reader and the women at the end of the Gospel.

Mark's positive portrait of Bartimaeus is not an end in itself, but instead it initiates a series of passages in which minor characters live up to the expectations of Jesus. Thus, the reader is encouraged to identify with a line of exemplary individuals that begins with Bartimaeus and continues until the women at the tomb. Within chs. 11–13 the wise scribe and the poor widow are commended by Jesus. Mark enhances the exemplary traits of these two individuals by setting them in contrast to the rich man. The wise scribe shows insight into the commandments and stands open to the kingdom of God, while the rich man possesses a shallow understanding of the commandments and refuses to enter into the kingdom. Unlike the rich man, the poor widow gives all that she owns. The wise scribe and the poor widow are also clearly different from the religious leaders. They acknowledge and reflect the values of Jesus at the same time that the religious leaders oppose Jesus and challenge his teaching. This contrast with the rich man and the religious establishment further encourages the reader's identification with these minor characters.

In the passion narrative (14.1–16.8) Mark presents several exemplary individuals as foils for the disciples, who have abandoned their responsibility to follow Jesus. Simon of Cyrene takes up the cross of Jesus. The centurion makes the confession that the disciples were never able to make, when he acknowledges the divine sonship of the crucified Jesus. Joseph of Arimathea cares for the burial of Jesus, which is a duty for disciples. Even before his death, the woman at

Bethany anoints Jesus' body for burial, while Mary Magdalene, Mary the mother of James and Salome seek to anoint the body of Jesus after his death. Thus, while the disciples fail, these minor characters continue to live up to the expectations of Jesus, and consequently the reader is encouraged to identify with them. All in all, Mark gives to the reader a series of unlikely heroes: a blind beggar, a scribe, a poor widow, a woman in the house of a leper, a passerby, a soldier, a member of the Sanhedrin and a group of women. Yet in this way, Mark's narrative confirms the teaching of Jesus that many who are first will be last and the last will be first (10.31).

Mark is particularly careful to encourage the reader to identify with the women followers.[1] He describes the women in positive terms in the crucifixion scene and the burial scene. Mark's initial portrayal of the women at the tomb on the first day of the week is also positive, but then at the very end of the Gospel he turns and presents the women as fearful and disobedient. Mark's final picture of the women at the tomb is thoroughly negative, and this negative characterization forces the reader to dissociate from the women. In the end, Mark designs the reader's relationship with the individuals from the crowd along the same lines as the previous relationship with the disciples: he encourages identification through a positive characterization followed by dissociation through a negative portrayal.

In Mk 8.34 Jesus calls together his disciples and also the crowd in order to instruct them about the demands of discipleship. Thus, following Jesus is not simply for the disciples, but it is also now open to others. Yet Jesus' words go out to a broader audience still, because they are directed at anyone who desires to follow him, and that 'anyone' includes the reader. Thus, the demands of discipleship reach beyond the disciples and beyond the members of the crowd out to the reader. However, along with the demands of following Jesus comes the potential for failure. The disciples are the first to be called to follow Jesus, but they abandon their call. In the face of possible suffering and sacrifice, they either run away or deny any relationship with Jesus. Jesus opens up his invitation to others, and some minor characters come to follow Jesus and begin to fulfill his demands. Yet the women at the tomb also fail by responding with fear and disobedience. This failure of the women moves the narrative and the potential for failure out toward the reader. Failure to follow Jesus and

---

1.   Boomershine, 'Apostolic Commission', pp. 231-33.

his demands is not simply a condition of the disciples before the resurrection. Fear, flight and disobedience are all potential hazards for followers of Jesus during the time between the resurrection and the parousia, that is, during the reader's own time. Once again, then, Mark's narrative moves beyond the disciples and beyond minor characters out to the reader.

For the reader, Mark's narrative is both a call and a caution. The call to follow Jesus is open to the reader, but it involves self-denial, sacrifice and a willingness to serve humbly. Through the failure of the disciples and then the failure of minor characters, Mark warns the reader that the demands that Jesus places upon his followers are difficult. Fear and disobedience are potential problems for any who choose to follow Jesus, including the reader. Mark's narrative, including his presentation of minor characters, carries a twofold message: 'anyone can be a follower, no one finds it easy'.[1]

Conclusion

In discussing past research on the subject of discipleship in the Gospel of Mark, Elizabeth Struthers Malbon states:

> Discipleship—that is, following Jesus—has been recognized as a central theme or motif in the Gospel of Mark. Understandably enough, the portrayal of the disciples in Mark has often been the focus of scholarly investigation of the theme of discipleship.[2]

Malbon points out that past scholarly investigations have been inadequate, because 'what Mark has to say about discipleship is understood in reference not only to the disciples but also to other Markan characters who meet the demands of following Jesus'.[3] If Mark's view of discipleship means his presentation of the proper response to Jesus and to his demands, then he does indeed use other means to communicate his understanding of discipleship beyond his depiction of the disciples. Mark's portrayal of the disciples may be the logical place to start an investigation of discipleship in Mark's Gospel, but it would be an improper place to end such a study. Mark's narrative includes certain minor characters who live up to the demands and ideals of Jesus, and

---

1.   Malbon, 'Fallible Followers', p. 46.
2.   Malbon, 'Fallible Followers', p. 29.
3.   Malbon, 'Fallible Followers', p. 30.

thus who serve to instruct the reader further in the proper response to Jesus. Simply put, Mark's narrative presents, in addition to the disciples, other followers of Jesus.

BIBLIOGRAPHY

Abrams, M.H., 'How to Do Things with Texts', *Partisan Review* 46 (1979), pp. 565-88.

Achtemeier, P.J., '"And He Followed Him": Miracles and Discipleship in Mark 10:46-52', *Semeia* 11 (1978), pp. 115-45.

Aland, K., 'Der Schluss des Markusevangeliums', in M. Sabbe (ed.), *L'Evangile selon Marc: Tradition et rédaction* (Leuven: Leuven University Press, 2nd edn, 1988), pp. 435-70, 573-75.

Alter, R., *The Art of Biblical Narrative* (New York: Basic Books, 1981).

—'A Literary Approach to the Bible', *Commentary* 60 (December 1975), pp. 70-77.

Anderson, H., *The Gospel of Mark* (NCB; London: Oliphants, 1976).

Anderson, J.C., 'Double and Triple Stories, the Implied Reader, and Redundancy in Matthew', *Semeia* 31 (1985), pp. 71-89.

—'Matthew: Gender and Reading', *Semeia* 28 (1983), pp. 3-27.

—'Matthew: Sermon and Story', in D.J. Lull (ed.), *Society of Biblical Literature Seminar Papers 1988* (Atlanta: Scholars Press, 1988), pp. 496-507.

Anderson, J.C., and S.D. Moore (eds.), *Mark and Method: New Approaches in Biblical Studies* (Minneapolis: Fortress Press, 1992).

Bachmann, H., and W.A. Slaby (eds.), *Concordance to the Novum Testamentum Graece* (Berlin: de Gruyter, 3rd edn, 1987).

Bagwell, J.T., 'Who's Afraid of Stanley Fish', *Poetics Today* 4 (1983), pp. 127-33.

Bar-Efrat, S., *Narrative Art in the Bible* (JSOTSup, 70; Sheffield: Almond Press, 1989).

Barton, S.C., 'Mark as Narrative: The Story of the Anointing Woman (Mk 14.3-9)', *ExpTim* 102 (1991), pp. 230-34.

Bassler, J.M., 'Mixed Signals: Nicodemus in the Fourth Gospel', *JBL* 108 (1989), pp. 635-46.

—'The Parable of the Loaves', *JR* 66 (1986), pp. 157-72.

Bauer, D.R., 'The Major Characters of Matthew's Story', *Int* 46 (1992), pp. 357-67.

—*The Structure of Matthew's Gospel: A Study in Literary Design* (JSNTSup, 31; Sheffield: Almond Press, 1988).

Beasley-Murray, G.R., *Jesus and the Kingdom of God* (Grand Rapids: Eerdmans, 1986).

Beavis, M.A., *Mark's Audience: The Literary and Social Setting of Mark 4.11-12* (JSNTSup, 33; Sheffield: JSOT Press, 1989).

—'The Trial before the Sanhedrin (Mark 14:53-65): Reader Response and Greco-Roman Readers', *CBQ* 49 (1987), pp. 581-96.

—'Women as Models of Faith in Mark', *BTB* 18 (1988), pp. 3-9.

Berlin, A., *Poetics and Interpretation of Biblical Narrative* (Bible and Literature Series, 9; Sheffield: Almond Press, 1983).

Best, E., 'Discipleship in Mark: Mark 8.22-10.52', *SJT* 23 (1970), pp. 323-37.

—*Following Jesus: Discipleship in the Gospel of Mark* (JSNTSup, 4; Sheffield: JSOT Press, 1981).

—*Mark: The Gospel as Story* (Edinburgh: T. & T. Clark, 1983).

—'The Role of the Disciples in Mark', *NTS* 23 (1977), pp. 377-401.

Betz, H.D., 'The Early Christian Miracle Story: Some Observations on the Form Critical Problem', *Semeia* 11 (1978), pp. 69-81.

Birdsall, J.N., review of *The Last Twelve Verses of Mark*, by W.R. Farmer, *JTS* 26 (1975), pp. 151-60.

Black, C.C., 'Depth of Characterization and Degree of Faith in Matthew', in D.J. Lull (ed.), *Society of Biblical Literature Seminar Papers 1989* (Atlanta: Scholars Press, 1989), pp. 604-23.

—*The Disciples according to Mark: Markan Redaction in Current Debate* (JSNTSup, 27; Sheffield: JSOT Press, 1989).

—'The Quest of Mark the Redactor: Why has it been Pursued, and what has it Taught Us?', *JSNT* 33 (1988), pp. 19-39.

Blomberg, C.L., 'Synoptic Studies: Some Recent Methodological Developments and Debates', *Themelios* 12 (1987), pp. 38-46.

Boomershine, T.E., 'Mark 16:8 and the Apostolic Commission', *JBL* 100 (1981), pp. 225-39.

Boomershine, T.E., and G.L. Bartholomew, 'The Narrative Technique of Mark 16:8', *JBL* 100 (1981), pp. 213-23.

Booth, W.C., 'A New Strategy for Establishing a Truly Democratic Criticism', *Daedalus* 112 (1983), pp. 175-92.

—*The Rhetoric of Fiction* (Chicago: University of Chicago Press, 2nd edn, 1983).

Boring, M.E., 'Mark 1:1-15 and the Beginning of the Gospel', *Semeia* 52 (1990), pp. 43-81.

Botha, J.E., 'Reader "Entrapment" as Literary Device in John 4:1-42', *Neot* 24 (1990), pp. 37-47.

Brawley, R.L., *Centering on God: Method and Message in Luke–Acts* (Literary Currents in Biblical Interpretation; Louisville, KY: Westminster Press/John Knox, 1990).

—'Paul in Acts: Aspects of Structure and Characterization', in D.J. Lull (ed.), *Society of Biblical Literature Seminar Papers 1988* (Atlanta: Scholars Press, 1988), pp. 90-105.

Broadhead, E.K., 'Mk 1,44: The Witness of the Leper', *ZNW* 83 (1992), pp. 257-65.

Brooks, J.A., *Mark* (New American Commentary; Nashville: Broadman, 1991).

Brown, R.E., 'The Burial of Jesus (Mark 15:42-47)', *CBQ* 50 (1988), pp. 233-45.

Brown, S., 'Reader Response: Demythologizing the Text', *NTS* 34 (1988), pp. 232-37.

Bultmann, R., *Die Geschichte der synoptischen Tradition* (FRLANT, 29; Göttingen: Vandenhoeck & Ruprecht, 3rd edn, 1957).

Burger, C., *Jesus als Davidssohn: Eine traditionsgeschichtliche Untersuchung* (FRLANT, 98; Göttingen: Vandenhoeck & Ruprecht, 1970).

Burnett, F.W., 'Characterization in Matthew: Reader Construction of the Disciple Peter' (paper presented at the Society of Biblical Literature Literary Aspects of the Gospels and Acts Group, 1985).

—'Characterization in Matthew: Reader Construction of the Disciple Peter', *McKendree Pastoral Review* 4 (1987), pp. 13-43.

—'Prolegomenon to Reading Matthew's Eschatological Discourse: Redundancy and the Education of the Reader in Matthew', *Semeia* 31 (1985), pp. 91-109.

Burton, E.d.W., *Syntax of the Moods and Tenses in New Testament Greek* (Chicago: University of Chicago Press, 3rd edn, 1898).

Busemann, R., *Die Jüngergemeinde nach Markus 10: Eine redaktionsgeschichtliche Untersuchung des 10. Kapitels im Markusevangelium* (BBB, 57; Königstein: Peter Hanstein, 1983).

Carter, W., 'The Crowds in Matthew's Gospel', *CBQ* 55 (1993), pp. 54-67.

Catchpole, D., 'The Fearful Silence of the Women at the Tomb', *Journal of Theology for Southern Africa* 18 (1977), pp. 3-10.

Chatman, S., *Coming to Terms: The Rhetoric of Narrative in Fiction and Film* (Ithaca, NY: Cornell University Press, 1990).

—'On the Formalist-Structuralist Theory of Character', *Journal of Literary Semantics* 1 (1972), pp. 57-79.

—*Story and Discourse: Narrative Structure in Fiction and Film* (Ithaca, NY: Cornell University Press, 1978).

Colwell, E.C., 'A Definite Rule for the Use of the Article in the Greek New Testament', *JBL* 52 (1933), pp. 12-21.

Cranfield, C.E.B., *The Gospel according to Saint Mark* (CGTC; Cambridge: Cambridge University Press, 4th edn, 1972).

Crossan, J.D., 'Mark and the Relatives of Jesus', *NovT* 15 (1973), pp. 81-113.

Culler, J., *On Deconstruction: Theory and Criticism after Structuralism* (Ithaca, NY: Cornell University Press, 1982).

—*Structuralist Poetics: Structuralism, Linguistics, and the Study of Literature* (Ithaca, NY: Cornell University Press, 1975).

Culpepper, R.A., *Anatomy of the Fourth Gospel: A Study in Literary Design* (FFNT; Philadelphia: Fortress Press, 1983).

—'Mark 10:50: Why Mention the Garment?', *JBL* 101 (1982), pp. 131-32.

Darr, J.A., *On Character Building: The Reader and the Rhetoric of Characterization in Luke–Acts* (Literary Currents in Biblical Interpretation; Louisville, KY: Westminster Press/John Knox, 1992).

Davis, P.G., 'Mark's Christological Paradox', *JSNT* 35 (1989), pp. 3-18.

Dewey, J., 'The Literary Structure of the Controversy Stories in Mark 2:1-3:6', *JBL* 92 (1973), pp. 394-401.

—*Markan Public Debate: Literary Technique, Concentric Structure, and Theology in Mark 2:1-3:6* (SBLDS, 48; Chico, CA: Scholars Press, 1980).

—'Point of View and the Disciples in Mark', in K.H. Richards (ed.), *Society of Biblical Literature Seminar Papers 1982* (Chico, CA: Scholars Press, 1982), pp. 97-106.

Dibelius, M., *Die Formgeschichte des Evangeliums* (Tübingen: Mohr [Paul Siebeck], 6th edn, 1971).

Dodd, C.H., *The Parables of the Kingdom* (London: Nisbet, 3rd edn, 1936).

Donahue, J.R., *Are You the Christ? The Trial Narrative in the Gospel of Mark* (SBLDS, 10; Missoula, MT: Society of Biblical Literature, 1973).

—*The Theology and Setting of Discipleship in the Gospel of Mark* (Milwaukee: Marquette University, 1983).

Droge, A.J., 'Call Stories in Greek Biography and the Gospels', in K.H. Richards (ed.), *Society of Biblical Literature Seminar Papers 1983* (Chico, CA: Scholars Press, 1983), pp. 245-257.

Dunn, J.D.G., 'The Messianic Secret in Mark', *TynBul* 21 (1970), pp. 92-117.

Dupont, J., 'L'aveugle de Jéricho recouvre la vue et suit Jésus (Marc 10,46-52)', *Revue Africaine de Théologie* 8 (1984), pp. 165-81.

Edwards, J.R., 'Markan Sandwiches: The Significance of Interpolations in Markan Narratives', *NovT* 31 (1989), pp. 193-216.

Edwards, R.A., 'Characterization of the Disciples as a Feature of Matthew's Narrative', in F. Van Segbroeck, C.M. Tuckett, G. Van Pelle and J. Verheyden (eds.), *The Four Gospels 1992* (Leuven: Leuven University Press, 1992), II, pp. 1305-23.

—*Matthew's Story of Jesus* (Philadelphia: Fortress Press, 1985).

—'Narrative Implications of Gar in Matthew', *CBQ* 52 (1990), pp. 636-55.

—'Reading Matthew: The Gospel as Narrative', *Listening* 24 (1989), pp. 251-61.

—'Uncertain Faith: Matthew's Portrait of the Disciples', in F. Segovia (ed.), *Discipleship in the New Testament* (Philadelphia: Fortress Press, 1985), pp. 47-61.

Elliott, J.K., 'The Text and Language of the Ending to Mark's Gospel', *TZ* 27 (1971), pp. 255-62.

Erlich, V., *Russian Formalism: History-Doctrine* (The Hague: Mouton, 3rd edn, 1969).

Farmer, W.R., *The Last Twelve Verses of Mark* (SNTSMS, 25; London: Cambridge University Press, 1974).

Fay, G., 'Introduction to Incomprehension: The Literary Structure of Mark 4:1-34', *CBQ* 51 (1989), pp. 65-81.

Fish, S., *Doing What Comes Naturally: Change, Rhetoric, and the Practice of Theory in Literary and Legal Studies* (Durham, NC: Duke University Press, 1989).

—*Is there a Text in this Class? The Authority of Interpretive Communities* (Cambridge, MA: Harvard University Press, 1980).

—*Self-Consuming Artifacts: The Experience of Seventeenth-Century Literature* (Berkeley: University of California Press, 1972).

—*Surprised by Sin: The Reader in Paradise Lost* (New York: St Martin's Press, 1967).

—'Why No One's Afraid of Wolfgang Iser', *Diacritics* 11 (Spring 1981), pp. 2-13.

Fisher, K.M., and U.C. von Wahlde, 'The Miracles of Mark 4:35-5:43: Their Meaning and Function in the Gospel Framework', *BTB* 11 (1981), pp. 13-16.

Focant, C., 'L'Incompréhension des disciples dans le Deuxième Evangile', *RB* 82 (1975), pp. 161-85.

Forster, E.M., *Aspects of the Novel* (New York: Harcourt Brace, 1927).

Fowl, S.E., 'Who's Characterizing Whom and the Difference this Makes: Locating and Centering Paul', in E.H. Lovering (ed.), *Society of Biblical Literature Seminar Papers 1993* (Atlanta: Scholars Press, 1993), pp. 537-53.

Fowler, R.M., *Let the Reader Understand: Reader-Response Criticism and the Gospel of Mark* (Minneapolis: Fortress Press, 1991).

—*Loaves and Fishes: The Function of the Feeding Stories in the Gospel of Mark* (SBLDS, 54; Chico, CA: Scholars Press, 1981).

—'Reader-Response Criticism: Figuring Mark's Reader', in J.C. Anderson and S.D. Moore (eds.), *Mark and Method: New Approaches in Biblical Studies* (Minneapolis: Fortress Press, 1992), pp. 50-83.

—'Reading Matthew Reading Mark: Observing the First Steps Toward Meaning-as-Reference in the Synoptic Gospels', in K.H. Richards (ed.), *Society of Biblical Literature Seminar Papers 1986* (Atlanta: Scholars Press, 1986), pp. 1-16.

—'The Rhetoric of Direction and Indirection in the Gospel of Mark', *Semeia* 48 (1989), pp. 115-34.

—'Thoughts on the History of Reading Mark's Gospel', *Proceedings of the Eastern Great Lakes Biblical Society and Midwest Society of Biblical Literature* 4 (1984), pp. 120-30.

—'Who is "the Reader" in Reader-Response Criticism?', *Semeia* 31 (1985), pp. 5-23.

Frei, H.W., *The Eclipse of Biblical Narrative: A Study of Eighteenth and Nineteenth Century Hermeneutics* (New Haven: Yale University Press, 1974).

—*The Identity of Jesus Christ: The Hermeneutical Bases of Dogmatic Theology* (Philadelphia: Fortress Press, 1975).

—'The "Literal Reading" of Biblical Narrative in the Christian Tradition: Does it Stretch or Will it Break?', in F. McConnell (ed.), *The Bible and the Narrative Tradition* (New York: Oxford University Press, 1986), 36-77.

Freund, E., *The Return of the Reader: Reader-Response Criticism* (London: Methuen, 1987).

Garvey, J., 'Characterization in Narrative', *Poetics* 7 (1978), pp. 63-78.

Genette, G., 'L'autre du même', *Corps Ecrit* 15 (1985), pp. 11-16.

—*Figures III* (Paris: Seuil, 1972).

Gibson, W., 'Authors, Speakers, Readers, and Mock Readers', *College English* 11 (1950), pp. 265-69.

Gnilka, J., *Das Evangelium nach Markus* (EKKNT; 2 vols.; Zürich: Benzinger Verlag; Neukirchen–Vluyn: Neukirchener Verlag, 1978–79).

Gould, E.P., *A Critical and Exegetical Commentary on the Gospel according to Saint*

Mark (ICC; New York: Charles Scribner's Sons, 1896).

Gowler, D.B., 'Characterization in Luke: A Socio-Narratological Approach', *BTB* 19 (1989), pp. 54-62.

—*Host, Guest, Enemy, and Friend: Portraits of the Pharisees in Luke and Acts* (Emory Studies in Early Christianity; New York: Peter Lang, 1991).

Grundmann, W., *Das Evangelium nach Markus* (THKNT; Berlin: Evangelische Verlagsanstalt, 9th edn, 1984).

Guelich, R.A., 'The Beginning of the Gospel: Mark 1:1-15', *BR* 27 (1982), pp. 5-15.

—*Mark 1-8:26* (WBC; Dallas: Word Books, 1989).

Gundry, R.H., *Mark: A Commentary on his Apology for the Cross* (Grand Rapids: Eerdmans, 1993).

Haenchen, E., *Der Weg Jesu: Eine Erklärung des Markus-Evangeliums und der kanonischen Parallelen* (Berlin: de Gruyter, 2nd edn, 1968).

Hahn, F., *Christologische Hoheitstitel: Ihre Geschichte im frühen Christentum* (FRLANT, 83; Göttingen: Vandenhoeck & Ruprecht, 1963).

Hawkin, D.J., 'The Incomprehension of the Disciples in the Marcan Redaction', *JBL* 91 (1972), pp. 491-500.

—'The Symbolism and Structure of the Marcan Redaction', *EvQ* 49 (1977), pp. 98-110.

Heil, J.P., *The Death and Resurrection of Jesus: A Narrative-Critical Reading of Matthew 26-28* (Minneapolis: Fortress Press, 1991).

—*The Gospel of Mark as a Model for Action: A Reader-Response Commentary* (New York: Paulist Press, 1992).

—'The Narrative Roles of the Women in Matthew's Genealogy', *Bib* 72 (1991), pp. 538-45.

—'Reader-Response and the Irony of Jesus before the Sanhedrin in Luke 22:66-71', *CBQ* 51 (1989), pp. 271-84.

Hochman, B., *Character in Literature* (Ithaca, NY: Cornell University Press, 1985).

Holub, R.C., *Reception Theory: A Critical Introduction* (London: Methuen, 1984).

Hooker, M.D., *The Gospel according to Saint Mark* (BNTC; Peabody, MA: Hendrickson, 1991).

Horst, P.W. van der, 'Can a Book End with ΓΑΡ? A Note on Mark XVI.8', *JTS* 23 (1972), pp. 121-24.

Howell, D.B., *Matthew's Inclusive Story: A Study in the Narrative Rhetoric of the First Gospel* (JSNTSup, 42; Sheffield: JSOT Press, 1990).

Hurtado, L.W., *Mark* (Good News Commentary; San Francisco: Harper & Row, 1983).

Iser, W., *The Act of Reading: A Theory of Aesthetic Response* (Baltimore: Johns Hopkins University Press, 1978).

—*The Implied Reader: Patterns of Communication in Prose Fiction from Bunyan to Beckett* (Baltimore: Johns Hopkins University Press, 1974).

—'Indeterminacy and the Reader's Response in Prose Fiction', in J. Hillis Miller (ed.), *Aspects of Narrative* (New York: Columbia University Press, 1971), pp. 1-45.

—'The Indeterminacy of the Text: A Critical Reply', *Comparative Criticism: A Yearbook* 2 (1980), pp. 27-47.

—'Interaction between Text and Reader', in S.R. Suleiman and I. Crosman (eds.), *The Reader in the Text* (Princeton: Princeton University Press, 1980), pp. 106-19.

—'Talk Like Whales: A Reply to Stanley Fish', *Diacritics* 11 (Fall 1981), pp. 82-87.

Johnson, E.S., 'Mark VIII. 22-26: The Blind Man from Bethsaida', *NTS* 25 (1979), pp. 370-83.

—'Mark 10:46-52: Blind Bartimaeus', *CBQ* 40 (1978), pp. 191-204.

Kawin, B.F., *Telling it Again and Again: Repetition in Literature and Film* (Ithaca, NY: Cornell University Press, 1972).

Keck, L.E., 'The Introduction to Mark's Gospel', *NTS* 12 (1966), pp. 352-70.

Kelber, W.H., *The Kingdom in Mark: A New Place and a New Time* (Philadelphia: Fortress Press, 1974).

—*Mark's Story of Jesus* (Philadelphia: Fortress Press, 1979).

Kertelge, K., *Die Wunder Jesu im Markusevangelium: Eine redaktionsgeschichtliche Untersuchung* (SANT, 23; Munich: Kösel, 1970).

Kingsbury, J.D., *The Christology of Mark's Gospel* (Philadelphia: Fortress Press, 1983).

—*Conflict in Luke: Jesus, Authorities, Disciples* (Minneapolis: Fortress Press, 1991).

—*Conflict in Mark: Jesus, Authorities, Disciples* (Minneapolis: Fortress Press, 1989).

—'The Gospel of Mark in Current Research', *RelSRev* 5 (1979), pp. 101-107.

—*Matthew as Story* (Philadelphia: Fortress Press, 2nd edn, 1988).

—'Reflections on "the Reader" of Matthew's Gospel', *NTS* 34 (1988), pp. 442-60.

—'The Religious Authorities in the Gospel of Mark', *NTS* 36 (1990), pp. 42-65.

Kirchschläger, W., 'Bartimäus—Paradigma einer Wundererzählung (Mk 10,46-52 par)', in F. Van Segbroeck, C.M. Tuckett, G. Van Pelle and J. Verheyden (eds.), *The Four Gospels 1992* (Leuven: Leuven University Press, 1992), II, pp. 1105-23.

Klauck, H.-J., 'Die erzählerische Rolle der Jünger im Markusevangelium: Eine narrative Analyse', *NovT* 24 (1982), pp. 1-26.

Knox, W.L., 'The Ending of St. Mark's Gospel', *HTR* 35 (1942), pp. 13-23.

Koch, D.-A., *Die Bedeutung der Wundererzählungen für die Christologie des Markusevangeliums* (BZNW, supp. 42; Berlin: de Gruyter, 1975).

Kümmel, W.G., *Introduction to the New Testament* (trans. H.C. Kee; Nashville: Abingdon Press, 1975).

—*Verheissung und Erfüllung: Untersuchungen zur eschatologischen Verkündigung Jesu* (Zürich: Zwingli-Verlag, 3rd edn, 1956).

Kurz, W.S., 'The Beloved Disciple and Implied Readers', *BTB* 19 (1989), pp. 100-107.

—'Narrative Approaches to Luke–Acts', *Bib* 68 (1987), pp. 195-220.

—'Narrative Models for Imitation in Luke–Acts', in D.L. Balch, E. Ferguson and W.A. Meeks (eds.), *Greeks, Romans, and Christians* (Minneapolis: Fortress Press, 1990), pp. 171-89.

—*Reading Luke–Acts: Dynamics of Biblical Narrative* (Louisville, KY: Westminster Press/John Knox, 1993).

Lagrange, M.-J., *Evangile selon Saint Marc* (EBib; Paris: Librairie Lecoffre, 8th edn, 1947).

Lane, W.L., *The Gospel according to Mark* (NICNT; Grand Rapids: Eerdmans, 1974).

—'The Gospel of Mark in Current Study', *Southwestern Journal of Theology* 21 (1978), pp. 7-21.

Lang, F.G., 'Kompositionsanalyse des Markusevangeliums', *ZTK* 74 (1977), pp. 1-24.

—'Sola Gratia im Markusevangelium: Die Soteriologie des Markus nach 9,14-29 und 10,17-31', in J. Friedrich, W. Pöhlmann and P. Stuhlmacher (eds.), *Rechtfertigung* (Tübingen: Mohr [Paul Siebeck], 1976), pp. 321-37.

Lategan, B.C., 'Current Issues in the Hermeneutical Debate', *Neot* 18 (1984), pp. 1-17.

Lightfoot, R.H., *History and Interpretation in the Gospels* (New York: Harper & Brothers, 1934).

Lincoln, A.T., 'The Promise and the Failure: Mark 16:7, 8', *JBL* 108 (1989), pp. 283-300.

Lohmeyer, E., *Das Evangelium des Markus* (Kritisch-exegetischer Kommentar über das Neue Testament; Göttingen: Vandenhoeck & Ruprecht, 17th edn, 1967).

Lohse, E., 'ῥαββί, ῥαββουνί', *TDNT*, VI, pp. 961-65.

—'υἱὸς Δαυίδ', *TDNT*, VIII, pp. 478-88.

Longman, T., *Literary Approaches to Biblical Interpretation* (Foundations of Contemporary Interpretation, 3; Grand Rapids: Zondervan, 1987).

Lührmann, D., *Das Markusevangelium* (HNT; Tübingen: Mohr [Paul Siebeck], 1987).

Luz, U., 'Das Geheimnismotiv und die markinische Christologie', *ZNW* 56 (1965), pp. 9-30.

Magness, J.L., *Sense and Absence: Structure and Suspension in the Ending of Mark's Gospel* (SBLSS; Atlanta: Scholars Press, 1986).

Mailloux, S., 'Learning to Read: Interpretation and Reader-Response Criticism', *Studies in the Literary Imagination* 12 (Spring 1979), pp. 93-108.

—'Reader-Response Criticism?', *Genre* 10 (1977), pp. 413-31.

√ Malbon, E.S., 'Disciples/Crowds/Whoever: Markan Characters and Readers', *NovT* 28 (1986), pp. 104-30.

—'Echoes and Foreshadowings in Mark 4-8: Reading and Rereading', *JBL* 112 (1993), pp. 211-30.

√ —'Fallible Followers: Women and Men in the Gospel of Mark', *Semeia* 28 (1983), pp. 29-48.

—'The Jewish Leaders in the Gospel of Mark: A Literary Study of Marcan Characterization', *JBL* 108 (1989), pp. 259-81.

—'Narrative Criticism: How Does the Story Mean?', in J.C. Anderson and S.D. Moore (eds.), *Mark and Method: New Approaches in Biblical Studies* (Minneapolis: Fortress Press, 1992), pp. 23-49.

—*Narrative Space and Mythic Meaning in Mark* (San Francisco: Harper & Row, 1986).

—'The Poor Widow in Mark and her Poor Rich Readers', *CBQ* 53 (1991), pp. 589-604.

Mann, C.S., *Mark* (AB, 27; Garden City, NY: Doubleday, 1986).

Marcus, J., *The Mystery of the Kingdom of God* (SBLDS, 90; Atlanta: Scholars Press, 1986).

—*The Way of the Lord: Christological Exegesis of the Old Testament in the Gospel of Mark* (Louisville, KY: Westminster Press/John Knox, 1992).

Margolin, U., 'Characterization in Narrative: Some Theoretical Prolegomena', *Neophilologus* 67 (1983), pp. 1-14.

—'The Doer and the Deed: Action as a Basis for Characterization in Narrative', *Poetics Today* 7 (1986), pp. 205-25.

Marshall, C.D., *Faith as a Theme in Mark's Narrative* (SNTSMS, 64; Cambridge: Cambridge University Press, 1989).

Marxsen, W., *Der Evangelist Markus: Studien zur Redaktionsgeschichte des Evangeliums* (FRLANT, 67; Göttingen: Vandenhoeck & Ruprecht, 1956).

Matera, F.J., '"He Saved Others; He Cannot Save Himself": A Literary-Critical Perspective on the Markan Miracles', *Int* 47 (1993), pp. 15-26.

—'The Incomprehension of the Disciples and Peter's Confession (Mark 6,14-8,30)', *Bib* 70 (1989), pp. 153-72.

—*The Kingship of Jesus: Composition and Theology in Mark 15* (SBLDS, 66; Chico, CA: Scholars Press, 1982).

—'The Prologue as the Interpretive Key to Mark's Gospel', *JSNT* 34 (1988), pp. 3-28.

—*What are they Saying about Mark?* (New York: Paulist Press, 1987).

McKnight, E.V., *The Bible and the Reader: An Introduction to Literary Criticism* (Philadelphia: Fortress Press, 1985).

—*Postmodern Use of the Bible: The Emergence of Reader-Oriented Criticism* (Decatur, GA: Abingdon, 1988).

Metzger, B.M., *The Text of the New Testament: Its Transmission, Corruption, and Restoration* (New York: Oxford University Press, 2nd edn, 1968).

—*A Textual Commentary on the Greek New Testament* (Stuttgart: United Bible Societies, 1971).

Meye, R.P., *Jesus and the Twelve: Discipleship and Revelation in Mark's Gospel* (Grand Rapids: Eerdmans, 1968).

Minear, P.S., 'Audience Criticism and Markan Ecclesiology', in H. Baltensweiler and B. Reike (eds.), *Neues Testament und Geschichte: Historisches Geschehen und Deutung im Neuen Testament* (Zürich: Theologischer Verlag, 1972), pp. 79-89.

Miscall, P.D., *1 Samuel: A Literary Reading* (Bloomington: Indiana University Press, 1986).

—'The Jacob and Joseph Stories as Analogies', *JSOT* 6 (1978), pp. 28-40.

—*The Workings of Old Testament Narrative* (Philadelphia: Fortress Press, 1983).

Moore, S.D., 'Are the Gospels Unified Narratives?', in K.H. Richards (ed.), *Society of Biblical Literature Seminar Papers 1987* (Atlanta: Scholars Press, 1987), pp. 443-58.

—*Literary Criticism and the Gospels: The Theoretical Challenge* (New Haven: Yale University Press, 1989).

—'Narrative Commentaries on the Bible: Context, Roots, and Prospects', *Forum* 3 (1987), pp. 29-62.

—'Negative Hermeneutics, Insubstantial Texts: Stanley Fish and the Biblical Interpreter', *JAAR* 54 (1986), pp. 707-19.

—'Stories of Reading: Doing Gospel Criticism as/with a "Reader"', in D.J. Lull (ed.), *Society of Biblical Literature Seminar Papers 1988* (Atlanta: Scholars Press, 1988), pp. 141-59.

Moore, W.E., '"Outside" and "Inside": A Markan Motif', *ExpTim* 98 (1986), pp. 39-43.

Moule, C.F.D., *An Idiom Book of New Testament Greek* (Cambridge: Cambridge University Press, 2nd edn, 1971).

Moulton, J.H., W.F. Howard and N. Turner, *A Grammar of New Testament Greek* (4 vols.; Edinburgh: T. & T. Clark, 1906–76).

Munro, W., 'Women Disciples in Mark?', *CBQ* 44 (1982), pp. 225-41.

Nineham, D.E., *Saint Mark* (Pelican Gospel Commentaries; Baltimore: Penguin Books, 1963).

Paul, A., 'Guérison de Bartimée: Mc 10,46-52', *AsSeign* 61 (1972), pp. 44-52.

Perrin, N., 'The Christology of Mark: A Study in Methodology', *JR* 51 (1971), pp. 173-87.

—*The New Testament: An Introduction* (New York: Harcourt Brace Jovanovich, 1974).

—'Towards an Interpretation of the Gospel of Mark', in H.D. Betz (ed.), *Christology and a Modern Pilgrimage: A Discussion with Norman Perrin* (Missoula, MT: Scholars Press, 1974), pp. 1-78.

—*What is Redaction Criticism?* (Guides to Biblical Scholarship; Philadelphia: Fortress Press, 1969).

Perry, M., 'Literary Dynamics: How the Order of a Text Creates its Meanings', *Poetics Today* 1 (Autumn 1979), pp. 35-64, 311-61.

Pesch, R., *Das Markusevangelium I. Teil* (HTKNT; Freiburg: Herder, 4th edn, 1984).

—*Das Markusevangelium II. Teil* (HTKNT; Freiburg: Herder, 3rd edn, 1984).

—*Naherwartungen: Tradition und Redaktion in Mk 13* (Düsseldorf: Patmos, 1968).

Petersen, N.R., 'The Composition of Mark 4:1-8:26', *HTR* 73 (1980), pp. 185-217.

—*Literary Criticism for New Testament Critics* (Guides to Biblical Scholarship; Philadelphia: Fortress Press, 1978).

—'"Point of View" in Mark's Narrative', *Semeia* 12 (1978), pp. 97-121.

—'The Reader in the Gospel', *Neot* 18 (1984), pp. 38-51.

—'When is the End not the End? Reflections on the Ending of Mark's Narrative', *Int* 34 (1980), pp. 151-66.

Phillips, G.A., 'History and Text: The Reader in Context in Matthew's Parable Discourse', *Semeia* 31 (1985), pp. 111-38.

—'"This is a Hard Saying, Who Can Listen to It?" Creating a Reader in John 6', *Semeia* 26 (1983), pp. 32-56.

Porter, S.E., 'Why hasn't Reader-Response Criticism Caught On in New Testament Studies?', *Journal of Literature and Theology* 4 (1990), pp. 278-92.

Powell, M.A., 'Direct and Indirect Phraseology in the Gospel of Matthew', in E.H. Lovering (ed.), *Society of Biblical Literature Seminar Papers 1991* (Atlanta: Scholars Press, 1991), pp. 405-17.

—'The Religious Leaders in Luke: A Literary-Critical Study', *JBL* 109 (1990), pp. 93-110.

—'Toward a Narrative-Critical Understanding of Mark', *Int* 47 (1993), pp. 341-46.

—'Types of Readers and their Relevance for Biblical Hermeneutics', *Trinity Seminary Review* 12 (1990), pp. 67-76.

—*What is Narrative Criticism?* (Guides to Biblical Scholarship; Minneapolis: Fortress Press, 1990).

Praeder, S.M., 'Jesus–Paul, Peter–Paul, and Jesus–Peter Parallelisms in Luke–Acts: A History of Reader Response', in K.H. Richards (ed.), *Society of Biblical Literature Seminar Papers 1994* (Chico, CA: Scholars Press, 1984), pp. 23-40.

Price, M., *Forms of Life: Character and Moral Imagination in the Novel* (New Haven: Yale University Press, 1983).

—'The Other Self: Thoughts about Character in the Novel', in M. Mack and I. Gregor (eds.), *Imagined Worlds* (London: Methuen, 1968), pp. 279-99.

Räisänen, H., *The 'Messianic Secret' in Mark* (trans. C. Tuckett; Edinburgh: T. & T. Clark, 1990).

Rand, J.A. du, 'The Characterization of Jesus as Depicted in the Narrative of the Fourth Gospel', *Neot* 19 (1985), pp. 18-36.

Rawlinson, A.E.J., *St Mark* (Westminster Commentaries; London: Methuen, 3rd edn, 1931).

Rendell, S., 'Fish vs. Fish', *Diacritics* 12 (Winter 1982), pp. 49-57.

Reploh, K.-G., *Markus—Lehrer der Gemeinde: Eine redaktionsgeschichtliche Studie zu den Jüngerperikopen des Markus-Evangeliums* (Stuttgart: Katholisches Bibelwerk, 1969).

Resseguie, J.L., 'Reader Response Criticism and the Synoptic Gospels', *JAAR* 52 (1984), pp. 307-24.

Rhoads, D., 'Narrative Criticism and the Gospel of Mark', *JAAR* 50 (1982), pp. 411-34.

Rhoads, D., and D. Michie, *Mark as Story: An Introduction to the Narrative of a Gospel* (Philadelphia: Fortress Press, 1982).

Rimmon-Kenan, S., *Narrative Fiction: Contemporary Poetics* (London: Methuen, 1983).

Robbins, V.K., 'The Healing of Blind Bartimaeus (10:46-52) in the Marcan Theology', *JBL* 92 (1973), pp. 224-43.

—*Jesus the Teacher: A Socio-Rhetorical Interpretation of Mark* (Philadelphia: Fortress Press, 1984).

—'Summons and Outline in Mark: The Three-Step Progression', *NovT* 23 (1981), pp. 97-114.

Robertson, A.T., *A Grammar of the Greek New Testament in the Light of Historical Research* (Nashville: Broadman, 1934).

Robinson, J.M., 'The Literary Composition of Mark', in M. Sabbe (ed.), *L'Evangile selon Marc: Tradition et rédaction* (Leuven: Leuven University Press, 2nd edn, 1988), pp. 11-20.

Rohde, J., *Die redaktionsgeschichtliche Methode: Einführung und Sichtung des Forschungsstandes* (Hamburg: Furche, 1966).

Roloff, J., *Das Kerygma und der irdische Jesus: Historische Motive in den Jesus-Erzählungen der Evangelien* (Göttingen: Vandenhoeck & Ruprecht, 2nd edn, 1973).

Schenk, W., 'Die Rollen der Leser oder der Mythos des Lesers?', *LB* 60 (1988), pp. 61-81.

Schenke, L., *Die Wundererzählungen des Markusevangeliums* (Stuttgart: Katholisches Bibelwerk, 1974).

Schmid, J., *Das Evangelium nach Markus* (RNT; Regensburg: Pustet, 4th edn, 1958).

Schmithals, W., *Das Evangelium nach Markus* (Ökumenischer Taschenbuchkommentar zum Neuen Testament; 2 vols.; Gütersloh: Gütersloher Verlagshaus/Gerd Mohn, 1979).

Schnackenburg, R., *Das Evangelium nach Markus* (2 vols; Düsseldorf: Patmos, 1966–71).

Scholes, R., *Elements of Fiction* (New York: Oxford University Press, 1968).

—*Textual Power: Literary Theory and the Teaching of English* (New Haven: Yale University Press, 1985).

Schrage, W., 'συναγωγή, ἐπισυναγωγή, ἀρχισυνάγωγος, ἀποσυνάγωγος', *TDNT*, VII, pp. 798-852.

Schreiber, J., 'Die Christologie des Markus Evangeliums', *ZTK* 58 (1961), pp. 154-83.

Schwartz, R., 'Free Will and Character Autonomy in the Bible', *Notre Dame English Journal* 15 (Winter 1983), pp. 51-74.

Schweizer, E., *Das Evangelium nach Markus* (NTD; Göttingen: Vandenhoeck & Ruprecht, 4th edn, 1975 [1967]).

—'The Portrayal of the Life of Faith in the Gospel of Mark', *Int* 32 (1978), pp. 387-99.

—'Die theologische Leistung des Markus', in R. Pesch (ed.), *Das Markus-Evangelium* (Darmstadt: Wissenschaftliche Buchgesellschaft, 1979), pp. 163-89.

—'Toward a Christology of Mark?', in J. Jervell and W.A. Meeks (eds.), *God's Christ and His People* (Oslo: Universitetsforlaget, 1977), pp. 29-42.

Scott, B.B., *Hear Then the Parables: A Commentary on the Parables of Jesus* (Philadelphia: Fortress Press, 1989).

—'How to Mismanage a Miracle: Reader Response Criticism', in K.H. Richards (ed.), *Society of Biblical Literature Seminar Papers 1983* (Chico, CA: Scholars Press, 1983), pp. 439-49.

—'The King's Accounting: Matthew 18:23-34', *JBL* 104 (1985), pp. 429-42.

—'A Master's Praise: Luke 16:1-8a', *Bib* 64 (1983), pp. 173-88.

Selvidge, M.J., 'And Those Who Followed Feared (10:32)', *CBQ* 45 (1983), pp. 396-400.

—*Woman, Cult, and Miracle Recital: A Redactional Critical Investigation on Mark 5:24-34* (Lewisburg, PA: Bucknell University Press, 1990).

Sinclair, S.G., 'The Healing of Bartimaeus and the Gaps in Mark's Messianic Secret', *Saint Luke's Journal of Theology* 33 (1990), pp. 249-57.

Smith, S.H., 'The Literary Structure of Mark 11:1-12:40', *NovT* 31 (1989), pp. 104-24.

Staley, J.L., *The Print's First Kiss: A Rhetorical Investigation of the Implied Reader in the Fourth Gospel* (SBLDS, 82; Atlanta: Scholars Press, 1988).

—'Stumbling in the Dark, Reaching for the Light: Reading Character in John 5 and 9', *Semeia* 53 (1991), pp. 55-80.

Stein, R.H., 'A Short Note on Mark XIV.28 and XVI.7', *NTS* 20 (1974), pp. 445-52.

—'What is *Redactionsgeschichte*?', *JBL* 88 (1969), pp. 45-56.

Steinhauser, M.G., 'The Form of the Bartimaeus Narrative (Mark 10:46-52)', *NTS* 32 (1986), pp. 583-95.

—'Part of a "Call Story"?', *ExpTim* 94 (1983), pp. 204-206.

Sternberg, M., *Expositional Modes and Temporal Ordering in Fiction* (Baltimore: Johns Hopkins University Press, 1978).

—*The Poetics of Biblical Narrative: Ideological Literature and the Drama of Reading* (Bloomington: Indiana University Press, 1985).

—'Time and Reader', in E. Spolsky (ed.), *The Uses of Adversity: Failure and Accommodation in Reader Response* (Lewisburg, PA: Bucknell University Press, 1990), pp. 49-89.

—'Time and Space in Biblical (Hi)story Telling: The Grand Chronology', in R. Schwartz (ed.), *The Book and the Text: The Bible and Literary Theory* (Oxford: Basil Blackwell, 1990), pp. 81-145.

Stibbe, M.W.G., *John as Storyteller: Narrative Criticism and the Fourth Gospel* (SNTSMS, 73; Cambridge: Cambridge University Press, 1992).

Stock, A., 'Chiastic Awareness and Education in Antiquity', *BTB* 14 (1984), pp. 23-27.

Strathmann, H., 'μάρτυς, μαρτυρέω, μαρτυρία, μαρτύριον', *TDNT*, IV, pp. 474-514.

Suleiman, S.R., 'Introduction: Varieties of Audience-Oriented Criticism', in S.R. Suleiman and I. Crosman (eds.), *The Reader in the Text: Essays on Audience and Interpretation* (Princeton: Princeton University Press, 1980), pp. 3-45.

—'Redundancy and the "Readable" Text', *Poetics Today* 1 (Spring 1980), pp. 119-42.

Sugirtharajah, R.S., 'The Widow's Mites Revalued', *ExpTim* 103 (1991), pp. 42-43.

Swete, H.B., *The Gospel according to St. Mark* (London: Macmillan, 3rd edn, 1909).

Swetman, J., 'Some Remarks on the Meaning of ὁ δὲ ἐξελθών in Mark 1,45', *Bib* 68 (1987), pp. 245-49.

Tannehill, R.C., 'The Composition of Acts 3-5: Narrative Development and Echo Effect', in K.H. Richards (ed.), *Society of Biblical Literature Seminar Papers 1984* (Chico, CA: Scholars Press, 1984), pp. 217-40.

—'The Disciples in Mark: The Function of a Narrative Role', *JR* 57 (1977), pp. 386-405.

—'The Gospel of Mark as Narrative Christology', *Semeia* 16 (1979), pp. 57-95.

—'Israel in Luke–Acts: A Tragic Story', *JBL* 104 (1985), pp. 69-85.

—*The Narrative Unity of Luke–Acts: A Literary Interpretation*. I. *The Gospel according to Luke* (Philadelphia: Fortress Press, 1986).

—*The Narrative Unity of Luke–Acts: A Literary Interpretation*. II. *The Acts of the Apostles* (Minneapolis: Fortress Press, 1990).

—*The Sword of His Mouth* (SBLSS, 1; Philadelphia: Fortress Press, 1975).

Taylor, V., *The Gospel according to Mark* (New York: St. Martin's Press, 2nd edn, 1966).

Telford, W. (ed.), *The Interpretation of Mark* (IRT, 7; Philadelphia: Fortress Press, 1985).

Theissen, G., *Urchristliche Wundergeschichten: Ein Beitrag zur formgeschichtlichen Erforschung der synoptischen Evangelien* (SNT, 8; Gütersloh: Gütersloher Verlagshaus/Gerd Mohn, 1974).

Thiselton, A.C., 'Reader Response Hermeneutics, Action Models, and the Parables of Jesus', in R. Lundin, A.C. Thiselton and C. Walhout (eds.), *The Responsibility of Hermeneutics* (Grand Rapids: Eerdmans, 1985), pp. 79-113.

Tolbert, M.A., 'How the Gospel of Mark Builds Character', *Int* 47 (1993), pp. 347-57.

—*Sowing the Gospel: Mark's World in Literary-Historical Perspective* (Minneapolis: Fortress Press, 1989).

Tompkins, J.P., 'An Introduction to Reader-Response Criticism', in *idem* (ed.), *Reader-Response Criticism: From Formalism to Post-Structuralism* (Baltimore: Johns Hopkins University Press, 1980), pp. ix-xxvi.

Trocmé, E., *La Formation de l'Evangile selon Marc* (Paris: Presses Universitaires de France, 1963).

Tuckett, C., 'Introduction: The Problem of the Messianic Secret', in *idem* (ed.), *The Messianic Secret* (IRT, 1; Philadelphia: Fortress Press, 1983), pp. 1-28.

Tyson, J.B., 'The Blindness of the Disciples in Mark', *JBL* 80 (1961), pp. 261-68.

Via, D.O., *Kerygma and Comedy in the New Testament: A Structuralist Approach to Hermeneutic* (Philadelphia: Fortress Press, 1975).

Vorster, W.S., 'Characterization of Peter in the Gospel of Mark', *Neot* 21 (1987), pp. 57-76.

—'Mark: Collector, Redactor, Author, Narrator?', *Journal of Theology for Southern Africa* 31 (1980), pp. 46-61.

—'The Reader in the Text: Narrative Material', *Semeia* 48 (1989), pp. 21-39.

Weeden, T.J., 'The Conflict between Mark and his Opponents over Kingdom Theology', in G. MacRae (ed.), *Society of Biblical Literature Seminar Papers 1973* (Cambridge: Society of Biblical Literature, II, 1973), pp. 203-41.

—'The Heresy that Necessitated Mark's Gospel', *ZNW* 59 (1968), pp. 145-58.

—*Mark—Traditions in Conflict* (Philadelphia: Fortress Press, 1971).

Wilson, R., 'The Bright Chimera: Character as a Literary Term', *Critical Inquiry* 5 (1979), pp. 725-49.

—'On Character: A Reply to Martin Price', *Critical Inquiry* 2 (1975), pp. 191-98.

Wittag, S., 'Formulaic Style and the Problem of Redundancy', *Centrum* 1 (1973), pp. 123-36.

Wrede, W., *Das Messiasgeheimnis in den Evangelien: Zugleich ein Beitrag zum Verständnis des Markusevangeliums* (Göttingen: Vandenhoeck & Ruprecht, 1901).

Wright, A.G., 'The Widow's Mites: Praise or Lament?—A Matter of Context', *CBQ* 44 (1982), pp. 256-65.

INDEXES

INDEX OF REFERENCES

INDEX OF AUTHORS